THE COMPLETE CRITICAL GUIDE TO
BEN JONSON

What is the historical context of Jonson's contradictory career and writings?

How do notions of history, power, gender and sexuality shape our readings of Jonson today?

So many questions surround the key figures in the English literary canon, but most books focus on one aspect of an author's life or work, or limit themselves to a single critical approach. *The Complete Critical Guide to Ben Jonson* is part of a unique series of comprehensive, user-friendly introductions which:

- offer basic information on an author's life, contexts and works
- outline the major critical issues surrounding the author's works, from the time they were written to the present
- leave judgements up to you, by explaining the full range of often very different critical views and interpretations
- offer guides to further reading in each area discussed.

This series has a broad focus but one very clear aim: to equip you with *all* the knowledge you need to make your own new readings of crucial literary texts.

'An excellent book: well-written, engaging and up-to-the-minute.'
Julie Sanders, *Keele University*

'I'm really impressed indeed with the scope, precision, conciseness, lucidity and comprehensiveness of this book. ... Bringing so much together in such a short space and making sense of it all is a major achievement.'
Sean McEvoy, *Varndean College,*
author of Shakespeare: the Basics

James Loxley is the author of *Royalism and Poetry in the English Civil Wars* (1997). He is lecturer in English literature at the University of Edinburgh.

THE COMPLETE CRITICAL GUIDE TO
ENGLISH LITERATURE
Series Editors
RICHARD BRADFORD AND JAN JEDRZEJEWSKI

Also available in this series:

The Complete Critical Guide to Samuel Beckett
David Pattie
The Complete Critical Guide to Robert Browning
Stefan Hawlin
The Complete Critical Guide to Geoffrey Chaucer
Gillian Rudd
The Complete Critical Guide to John Milton
Richard Bradford
The Complete Critical Guide to Alexander Pope
Paul Baines

Forthcoming:

The Complete Critical Guide to Charles Dickens
The Complete Critical Guide to D. H. Lawrence
The Complete Critical Guide to William Wordsworth

Visit the website of *The Complete Critical Guide to English Literature*
for further information and an updated list of titles
www.literature.routledge.com/criticalguides

THE COMPLETE CRITICAL GUIDE TO
BEN JONSON

James Loxley

London and New York

First published 2002
by Routledge
11 New Fetter Lane, London EC4P 4EE

Simultaneously published in the USA and Canada
by Routledge
29 West 35th Street, New York, NY 10001

Routledge is an imprint of the Taylor & Francis Group

© 2002 James Loxley

Typeset in Schneidler by
HWA Text and Data Management, Tunbridge Wells
Printed and bound in Great Britain by
Biddles Ltd, Guildford and King's Lynn

British Library Cataloguing in Publication Data
A catalogue record for this book is available from the British Library

Library of Congress Cataloging in Publication Data
Loxley, James, 1968–
The complete critical guide to Ben Jonson / James Loxley.
p. cm. (The complete critical guide to English literature)
Includes bibliographical references and index.
1. Jonson, Ben (1573?–1636 – Criticism and interpretation –
Handbooks, manuals, etc.
I. Title II. Series
PR2638 .L69 2001
822´.3–dc21   2001034889

ISBN 0–415–22227–3 (hbk)
ISBN 0–415–22228–1 (pbk)

CONTENTS

CONTENTS

SERIES EDITORS' PREFACE

The Complete Critical Guide to English Literature is a ground-breaking collection of one-volume introductions to the work of the major writers in the English literary canon. Each volume in the series offers the reader a comprehensive account of the featured author's life, of his or her writing and of the ways in which his or her works have been interpreted by literary critics. The series is both explanatory and stimulating; it reflects the achievements of state-of-the-art literary-historical research and yet manages to be intellectually accessible for the reader who may be encountering a canonical author's work for the first time. It will be useful for students and teachers of literature at all levels, as well as for the general reader. Each book can be read through, or consulted in a companion-style fashion.

The aim of *The Complete Critical Guide to English Literature* is to adopt an approach that is as factual, objective and non-partisan as possible, in order to provide the 'full picture' for readers and allow them to form their own judgements. At the same time, however, the books engage the reader in a discussion of the most demanding questions involved in each author's life and work. Did Pope's physical condition affect his treatment of matters of gender and sexuality? Does a feminist reading of *Middlemarch* enlighten us regarding the book's presentation of nineteenth-century British society? Do we deconstruct Beckett's work, or does he do so himself? Contributors to this series address such crucial questions, offer potential solutions and recommend further reading for independent study. In doing so, they equip the reader for an informed and confident examination of the life and work of key canonical figures and of the critical controversies surrounding them.

The aims of the series are reflected in the structure of the books. Part I, 'Life and Contexts', offers a compact biography of the featured author against the background of his or her epoch. In Part II, 'Work', the focus is on the author's most important works, discussed from a non-partisan, literary-historical perspective; the section provides an account of the works, reflecting a consensus of critical opinion on them, and indicating, where appropriate, areas of controversy. These and other issues are taken up again in Part III, 'Criticism', which offers an account of the critical responses generated by the author's work. Contemporaneous reviews and debates are considered, along with opinions inspired by more recent theoretical approaches, such as New Criticism, feminism, Marxism, psychoanalytic criticism, deconstruction and New Historicism.

The volumes in this series will together constitute a comprehensive reference work, offering an up-to-date, user-friendly and reliable account of the heritage of English literature from the Middle Ages to the twentieth century. We hope that *The Complete Critical Guide to English Literature* will become for its readers, academic and non-academic alike, an indispensable source of information and inspiration.

RICHARD BRADFORD

JAN JEDRZEJEWSKI

ACKNOWLEDGEMENTS

The debts, as usual, are substantial. I am grateful to Oxford University Press for permission to reprint copyright material. Discussions with Martin Butler and David Lindley during a spell at the University of Leeds helped to generate an interest in Jonson substantial enough to issue, for starters, in an enterprise such as this. I have profited immensely from many conversations with James Knowles and from his careful reading of part of the text, while the three readers for Routledge rescued me from many errors and infelicities. Both Dr Knowles and Professor Butler kindly allowed me to read work then in press. My colleagues at Edinburgh, particularly Suzanne Trill, Lee Spinks and Penny Fielding, have provided an environment both supportive and – at times – necessarily distracting. To Joanna, my fortune and my star, I am obliged beyond the bounds of the calculable.

ABBREVIATIONS AND REFERENCING

Throughout the text, references to Jonson's plays are from *The Complete Plays*, ed. G. A. Wilkes, 4 volumes (Oxford: Oxford University Press, 1981–2). The texts therein are based on the monumental *Ben Jonson*, ed. C. H. Herford, Percy Simpson and Evelyn Simpson, 11 volumes (Oxford: Oxford University Press, 1925–52), abbreviated as *HSS*. References to the poems, *Timber, or Discoveries* and *Conversations with Drummond and Hawthornden* are from *The Oxford Authors: Ben Jonson*, ed. Ian Donaldson (Oxford: Oxford University Press, 1985), while those to the masques are from *The Complete Masques*, ed. Stephen Orgel (New Haven: Yale University Press, 1969). References to the plays are given as act, scene (where appropriate) and line numbers. References to all other works are to line numbers.

The choice of Wilkes's edition in particular merits a word or two of explanation, since there are many editions of single plays or selections from the corpus which follow more up-to-date editorial procedures and contain fuller introductions and apparatus, and in which readers are most likely to encounter the plays. Wilkes, however, is the only modern spelling edition of all the extant plays currently in circulation, and ease of reference thus requires its use in a synoptic work such as this. The complete publication of Jonson's dramatic *oeuvre* in the excellent Revels Plays series is keenly awaited, as is the appearance (scheduled for 2005) of the new Cambridge edition of the complete works currently being prepared under the editorship of David Bevington, Martin Butler and Ian Donaldson.

Cross-referencing between sections is one of the features of this series. Such references are to relevant page numbers and appear in bold type and square brackets e.g. **[37]**.

INTRODUCTION

This book examines the life, works and critical reception of Ben Jonson. A former bricklayer and convicted murderer who became James I's 'poet laureate', the loyal servant who simultaneously asserted his own poetic authority, and the writer of elevated court entertainments whose works are also shaped by the rhythms of urban popular culture, Jonson's contradictory career and complex literary inventions have been sources of both pleasure and bewilderment for four hundred years. And while he has at times been on the wrong end of an invidious comparison with Shakespeare, his friend and rival, recent developments in literary criticism and the renewed attentions of theatrical practitioners have ensured that the seemingly strange shapes and textures of his works continue to fascinate.

Part I of this book offers a concise narrative of Jonson's life and literary career, from his inauspicious beginnings in the bustling environment of early modern London, through his adventures and misdemeanours as bricklayer, soldier and novice playwright, his emergence as a central literary figure of his generation, to the final burst of dramatic productivity in the straitened circumstances of his last years. Part II provides clear outlines of all the extant plays, accounts of their major thematic concerns and indications of particular points of critical attention or controversy. It also details in more general terms Jonson's work as non-dramatic poet and as an innovative writer of entertainments for the festive rituals of the Stuart monarchy. Part III traces the most significant trends in criticism of Jonson's work in recent decades, showing in particular how the focus in contemporary criticism on issues such as history, power, gender and sexuality has shaped our readings of Jonson.

The Complete Critical Guide to Ben Jonson presents an overview of Jonson's life, writing and the critical responses it has evoked. It may be read through as a handbook to the field, if readers so wish; or those with interests in particular areas may consult the relevant part of any section, and use the cross-references and 'Further reading' subsections to find relevant material elsewhere.

PART I
LIFE AND CONTEXTS

(a) INTRODUCTION

This section provides an account of Jonson's life and literary career, giving details both of his personal circumstances and the development of his reputation as a writer. It draws substantially on the biographies mentioned in 'Further reading' for its account. We ought to note, though, that none of these biographies agree on every point, and the frequently ambiguous evidence is interpreted in conflicting ways. This section seeks to represent points of consensus, but it should be remembered that there cannot be consensus on every aspect of Jonson's life. Readers in search of greater detail are directed to the works listed in 'Further reading'. The section also locates Jonson in contexts which are of particular significance to his works and for the criticism they have generated. For that reason, the narrative of the poet's life is punctuated by subsections dealing with early modern London, Renaissance humanism, the theatres of Jonson's city, and the political structures and issues of the Elizabethan and early Stuart periods. The accompanying chronology provides a clear sequence of events for reference purposes.

(b) JONSON'S CITIES

In the last quarter of the sixteenth century London was already a thriving metropolis. The lack of anything resembling census information means that indisputable population figures will never be forthcoming, but it has been estimated that by 1550 its population stood at perhaps 50,000, many times that of any other English city. And it was growing fast. By 1565 it had 85,000 inhabitants; by 1603, perhaps as many as 180,000 in the city and its suburbs, and it continued to swell at as high or a higher rate (Porter 1994: 42). This was not, though, the result of some particularly industrious breeding – in fact, the death rate outstripped the birth rate over these years. Rather, London was a city into which immigrants from the countryside poured at a great rate, and the influx produced a radical transformation of the place to which they came. It had long since slipped the confines of its medieval walls: to the north, west and east speculative building was proceeding apace, generating new suburbs. To the south, over the Thames, Southwark was connected to the city by London Bridge and was itself becoming a place to which Londoners resorted in their thousands in search of entertainment.

In this expansion, two cities were gradually being merged. London, with the Tower at its south eastern corner and the gothic St Paul's cathedral on a hill at its centre, had always been matched by West-minster, lying westwards and round a bend in the river, the site of an abbey, a hall in which Parliament met and increasingly the settled base of royalty. Facing it over the Thames stood Lambeth palace, the resid-ence of the Archbishop of Canterbury. Over the course of the Tudor period the area immediately north of Westminster towards London had become – as Whitehall palace – the main residence of the monarch and the court during their regular spells in the capital, and as it came closer to being the constant administrative centre of the kingdom so it drew in increasing numbers of petitioners, office-seekers and servants. Further eastwards, abutting the western edge of the city itself, stood the Inns of Court, populated during the legal terms by lawyers, their dependants, and a class of young men not destined for the law but for whom the Inns functioned as a kind of finishing school. The area in between here and Whitehall, along a wide road known as the Strand, was attracting noblemen in search of impressive riverside dwellings (conveniently located close to both court and city), and a gentry prepared to settle for slightly less impressive lodgings. The sixty years around 1600 were to see intensive building in this area, including the development on the Earl of Bedford's land at Convent (or Covent) Garden of terraced townhouses and a grand, Italianate piazza. In a variegated but unbroken sprawl, London now stretched from the docks and manufacturing industries of its eastern fringes to the grandeur of royal dwellings in the west.

The governmental structures of the city had not kept up with this rapid development. The area within the city walls, along with a few adjoining districts, fell under the jurisdiction of the Lord Mayor and his Common Council, a civic oligarchy which gave London its official voice. This voice might be heard in the street theatre of the Lord Mayor's annual pageant, or in the civic entertainments provided periodically for the monarch, or reflected in works such as John Stow's historical *Survey of London* (1598). The suburbs on both sides of the Thames, though, were not answerable to this organisation and did not contribute to this voice, and the institutions of court and church were similarly outside the purview of the city. The Reformation of the Church in the mid-Tudor period also complicated matters. Ecclesiastical property within the city limits had always been exempt from control by civic authorities; when such property was expropriated by Henry VIII, and sold on to secular owners, that exemption was sold with it. These areas – perhaps the best known was the Blackfriars, down by the Thames – were called 'liberties', and had the slightly dubious reputation that their marginal status might lead us to expect.

The complexity of its governmental structures was also evident in the related organisation of London's economic life. As was common in English towns, the medieval city had organised its many trades and industries into monopolistic institutions known as 'guilds'. Guild membership was an essential prerequisite for anyone attempting to practise a recognised trade in the city; the guilds also oversaw both the induction, training and discipline of apprentices, and their passage into full membership. From the ranks of these 'freemen' came the city's governing elite. Yet not all guild members were alike – while some were journeymen, and some managed their own craft businesses, others grew rich through their participation in trade, both national and international. Some guilds, too, were more wealthy and influential than others. Keeping the system in place required the incorporation into the guild structure of new trades made possible by technological advances. In 1557, for example, the Stationers' Company was established to organise and control the production of printed books.

Other institutions, though, began to threaten the displacement of the system. By 1550, London was already handling 90 per cent of the nation's trade, and the religious and political turmoil that afflicted such established international mercantile centres as Antwerp in ensuing decades provided the opportunity for the city to establish itself as northern Europe's foremost commercial site. Hitherto, the Mercers' Company, organising the cloth trade, had dominated such activity; but in 1555 the Russia Company was established as a joint-stock venture seeking to profit from international commerce, followed by the Levant Company (1581), the East India Company (1600), the Virginia Company (1606) and others. In 1570, the Royal Exchange – a commodities trading centre – was opened in the city, financed by the prominent merchant Thomas Gresham. London was becoming a financial centre, a place for the pursuit of the kind of commercial schemes put forward by the 'projectors' of the early Stuart period.

London, in other words, was getting rich. Its expansion was due in no small part to the city's mercantile development and to Westminster's consolidation of its status as the kingdom's administrative centre. The nobility and gentry who flocked to the court mingled with the city's great merchants, each attracted to the opportunities represented by the other. To them were drawn all the service industries necessary to keep them supplied with provisions, dressed, housed, mobile and entertained. And so the city's economic life supported those employed outside the guilds as well as masters, journeymen and apprentices, and attracted those in search of work to its ever-expanding suburbs.

This expansion was a constant source of concern both to monarch and civic authorities, and both sought in differing ways to prevent the new metropolis from coming into being. Clearly, it put the established civic institutions and infrastructures under increasing strain. The narrow streets were already crowded, the rivers and streams filling up with refuse, making this an unparalleled breeding ground for plague – which struck with monotonous but horrifying regularity – and the other diseases which helped keep the urban death rate dizzyingly high. Other ills were also the focus for the authorities' concern. Prostitution was rife, and property crime widespread. The pamphlet literature of the period is populated by a cast of criminal types: the pimp, whore, cutpurse and conman who constitute a shadowy urban underworld. They are even credited with their own dialect, the language of 'canting'. Yet they were not the only source of disorder. The city's apprentices could prove a volatile crowd, especially during their annual Shrovetide festivities, as their propensity to riot against matters as diverse as high prices and foreigners demonstrated. London was also a prime centre of Protestant radicalism, sustaining artisanal, 'Puritan' congregations and contacts with co-religionists on the continent. These were not – or not yet – in unison with the official voices of the city, but they were nevertheless clearly audible.

This was Jonson's London, the city of his childhood and his adult life. He was born, it is thought, on June 11 1572, the posthumous son (so he claimed, in conversation with the Scottish poet William Drummond) of a minister. Of his father no definitive trace has been found – Johnson was hardly an uncommon name, and the distinctive spelling which has marked out Benjamin for four centuries was his own doing. His mother was remarried in his infancy, to a bricklayer named Robert Brett, and Jonson's early years were spent living in his stepfather's household in Hartshorn Lane, off the Strand near Charing Cross. Brett was by no means an impoverished labourer, but a bricklayer could not claim the same affinity with gentility that might accrue to a clergyman. He was literate, nevertheless, and his stepson was educated from an early age: first at a private school in the nearby St Martin's church, and then, at some point after he reached seven years of age, at the prestigious Westminster school on the other side of Whitehall palace.

(c) HUMANISM AND EDUCATION

The education Jonson received was not to be prolonged, but it was to be decisive. It served to inculcate in him the humanist culture that provided crucial resources for the political, religious and philosophical disputes of the age. At the heart of the humanist project were the writings of classical philosophers, poets, historians and statesmen, writings which had inspired influential early sixteenth century scholars such as Juan Luis Vives, Desiderius Erasmus and Sir Thomas More. These texts, some only recently rediscovered, had been fused with biblical authority in humanist writing to offer a distinctively if tentatively secularised body of knowledge through which political and ethical principles might be challenged and reorganised. Humanist learning enjoyed a complex relationship with the project of ecclesiastical Reformation which confronted the Catholic church at the same time. It provided succour to the Protestant reformers in their attacks on a hidebound and dogmatic church. Yet, the sophisticated (some said sophistical) relationship to the scriptures that Christian humanism of necessity engendered was regarded with some suspicion by many Protestants.

Among the deepest concerns of figures such as Vives and Erasmus were the educational programmes of their own societies. One of the crucial motifs they took from their reading of Roman sources such as Cicero, was the integration of learning and public life, the insistence that knowledge should be *responsible*. And this public life, for them, was not simply the province of the church: learning was not just for clerics. So they placed great emphasis on pedagogical provision beyond ecclesiastical parameters and purposes, and their followers undertook to reform and reinvigorate education wherever they could. The sixteenth century in England saw just such a humanist-inspired revision of institutions and syllabuses, and the establishment of new foundations capable of delivering the requisite schooling. The accomplishment that was the initial goal of all such teaching was a familiarity with Latin, the language not only of the classical authorities but also of much contemporary intellectual debate, and this goal dominated the curricula of the grammar schools. From an early age boys were required to read their way through selected classical texts (this was an education aimed at boys only; since girls were not expected to participate in public life when they grew up, providing such an education for them would by most have been thought superfluous), or through the kind of textbooks which not only provided examples of Latin usage but also, in their thematic content, introduced their readership to the ethos of Christian humanism. As they progressed, so the difficulty of the texts they read and the complexity of the tasks they were required to perform increased. Eventually, they would be expected to conduct grammatically and rhetorically exacting debating exercises, as well as being proficient in translation. And since Greek was the language of some classical literature and (especially) philosophy, texts that the Roman authorities cited as their own authorities, so a familiarity with Greek formed an important element in the curriculum of older boys.

(d) 1572–1597

It was this curriculum that Jonson followed at Westminster, his fees paid by a patron whose identity we do not know. He was taught by the school's then second master, William Camden, a hugely respected teacher and writer, who in 1586 (during Jonson's time at his school) published his great work *Britannia*, a region-by-region history of England, Scotland and Ireland. Jonson was later to claim that to Camden he owed 'All that I am in arts, all that I know' (*Epigrams* 14, 2), and, even allowing for hyperbole here, his influence was clearly crucial. Under his tutelage the young 'town-boy' (as the day students were known) encountered works which were to stay with him for the rest of his life, forming a reservoir on which his own work drew exhaustively. In his biographical study of Jonson's work, David Kay has outlined the list of texts to be studied, drawn up when the school's statutes were revised in 1560 (Kay 1995: 3). In their first years at the school pupils would have been reading Erasmus' compilation of extracts, as well as *Aesop's Fables* and the works of the Roman comic dramatist Terence (whose plotting and character types, like those of his contemporary Plautus, provided a model for Jonson's earliest comedies [43]). In subsequent years, they would have read Cicero's treatises and orations, the Roman histories of Sallust (both central to Jonson's Roman tragedy *Catiline* [61]; Cicero's *De Officiis*, [On Duty] provided a discourse on ethical obligation which finds frequent echoes in Jonson's verse), the poetry of Horace, Virgil and Ovid (all invoked in *Poetaster* [54]; Horace was to be Jonson's enduring poetic ideal), among many other works. Their notebooks would have been filled with extracts and examples, translated and in the original Latin.

In fact, the humanist techniques of learning that Jonson acquired here not only helped to furnish the content of his later writing, but also informed its structure, as a work such as *Timber, or Discoveries* strikingly reveals [113]. Translating, copying out and memorising passages were staple methods of mastering the text, and in so doing of becoming a *vir civilis* [civilised man], attuned to the responsibilities of public life; where Jonson's own works translate, paraphrase or incorporate classical authorities (which is often), or call attention to their affinity with such humanist educational techniques (which is also often), they are not necessarily displaying a merely – as we would say – academic learning. Instead, they are negotiating a relationship with the processes of producing responsible knowledge. Jonson's classicism, in other words, is not the enemy of his relevance but the means by which it is claimed. It shapes crucial critical debates about the possibility and nature of any political work his texts might have performed then – or, indeed, be able to perform now **[131]**.

Jonson told Drummond that he was 'taken from' his education, 'and put to another craft' (196). Biographers have disagreed over the date of this interruption, but it may not mean that he was forced to leave school much or at all before the age at which this stage of his education would have anyway come to an end (see Kay 1995: 6). What seems certain is that he did not go on to study at university. Instead, he found himself apprenticed to his stepfather, working as a bricklayer – for a time, according to seventeenth century accounts, on the walls of Lincoln's Inn near Holborn. The apprenticeship was itself interrupted before Jonson had completed his full eight year term, though, and at some time before late 1594 he had a spell as a soldier in the Netherlands. He probably served in one of three towns garrisoned by English soldiers during the conflict between Protestant states and the Catholic Spanish, whose rule in this area was now under continuous challenge. To Drummond, he spun an unlikely tale of a single combat 'in the face of both the camps' (199–200) in which he killed his enemy.

This military career did not last, however, and we can be sure that he had returned to London by the end of 1594, for on 14 November that year evidence suggests that he married a woman called Anne Lewis. Nothing is known of her save Jonson's dismissive comment to Drummond that she was 'a shrew yet honest' (208). The latter was not an epithet that could be applied to her husband, who also confessed to Drummond that he was 'in his youth given to venery' and 'thought the use of a maid nothing in comparison to the wantonness of a wife' (238–9). How many children the marriage produced is unknown: his eldest son and daughter, Benjamin and Mary, are elegised in the *Epigrams* **[108]**, a second son named Joseph was christened in 1599, and a third boy, also named Benjamin, was born in early 1608. To these four could perhaps be added Elisabeth and another Benjamin, both baptised within two weeks of each other at different ends of the city in the spring of 1610, and both credited to a man of the poet's name in the respective parish registers. It is just about plausible that these might be twins, or else born to different women, but the fact that Jonson's name (spelling apart, and that in a time of orthographic uncertainty) was not particularly uncommon means that his paternity is likely to remain unproved in these cases. What we do know is that all his offspring predeceased him, most probably in early childhood. Such misfortune aside (and his elegies for his eldest children suggest that their deaths were keenly felt), his marriage may not have been a happy one. To support this suggestion we have not only the unflattering description of Anne quoted above but also his statement, again to Drummond in 1618/19, that he had not 'bedded with her' (209) for a period of five years (when exactly this might have been is uncertain), and the suggestion of an ongoing separation between them in legal depositions of 1606.

Married, with very young children, Jonson's prospects cannot have looked too good: his marriage, as well as his military adventure, had left him in breach of his apprenticeship. Nonetheless, it seems that he joined the Tylers and Bricklayers company in 1595 (presumably by buying his freedom), and was still paying his dues as late as 1611 – a much longer connection with this 'other craft' than might have been expected. But at this time, too, his involvement in the theatre also begins, though once again the details are somewhat sketchy. He probably began as an actor, perhaps touring with the not overly successful Pembroke's Men as early as 1595/6. By 1597 he had clearly also begun to write for the company, perhaps first penning *The Case Is Altered* **[43]** for them. But the definitive evidence of his involvement comes from surviving records of a brush with the law that led the company into a catastrophic dissolution and put Jonson in jail.

(e) THEATRE, COMMERCE, AND THE LAW

The simultaneous development of the Royal Exchange and the first dedicated, professional theatres has been thought noteworthy since the time of their construction. Both have been taken to be indicative of London's emergence as a modern commercial centre – and it is clear that the growing population and wealth of the city produced a ready market for the kind of specialised leisure industry that theatre on this scale was to become. Prior to the construction of the first purpose-built arena or amphitheatre in 1567, commercial theatre had by and large been confined to the innyards of the city; it was perhaps the civic authorities' attempts at prohibition in 1559 and 1574 that fostered the theatres' development, as they were all built on land outside their jurisdiction. Over the next forty or so years entrepreneurs including

Richard Burbage and Philip Henslowe were responsible for the construction of such celebrated playing spaces as the Rose and the Globe, both of these on the south of the Thames at Bankside. This was already home to popular entertainments like bear-baiting, and although the earliest arenas were constructed to the north and east of the city, this convenient riverside site became the customary locale for this kind of theatre after the 1580s.

The arenas were outdoor theatres, circular galleried buildings constructed round a stage which jutted out into a central space open to the elements. The largest of them could accommodate 3,000 spectators, who by the turn of the century were flocking to daily, afternoon performances of a large and ever-changing repertoire. The players were organised into separate companies, under the nominal patronage of a member of the aristocracy (later of the royal family), leasing the theatres in which they played. They were customarily run by a group of principal actors, 'sharers', who jointly owned the company and all its properties (including the rights to plays), and who hired other actors and musicians as necessary. Shakespeare made a very good living out of his share in the Lord Chamberlain's Men, for whom he wrote and acted exclusively; Jonson, on the other hand, was never a sharer. While the players may have had different levels of investment in the structures of the companies, they had their gender in common. Only in foreign companies visiting London were actresses to be found at this date – all the female parts in the repertoire of the domestic companies were played by boys, a convention exploited to particular effect by Jonson in *Epicene* and *The New Inn* **[74, 94, 143]**.

Their clientele was socially diverse, the cheapest seats being in fact standing room in front of the stage, while 'gentlemen's rooms' – the forerunners of private boxes – were available in the galleries above for the wealthier element. Among the best places in the auditorium, it seems, were seats at the side of the stage itself, where the spectator was as much in view as the actors themselves. Clearly, going to a play was for some a matter of being seen as much as of seeing – Jonson makes much of this in his own rendering of the experience of drama as a thematic focus of his plays. And even though they weren't to be found on the stage, women were certainly present in the audience – to the horror of anti-theatrical preachers, who joined the Common Council in looking on theatre as primarily a threat to social order. Such mixed crowds could only be a fertile terrain for crime, immorality and disease. Indeed, during the plague's regular visitations on the city the theatres were closed, sometimes for months at a time, on both public health and spiritual grounds, and any company that did not tour would face serious financial difficulties. As far as the authorities were concerned, afflictions such as plague called for penance, and the stifling of a morally dubious activity like playgoing could only be an aid to gaining God's mercy on the sufferings of the city.

In 1596 Burbage secured some space in the precincts of the erstwhile monastery at Blackfriars, across the river from Bankside. A prime attraction of the site was its location in one of the liberties, an area exempt from the edicts of the Common Council (a status that lasted until 1608). Here he planned to open a theatre, but was foiled by protests from outraged locals. The residents' respite was brief: only four years later a theatre did open on the site. This was not, though, an arena of the sort to which London was by now accustomed. For a start, it was an indoor auditorium, and much smaller than any of its rivals on Bankside with a capacity of about 500. The lack of capacity was offset by the higher admission price, the cheapest seats costing sixpence (more than a day's wages for the less well-off artisan), which consequently ensured a more socially restricted audience watching in greater comfort and luxury than could be found on the opposite bank of the Thames. Indeed, the Blackfriars and other similar indoor theatres came to be known as 'private' rather than 'public' theatres. The company that played here was also very different from those playing in the public arenas: the actors were all boys. Such companies had existed before, providing private entertainments and performances at court, and had also utilised a small space on the Blackfriars site between 1576 and 1584 for perhaps twice weekly performances to very small audiences. Now the boys' companies were revived on a more commercial basis, able to offer a 'sophisticated' alternative to the forms of drama characteristic of the arenas. They thrived for about a decade, before the King's Men (formerly the Chamberlain's Men) took over the lease on the Blackfriars and began to use it as their winter house, and the boys' companies merged or were absorbed into the dominant adult companies.

Throughout this period, then, playwrights could be writing for adults or boys, for public or private stage, and we might expect such different circumstances to leave some mark on the texts they produced. It has been suggested, for example, that the more obvious artifice evident in having children playing adults' roles contributed to a greater distance from naturalism or realism in the plays written for the boys' companies, a lesser regard for narrative or characterisation (though the simple invocation of such modern categories for the delineation of early modern drama is not necessarily unproblematic). It has also been claimed that the social differentiation between the audiences of the public and the private theatres would have found a reflection in the greater erudition and sophistication on offer in the repertoire of the latter. This, too, cannot be anything other than a problematic argument – not only because it depends on the assumption that the modern, complex opposition between elite and mass culture is necessarily translatable to the Tudor theatre, but also because it assumes too hard and fast a distinction between the 'public' and 'private' repertoires. The boys' companies drew on the existing stock of plays written for adult players, for a start, and plays were not necessarily written for a single environment or audience. *Bartholomew Fair*, for example, received its first performance on 31 October 1614 at the Hope theatre on Bankside, a venue which also hosted bear-baiting; the very next night, it was performed before the King and court at Whitehall. This double origin marks the text in its inclusion of two different kinds of framing device **[88]**, but substantially the same play entertained both the groundlings in the arena and the monarch in his Westminster home.

All theatre companies, of whatever stripe, had to negotiate the space in which to make a living with the governments of their day. This was not necessarily a simple procedure, either for them to follow or for us to trace today. London players and theatre owners had to deal with the hostility of the civic authorities, a fairly consistent force throughout the late Tudor and early Stuart periods, and if the city fathers were not legislating against playing on territory under their jurisdiction they were often importuning the monarch's government to take action. Yet these same authorities were not averse to commissioning theatrical professionals to assist them in producing often lavish civic celebrations and entertainments for royalty, such as Lord Mayor's pageants and ceremonial interludes to mark King James's official entry into London in 1604. The attitude of the Privy Council, the government of the realm, is more complex still. It could at times issue harsh edicts against drama, such as the 1597 prohibition on both playing and playhouses (though such commandments were only fitfully or temporarily enforced). But the government did not simply try to control drama negatively. It also sought to police it by sponsorship and selective support, offering it some exemption from the more censorious attentions of local, civic authorities, and reflecting royal authority's own use of theatricality for court ceremonial and entertainment.

Over the course of Jonson's early life the government gradually exerted its authority by bringing the theatre companies under dependable patronage. Only licensed companies were allowed to perform: by the early years of James's reign, the companies playing in the London amphitheatres were under direct royal patronage, operating as the

King's Men and the Queen's Men. The children's companies were also under similar patronage. These arrangements were complemented by the simultaneous emergence of the monarch's Master of the Revels as a crucial figure in the licensing and control of drama. Originally a court official with the responsibility for organising household entertainments and festivities, and thus involved in drawing together groups of players and commissioning performances, during the three decade tenure of Edmund Tilney (beginning in 1581) the Master of the Revels also became the figure whose 'allowance' was required for the performance of any play on the London stage. Yet this process of 'allowing' might not be easily understood as political censorship in our modern sense, since it is by no means apparent that it was primarily concerned to prevent heterodox opinion or doctrine from reaching the stage (Dutton 1991: 89). The rather different early modern practice of politics motivates a rather different process of censorship. Through the Master of the Revels, and royal patronage of theatre companies, authority and drama were integrated in a particularly distinctive manner.

(f) 1597–1601

Jonson could hold himself at least partially responsible for the Privy Council edict of 1597, since it was a play on which he had collaborated with Thomas Nashe – the now lost *Isle of Dogs* – that provoked the complaints against the theatre and government action in response. The play was held to be 'lewd', containing 'seditious and slanderous matter' (Kay 1995: 18), though, lacking a text, we can only guess what might have prompted such a response. While Nashe fled to Norfolk, Jonson and two of the company's players – Gabriel Spencer and Robert Shaw – were arrested and imprisoned by order of the Privy Council, questioned and held for up to two months. The company did not recover from this intervention, but Jonson did. After his release he began to work as a writer for the impresario Philip Henslowe, collaborating on a number of plays during 1598 and 1599 (not one of these collaborations was preserved by Jonson in his editions of his own works; none have survived by other means). At the same time, since he was a freelance writer, he penned *Every Man In His Humour* for the Lord Chamberlain's Men (later the King's Men) in the late summer of 1598 **[45]**, and *Every Man Out of His Humour* a year later for the same company **[48]**.

As his writing career took off, Jonson's troubles on other fronts multiplied. Only days after the first performance of *Every Man In* he committed a murder, killing the same Gabriel Spencer with whom he had been imprisoned the previous year. In conversation with Drummond, Jonson depicted Spencer as the aggressor, suggesting that the actor had effectively challenged him to a duel. He did not, though, provide any reason for the dispute between them, and other sources do not help us to establish its basis. What is known is that Jonson was tried, convicted and found himself facing execution: murder was of course a capital offence. He was able, however, to plead 'benefit of clergy' – a loophole in the law that allowed the literate to escape hanging. Instead, his goods were forfeit and he was branded on the thumb with a 'T' for Tyburn, the place of execution. The brand was a visible mark of his felony; should he re-offend in like manner it would also ensure that he did not escape the gallows a second time. He probably carried it for the rest of his life; its existence adds a peculiar resonance to those moments when Jonson evokes such judicial inscription as an analogue for his own poetic endeavour [50, 69]. But his release was not to be the end of his difficulties. The confiscation of his goods had left him and his family penniless, and the writing in which he engaged during 1599 clearly did not bring in enough money. It is possible that the series of back payments to the Bricklayers' Company made at this time mean that he actually returned to the practice of his other craft; he was certainly forced to borrow money. Unable to repay it, though, he found himself imprisoned for the third time in as many years, until he somehow acquired funds sufficient to cover the debt and procure his release early in 1600.

During his second spell in jail, perhaps when faced with the threat of imminent execution, he converted to Catholicism. Whatever the spiritual solace such a conversion offered, in the England of the 1590s it could only be a rash or brave move – particularly for a figure who had already once been in trouble over 'seditious matter'. Only a few years after the Spanish Armada of 1588, with religious conflict endemic in Europe, to be Catholic in England was to be highly suspect. Faith was political, and English Catholics were universally suspected not just of doctrinal or theological heresies but of compromised loyalties at best, and often of outright treason. Nonetheless, it was obviously an important step for Jonson, and one he took very seriously. His faith colours his elegy for his eldest daughter, Mary [108], and perhaps even influenced his choice of name for her – certainly, when the two most prominent Marys of the age had been the stridently Catholic queens of England and Scotland, both of them at different stages antagonists of the current monarch, the name could not be without resonance within contemporary conflicts as well as in broader doctrinal traditions.

And he managed to remain a Catholic, he told Drummond, for twelve years, through all the religious tensions and pressures of the decade which witnessed the troubled end of the long rule of Elizabeth and the establishment of a new Stuart dynasty. This was also precisely the period of the spectacular Gunpowder Plot, the audacious attempt by disaffected English Catholics to regain the country for Rome by wiping out King, Lords and members of the House of Commons when they gathered at Westminster in November 1605. And despite his Catholicism, despite his frequent and continuing difficulties with the authorities, it was also the period in which Ben Jonson established himself as a central figure in the literary and court culture of the age.

(g) RELIGION, GOVERNMENT AND REBELLION

Both Jonson's troubles and his simultaneous success can best be understood in the light of the ways in which royal government operated at this period. This was a time of intense political and religious conflict, a century in which differences of faith mapped onto the disputes between European empires and the rebellions against their rule. Conflicts such as the late sixteenth century Dutch revolt against Spanish power in the Netherlands was understood, if very simplistically, as a struggle between a Catholic monarchy and a Protestant people. To Protestants, the Catholic church was a corrupt institution which had lost sight of true Christianity; its leaders were remote and self-interested, more concerned to make a worldly profit for themselves than to act as good shepherds for their flock. To some the church was even anti-Christian, the very force that needed to be destroyed if God's will was to prevail on earth and Christ was to come again. It was certainly failing ordinary believers, leading them not to salvation but into a fog of doctrinal error, superstition and image-worship or idolatry. The Reformed church offered a chance to sweep all this away and start again with a purified and resanctified community of believers, founding their faith not on the authority of corrupt priests, bishops and popes but on the revealed truth of the Scriptures. To Catholics, the Reformers were simply destroyers, heretics who had been led by their own arrogance into catastrophic misreadings of the Bible and misunderstandings of doctrinal positions. Their wrong-headed schism meant turning their backs on the church as instituted by St Peter, a church descended lineally from Christ's own ministry on earth. It was thus a rebellion against divinely authorised Papal government. In general terms, then, and also in specific examples such as the Dutch revolt, a war between religious alternatives became explicable in the political language of a revolt against tyranny, on the one hand, or that of an anarchic rebellion against legitimate authority, on the other. The discourses of politics and religion were in practice inseparable.

Within states this ensured that differences of religion could not simply be left at that. The Protestants of France had been massacred in Paris in 1572 on the orders of their own government: here, the doctrinal disputes set in train by the Reformers of the early sixteenth century had coalesced into vicious factional struggles between powerful regional rulers. In England, meanwhile, Queen Elizabeth had continued the process of reform set in train by her father, Henry VIII, and her brother, Edward VI, and partially reversed by Mary, her elder sister. Yet because Henry's Reformation had been concerned more with Papal supremacy than with the other components of the Protestant programme, the Anglican church which his younger daughter eventually inherited was not nearly as 'reformed' as some of the continental churches established at the same time. The whole institution maintained the 'episcopal' framework of government by bishops and archbishops, and although the Protestant emphasis on Scripture was certainly made evident, many of the forms of worship to be seen in English churches kept the ceremonial aspect associated by Protestant militants with Catholicism. Within the one church, then, some of the disputes of the Reformation continued in miniature, and the history of the Church of England in this period is a history of conflict and compromise, of worries that the reform had gone too far and anxieties that it had not gone far enough. And as this was a *state* church, presided over by the monarch as its supreme governor, such differences were of necessity political issues.

Given, too, that Europe was riven by religious turmoil, English ecclesiastical disputes merged with questions of foreign or international policy. It was the aggressively Protestant factions among the English elite who were most strongly in favour of an increased colonisation in Ireland, for example, seeking to transplant the Reformation with a new wave of settlers and bring the Catholic Irish firmly under Protestant English control. But to these factions and many other English Protestants it was the Spanish, busy dealing with their rebellious Protestant subjects in the Netherlands, who were the most feared and hated enemy. The more militant sought an aggressively anti-Spanish policy, intervening to help the Dutch United Provinces, securing anti-Spanish alliances, seeking to challenge Spanish supremacy in the New World. Those who were not so committed might see the virtues instead of pursuing a less warlike programme, willing to countenance an accommodation with the larger, more staunchly Catholic powers in western and central Europe. To argue for such a policy did not make one a Catholic, of course, though opponents would be happy to insinuate that such advocacy demonstrated a suspicious lack of the proper hostility. The existence of a perfectly Protestant peace party only serves to remind us that religious differences did not constitute the only considerations which might be advanced in the determination of policy. Not everyone who wished England to supplant Spain as the chief plunderer of the Americas was necessarily motivated by Protestant zeal, either. Equally, some English Catholics saw no contradiction between their faith and loyalty to a Protestant monarch, thinking the disconnection of religion from patriotism entirely feasible. Nonetheless, religious considerations *were* crucial to the terms and substance of debate.

It is important also to be aware of the frameworks within which any debate might take place. As we might expect, there could be discussions in Parliament when it was in session – but that was not necessarily very often. England was a monarchy, governed by a Queen until 1603 and Kings thereafter who had the power to make and enforce laws without calling any kind of Parliament. The monarchy, however, had to fund the costs of government from its own revenues, and during the reigns both of Elizabeth and her successors expenditure always managed to outstrip income. According to precedent, financial matters *were* the business of a Parliament. It could agree to levy revenue for the government's requirements, but would not often do so without asking the monarch to take due account of its members' concerns. The monarch might promise to do so once supply had been voted; the Parliament might promise to levy taxes once its concerns had been addressed. The whole system required a certain amount of bargaining and brinkmanship, but its stability was not enhanced by the fact that the nature of monarchical sovereignty and the extent of parliamentary authority were persistently moot points throughout this period – eventually disastrously so. Whatever these uncertainties, though, no Parliament was able to embody anything like an executive function. Power was exercised through the Privy Council, a committee of nobles, administrative officials and other important figures, and through the appointed offices of state.

The court, then, and not Parliament, was the political heart of the realm, and causes and careers could only be advanced through the assiduous currying of royal favour and through the cultivation of those who already had both positions of power and the monarch's ear. Yet those in office could not rest content at night, their own continuing success being dependent on the continuation of the monarch's patronage. For the monarch – governing without any real independent power base and without an army or police – the goal was to rule through dependable lieutenants without allowing those lieutenants to become any kind of threat to one's own sovereignty, and without alienating or excluding other powerful subjects to the extent that they might threaten the integrity of the governmental system. Nobles and their factions needed to be managed, played off against one another, their loyalty maintained in pursuit of their own self-interest. Court was therefore a place of perpetual intrigue and jockeying for position, of royal favourites and repeated attempts to supplant them or otherwise bring about their disgrace. Any *ideological* dispute that might affect government – between militant and pacific strands of Protestantism, for example – could thus only take place in a structure of factional conflict which was not of necessity an index of differences in belief. For those lower down the hierarchy, similar rules applied. Getting on meant seeking out patronage from those with power and influence, and maintaining their goodwill. A writer, for example, might well address himself to a courtier with similar religious convictions, and attempt to forge a bond on that basis. But if a writer did not have other financial means – and in this period few were able or wished to sustain themselves solely by writing for the market, literary or theatrical – his own well-being would be dependent on his patron's star remaining in the ascendant. Better, perhaps, to cultivate patrons across different factional groupings, and try in that way to insulate oneself from the effects of a change in the political climate.

The climate was certainly prone to change during Jonson's adult life, perhaps most clearly at exactly the moment that the poet chose to look to the denizens of the court, rather than the business of theatre, as his route to success. The 1590s were not the happiest period in Elizabeth's reign, marked particularly by the perception of economic crisis and further fears of Spanish invasion following the disintegration of the Armada. The question of the succession was also increasingly pressing, as the Virgin Queen – naturally enough – had no direct heirs, and there existed no sure-fire mechanism to select a sovereign to follow her. The strongest candidate was to all intents and purposes a foreigner, James VI of Scotland, whose own reign north of the border had not so far been without potentially troubling incident. The uncertainty of Elizabeth's last years was provoked and heightened by an unforgiving struggle for primacy between her chief courtiers and favourites, particularly Sir Walter Ralegh, Sir Robert Cecil and the Earl of Essex. While Essex was leading an expedition to Ireland his rivals sought to blacken his name with the Queen, and on his early and unauthorised return the Earl found his standing at court fatally compromised. He only compounded his 'offence' in foolishly trying to speak directly to his sovereign, but his status as a pole of opposition to the venality at the heart of government was by the same token enhanced. He was able to draw support from an apparently unlikely coalition of the politically excluded, including both radical Protestants and Catholics as well as those simply outmanoeuvred by the scheming Cecil. Incensed at his own marginalisation he instituted a doomed revolt against the government of his rivals in February 1601, but was swiftly defeated and executed the very same month. Interestingly, literature played a significant part in these political struggles. The reaction to *The Isle of Dogs* and the ever more refined regulation of the drama showed the extent to which difficult times for the government could translate into spectacular if inconsistent bouts of repressive action. In 1599, faced with an explosion of controversial satiric writing, often published in pamphlet form, the Archbishop of Canterbury and the Bishop of London jointly issued an order requiring the burning of a number of books and the prohibition of any further satires or epigrams. And on the eve of his rebellion, a group of Essex's supporters paid the Chamberlain's Men to put on a one-off performance of an old play (probably Shakespeare's) about the deposition of Richard II, as if to justify by analogy the Earl's own rising against Elizabeth's ministers.

Cecil, the son of Elizabeth's great minister Lord Burghley, survived all these factional machinations unscathed and managed to secure for himself a leading role in the government of the new Stuart monarchy when James VI, as James I of England, eventually succeeded Elizabeth in 1603. Reassuringly – and unlike his mother, Mary, Queen of Scots – James was a staunch Protestant, and he brought with him not only religious continuity, Protestant heirs and the prospect of a united 'British' kingdom but also a complement of Scottish aristocrats and gentry to add to the factional stew of the English court. But although the succession was smooth, the early years of the new reign were inevitably a period of political uncertainty and paranoia, the shape of the new sovereign's government not yet fully established. Furthermore, the existence of a royal family now meant that there were three royal households to negotiate, as the Queen, Anne of Denmark, and her eldest son, Prince Henry, gathered together courts of their own. While these households were clearly subordinate to that of James himself, they nonetheless might offer the space for the articulation of alternatives to the dominant ethos and policies of the King's court. Anne, for instance, had been a committed if unobtrusive Catholic since the 1590s.

At this early stage, though, the uncertainties about the direction and personnel of the new regime made caution a wise move: courtiers and their clients needed to watch their step, while writers and dramatists had to be careful what was said on the stage or appeared in print. Just two years into the new king's reign, the Gunpowder Plot seemed to bear out all the government's worst fears.

In 1605 Jonson – Catholic, bricklayer and murderer, his transgression recorded in scar tissue on his thumb – was employed to write a masque for performance at court during Christmas festivities. It was such a success that he was invited back the following year, in the aftermath of the Gunpowder Plot, to write another, and so began a career as masque writer that was to lead directly to a royal pension and the unofficial title of laureate. On one level this seems incomprehensible, particularly when we take into account the fact that government willingly acknowledged that literature was not a realm entirely separate from political action, that it was – in our idiom – *relevant*. How could such a dubious figure have made it as a court artist, given the fraught circumstances at the outset of James's reign? Perhaps a definitive answer will not be forthcoming, but clues surely lie both in Jonson's cultivation of his patrons and his ability to be of real use to them in their endeavours.

(h) FRIENDS, PATRONS AND RIVALS: 1601–1606

At the turn of the century, we find Jonson keeping contact with a like-minded group centred on the Middle Temple, one of the Inns of Court, educated and able men whose talents were often turned to politically charged ends. Their knowledge of the law might make them useful agents of royal power in its occasional if regular confrontations with Parliament; conversely, such knowledge might be deployed in the same circumstances to assert the limits of monarchical authority. Prominent among them were Sir Robert Cotton, Richard Martin, John Selden, Thomas Overbury, Richard Hoskins and Benjamin Rudyerd, though John Donne, the architect Inigo Jones and the poet John Marston all had strong connections to members of this network. Not all of these men were well-disposed towards the dominant forces in Elizabeth's court – indeed, a number of them manifested pronounced Essexian tendencies. Some prominent Catholics were also to be found in such 'oppositional' circles, including William Parker, Lord Monteagle – to whom Jonson later addressed *Epigrams* 60, and who may well have provided some measure of patronage to the aspirant writer. At this time Jonson was also directing his attentions to other plausible patrons, including the Earls of Bedford and Rutland, both of whom were in some sympathy with Essex. He may already have been cultivating the group to whom the bulk of the poems later gathered together as *The Forest* are addressed **[101]**, the Sidney family and their relations. Sir Philip Sidney had died fighting for the cause of European Protestantism in 1586, and his surviving relatives maintained similar ideological inflections. Sir Philip's brother, Sir Robert, occupant of the family estate at Penshurst **[102]**, and his nephew William Herbert, Earl of Pembroke, were associated with Essex and Ralegh more than with any other faction at the court of the declining Queen.

Jonson's early connections, therefore, seem both particularly elevated for one of his background and also to be mainly with figures who might be considered in some sense oppositional. It was probably his Westminster schooling and its connection to Camden that offered him contact with the erudite circles of the Inns, and the friends he acquired there no doubt made the possibility of eventual access to grandees such as the Sidney circle less far-fetched. He also had his talent to recommend him, of course, and in reflecting their own interests his writing could be useful to possible patrons. In the anti-court satire of *Cynthia's Revels*, his 1600 play for the children at the Blackfriars **[52]**, or the sideswipes in *Poetaster, or His Arraignment* (1601) at the kind of political machinations which many Essexians saw as the cause of the former favourite's downfall **[55]**, we might think to find evidence of these kind of connections. That he sent a specially dedicated copy of *Cynthia's Revels* to the Countess of Bedford in 1601 seems to support such a suggestion. Yet *Poetaster, or His Arraignment* also encodes other kinds of contemporary reference, speaking not of the relations between patron and client but of those between rival clients. Jonson's characterisation of himself as the noble poet Crites in *Cynthia's Revels* provoked a satiric response in his fellow writer John Marston's 1601 play *What You Will*, written for the rival boy company at St Paul's. With this play, Marston began what theatre historians have long referred to as the 'War of the Theatres' **[54]**. The quarrel escalated with a planned intervention by a third writer, Thomas Dekker, whose *Satiromastix, or The Untrussing of the Humourous Poet*, aimed to incorporate a further, unflattering portrayal of Jonson. Before Dekker's work could be performed, though, Jonson launched a pre-emptive strike with *Poetaster*, in which both Marston and Dekker are transparently and viciously lampooned as intellectually feeble, craven and unscrupulous peddlers of sub-literary trash **[55]**. *Satiromastix* was rewritten to take account of this new salvo; similarly,

Poetaster was augmented with an 'Apologetical Dialogue' responding to Dekker's attack and complaining of the author's treatment at the hands of his rivals, only once spoken on stage. The quarto edition of the play, published in 1602, contained a paragraph noting that 'Authoritie' had prevented its inclusion in the printed text (it eventually appeared in the *Works* of 1616). By this time (contrary to the assumptions of nineteenth century theatre historians [128]) the 'War' between the rivals had come to an end, though perhaps not without a much-debated but never convincingly identified interjection from Shakespeare.

The years that follow offer two almost opposed narratives of Jonson's development. On the one hand, we find increasing professional success. A play for Henslowe in 1602 (the now lost *Richard Crookback*, presumably a version of the history of Richard III) was followed by the tragedy *Sejanus*, initially written with George Chapman and performed by the King's Men in 1603 [57]. Although it may not have been an outstanding success in performance, the publication in 1605 of a revised text solely by Jonson secured its author a wide and generally admiring readership. In that year he also collaborated with Chapman and Marston (with whom he had by now made his peace) on a striking new comedy for the boy players, *Eastward Ho!* [66]. The accession of a new monarch also brought him his first commissions to write courtly entertainments for special occasions, beginning with the performance before Queen Anne and Prince Henry of *A Particular Entertainment at Althorp* on 25 June 1603. This was swiftly followed by *The Entertainment at Highgate*, this time for a reception of the new King as well as his Queen, as well as the 1604 Lord Mayor's pageant and a major role in the construction of the spectacular greeting given to James on his formal entry into London earlier the same year. The commissions from the new court for Twelfth Night masques for 1605 and 1606 might just seem to be the culmination of a simple narrative of success and recognition.

But these self-same years can look very different from another perspective. 1603 was also a year of personal tragedy for Jonson, as his eldest son and namesake died during an outbreak of plague. To Drummond he related a troubling story of a vision of his boy 'with the mark of a bloody cross on his forehead, as if it had been cutted with a sword' (217–18). Something about *Sejanus*, either in performance or at its publication, gave offence to the powerful courtier Henry Howard, Earl of Northampton, and led to Jonson being accused of 'popery and treason' before the Privy Council. No action was taken, as far as we know, but Jonson was not to be so lucky with *Eastward Ho!*. The text performed in 1605 not only contained satiric references to Scots at court – perhaps even to James himself – but had somehow failed to gain the allowance of the Master of the Revels. The judicial response was harsh: the printed edition was censored, and Jonson and Chapman were thrown into jail. Both penned anxious letters to courtiers and patrons who might intervene to forestall any further punishment. Jonson felt able to address his suit to Thomas Howard, Earl of Suffolk, a relative of his erstwhile accuser, as well as to both Cecil (now Lord Salisbury) and Pembroke, which demonstrates that his network of patrons was by then not only quite extensive but also crossed factional boundaries. In this instance, too, he was able to address himself to Esmé Stuart, Lord d'Aubigny, a 'close and dear' relation of the King, one of his Gentlemen of the Bedchamber, and also a practising Catholic – an invaluable contact for someone like Jonson (Donaldson 1997: 61). According to the records of his conversations with Drummond (208–9), the poet even lodged with him for a number of years at some point prior to 1618, during the separation from his wife. The letter-writing paid off, and the errant playwrights were released – probably as a result of Cecil's intercession, who was particularly well-placed to effect such a move.

But Jonson's difficulties were still not over. The Gunpowder Plot brought a new wave of repression down upon England's Catholics. Jonson, as a Catholic with a seemingly Essexian past, might have been looked upon particularly suspiciously – a number of the conspirators had participated in Essex's rising four years previously. Indeed, Jonson was present at a dinner with these very people only about a month before the attack. Could he have known of the plot? Was he perhaps a spy for Cecil? He certainly agreed afterwards to act as a go-between for Salisbury and a Catholic priest who apparently wanted to provide information helpful to the government, but we perhaps only need to class him with his co-religionist Lord Monteagle, who blew the whistle on the Plot when forewarned by letter. In early 1606 Jonson found himself called upon to account for his failure to take Anglican communion, as required by law. His allegiance to Catholicism shaken by the Plot, he undertook to consult with learned divines on doctrinal matters, and thus began the journey back to Anglicanism that was apparently completed by 1610.

Repeatedly in trouble, and yet increasingly successful – the fact that Jonson could be both simultaneously between 1597 and 1606 forces us to reconsider the operations of government in the early seventeenth century. While monarchs may have claimed a divinely acquired right to govern absolutely, and while such an ideology was clearly an important element in the court culture of the age, the actual processes of government seem far less univocal than the theory of absolutism might suggest. Capable of responding with breathtaking violence to the most minor infractions, the state seems only to have applied this force discontinuously, and – perhaps because of the delicate factional balance at court, the differentiation between rival if unequal royal households and the lack of integration between different elements of government – rarely to have acted as a monolithic entity. It was this multiplicity that allowed Jonson to become an important voice in the culture of the very court that, looking from another perspective, could regard him with deep suspicion. Cultivating the patronage of important court figures such as Aubigny could not only protect him from the displeasure, however motivated, of other powerful courtiers or elements of government (the Earl of Northampton, who had accused Jonson of 'popery and treason' over *Sejanus*, was also 'his mortal enemy', he told Drummond, 'for brawling, on a St George's Day, one of his attenders' (271–3)). Such cultivation could also provide him with his own channels of communication to figures at the very top of the hierarchy. Queen Anne seems to have been most strongly behind the early Stuart masques, and she was someone for whom the writer's Catholicism would not have been quite so much of a problem. The fact that the responsibility for assisting the Queen in the preparation of entertainments fell to the Countess of Bedford, one of Anne's ladies-in-waiting and the recipient of a personalised copy of *Cynthia's Revels* a few years earlier, no doubt contributed to the poet's elevation into the royal orbit, even if this made him only one of a number of writers on whom the court might call.

Whatever the source of the first commissions, Jonson nonetheless demonstrated his worth to the dominant court factions as a whole in their execution. The masque for 1606, *Hymenaei*, celebrated the dynastic marriage between the young Earl of Essex, son of the executed favourite, and Lady Frances Howard, daughter of the Earl of Suffolk. This match was clearly performed on the Howards' terms, and in his celebration of the young couple's 'union' Jonson carefully reflected the balance of factional power that underpinned it. Such delicate handling was enough to win him regular masque commissions from then on (as Lord Chamberlain, Suffolk had an important say in the production of court entertainments), as well as the impressive but clearly troubling patronage of as elevated a courtier as the now ennobled Cecil, Lord Salisbury **[106]**. When the latter needed to entertain the royal family in the next few years, it was Jonson to whom he turned for a text **[120]**. Such success, though, also had its downside. As the masque was in essence a composite event, consisting of dance, drama, song and visual spectacle, it could not be the sole work of the poet. He was required to collaborate with the innovative court architect Inigo Jones, an equally talented if similarly self-opinionated artist who went on to design such striking classicist buildings as the Banqueting House at Whitehall, a venue purpose-built for royal festivities which is now the only surviving part of the old palace. Their collaboration was not only mutually advantageous, but also became the source of enduring friction and rivalry, as each claimed the major part in the successful court entertainments they produced together **[116]**. While the partnership lasted for over a quarter of a century, it was also for much of that time perhaps the most fraught professional relationship Jonson endured – poems such as *Epigrams* 115, 'On the Town's Honest Man', which denounces its unnamed but only thinly veiled subject as 'her arrant'st knave' (34) demonstrate as much.

(i) TOWARDS LAUREATESHIP: 1606–1616

By 1607, then, Jonson was an established court artist, enjoying more of the patronage than the hostility of the most powerful factions at the now-established Jacobean court. He was able to take up residence in the fashionable Blackfriars district, where Aubigny himself had a house, and near the theatre in which his earliest bids for such authoritative status had been staged. He was also by now the author of a roaring success in the public theatre, performed by the King's Men in 1606 and then played to continuing approbation at the universities of Oxford and Cambridge. *Volpone, or The Fox* **[70]** made good the damage done by *Sejanus*'s failure in performance and *Eastward Ho!*'s provocation of judicial wrath. The publication of the two former plays and of his masque texts made sure that this success was reinforced by a claim to the kind of intellectual seriousness that would set Jonson apart, in his own mind, from mere playwrights or peddlers of court frippery, and associate him firmly with the gentlemen and wits he felt to be his proper *milieu*. *Sejanus* appeared encrusted in an apparatus of notes and quotations from its classical sources **[136]**, while *Volpone* was printed both with a dedication to the universities where it had been performed and with an 'Epistle Dedicatory' which provided a learned critical justification of the work **[64]**. *Hymenaei*, too, was printed with a similar validation in classical terms **[117]**. In 1609 his comedy *Epicene, or The Silent Woman* **[74]** was performed by the Children of the Queen's Revels, while the following year *The Alchemist* **[79]** was staged at the Blackfriars by the King's Men. The fact that James's cousin, Lady Arbella Stuart, took offence at a possibly unwise allusion to her personal circumstances in the former play did not hinder Jonson's progress: he secured a commission to provide the *Speeches at Prince Henry's Barriers*, an entertainment to accompany the feats of arms performed by the young Prince, heir to the throne, at Twelfth Night celebrations in 1610. Once again, a delicate balancing of political interests was called for, and evidently delivered. Jonson managed to reconcile Henry's identification with an aggressive, patriotic Protestantism with the King's own pursuit of a more pacific foreign policy, tactfully accommodating such differences in a work celebrating Henry's forthcoming investiture as Prince of Wales. The following year Jonson made a further attempt at writing tragedy, penning *Catiline* for performance by the King's Men **[61]**. A political tragedy which harks back to the problems explored in *Poetaster* and *Sejanus*, as well as inevitably evoking memories of the Gunpowder Plot and the recent regicide of Henri IV of France, it did not meet with the same degree of popular acclaim as either *Volpone* or *The Alchemist*.

The next year, Jonson left London for a while. He had been employed by the still imprisoned Sir Walter Ralegh as tutor or governor to his somewhat wayward son, and accompanied the young Wat Ralegh on a tour of France and the Netherlands. Jonson took the opportunity to make the acquaintance of European men of letters, demonstrating to his own satisfaction his fitness for such erudite company. Ralegh's son seems to have been more concerned with less elevated matters, inveigling the drunk and only recently re-converted Jonson into some dangerous anti-Catholic tomfoolery in Paris. On his return to England in the first half of 1613, the poet found his world much changed. Both Salisbury and Prince Henry had died the year before, and the Howard family was now even more clearly in the ascendant. The Howards sought to reinforce their position by cementing a connection with the King's current favourite. James's fondness for handsome young men was no secret, and his high estimation of Robert Carr, Viscount Rochester, ensured that Carr's allies would be equally secure in royal estimation. Frances Howard, daughter of the Earl of Suffolk, who had been married to the Earl of Essex in 1606, was in love with Carr; if a divorce could be secured, their marriage would cement a perhaps unassailable Carr-Howard alliance at the apex of the Jacobean court. Following his favourite's wishes James threw his weight behind the campaign to procure a divorce, on the humiliating grounds of Essex's impotence. There was particularly strong opposition to the proposed match from others at court, including Pembroke, the Archbishop of

Canterbury and Carr's own secretary, Sir Thomas Overbury. This latter found himself imprisoned for his pains, and later died – in circumstances which were to prove as deadly in the end to the ambitions of both Carr and the Howards (see Lindley 1993).

In the meantime the divorce was obtained and Viscount Rochester elevated to the position of Earl of Somerset, so that his bride should suffer no diminution in her status on her remarriage. When the wedding itself took place, Jonson and a fair number of his fellow writers contributed celebratory poems and entertainments. *A Challenge at Tilt* inevitably recalls the masque Jonson had produced only eight years previously for Frances's first marriage, and the poet needs to handle the situation with particular delicacy **[199]**. But Somerset's triumph was to be short-lived. Northampton died in 1614, and Pembroke and his allies had found in the handsome young figure of George Villiers a man to challenge Carr in James's affections. Jonson's masque for the Christmas season 1614/15 offered an opportunity for Villiers to excel in the very skill – dancing – which would most obviously demonstrate his attractiveness to the King. During 1615, when the allegation that Overbury had met his death at the instigation of Lady Somerset and her husband was first made public, Somerset's position was sufficiently in jeopardy to ensure that neither he nor his allies could prevent a judicial inquiry. Convicted of Overbury's murder, the disgrace of the erstwhile favourite and his wife was assured, even though Frances's death sentence was quickly commuted and Carr himself was eventually pardoned. This further shift in the balance of power at court was celebrated in *The Golden Age Restored*, Jonson's masque of early 1616.

Jonson's masques are one of the few consistent features of this period of scandal and factional turmoil. He had proved his serviceability to all the competing groups and thus, perhaps like the King, his elevation above such scrabbling for position. It is perhaps fitting, then, that February 1616 should see him awarded a yearly pension of sixty six pounds by order of the monarch, effectively establishing him – in the words of the grant – as the King's 'well-beloved servant' and the first salaried, if *de facto*, laureate. When Jonson published his collected *Works* later that same year, in an elegant and prestigious format, it too seemed to confirm his elevated status **[37]**. Here were to be found his occasional poems to friends and patrons, demonstrating both his links to courtiers and gentry and his right to dwell in the company of scholars and wits. Here he published his masques, stripped of embarrassing details which might only serve to recall the factional struggles from which they emerged. Here, also, integrated into his other work and dedicated to noble or esteemed patrons, were his plays for the public and private theatres. Some early and collaborative works, as well as the perhaps too recent *Bartholomew Fair* (1614) **[84]**, were omitted, but the *Works* went some way to establishing the clear outlines of a Jonsonian canon which would, the volume implied, bear comparison with the classical literature on which so much of it drew.

(j) A JACOBEAN SUMMER: 1616–1625

The years that followed have often been painted as the beginnings of a decline. It is true that Jonson's later dramas failed to win the unqualified approbation of subsequent critics, and worth noting that only two further plays – *The Devil is an Ass* (1616) **[89]** and *The Staple of News* (1626) **[91]** – were written between 1614 and 1629. But rather than an indication of decline, such low productivity for the public stage is a mark of Jonson's secure place at the heart of Jacobean court culture. His efforts and energies were directed elsewhere, towards poetry and towards the masque – a genre that criticism has not customarily regarded as highly as drama but which should not necessarily be regarded as inherently less challenging. Between 1616 and the end of James's reign he produced some of his most elaborate and pioneering masques, making full use of the range of anti-naturalistic possibilities such an art form offered and extending its scope way beyond that of an ornate frame for courtly dancing **[115]**. Perhaps the most striking proof of this is the long masque commissioned by Villiers (now, by the King's favour, Marquis of Buckingham) in 1621, and performed before James no less than three times between August and September that year. *The Gypsies Metamorphosed* **[119]** cast Buckingham and his friends and family as gypsies who tell the fortunes of their royal audience before being transformed by the King's presence into their own, noble personages. Buckingham and his fellow masquers have elaborate speaking parts, and regale the King with sly, private jokes which would only really be appreciated by those on the inside of this elevated coterie. Jonson was paid the sum of one hundred pounds by Buckingham, but it was clearly money well spent. James loved the masque, and as a mark of his favour offered Jonson the reversion of (essentially, a place in the queue for) the job of Master of the Revels. The poacher of 1605 could now look forward to a gamekeeping future – although, in the end, Jonson died before the man he was to succeed.

Jonson was by now something of a public celebrity, too. He was dignified with honorary degrees by both Oxford and Cambridge, and delivered lectures in rhetoric at London's Gresham College. His name was among those put forward for membership of a proposed 'Academy Royal' first mooted to Parliament in 1621. In 1618 he set out to walk to Scotland, his arrival in Edinburgh being marked by a banquet in his honour. He stayed until January 1619, finding hospitality at the house of William Drummond of Hawthornden, a poet whose records of his conversations with Jonson have proved invaluable to subsequent biographers. Drummond does not seem to have approved entirely of his guest, and his pithy concluding judgement on the King's poet deserves to be quoted in full for the complex portrait it paints:

> He is a great lover and praiser of himself, a contemner and scorner of others, given rather to lose a friend than a jest, jealous of every word and action of those about him (especially after drink, which is one of the elements in which he liveth), a dissembler of ill parts which reign in him, a bragger of some good that he wanteth, thinketh nothing well but what either he himself or some of his friends and countrymen hath said or done. He is passionately kind and angry, careless either to gain or keep, vindicative, but, if he be well answered, at himself.
>
> (605–12)

Here, certainly, is a picture of a man with a lively sense of his own worth and achievements – especially, perhaps, in his fears that they might go unrecognised. Back home in London Jonson installed himself at the centre of a social network predicated on the repeated recognition of his talents. Grown hugely fat after many years of convivial suppers and drinking sessions held with friends at the Mermaid Tavern in Bread Street, the poet oversaw a change of venue for such events in the early 1620s to the Apollo Room at the Devil and St Dunstan Tavern, near Temple Bar on the boundary between the city and Westminster. The sessions held there symbolised the coming together of the 'Tribe of Ben' [110], the poet laureate now gathering around himself a community of 'sons' who not only shared his fondness for wine and wit, but also placed themselves self-consciously in his train. Among them were such coming men as Robert Herrick, James Howell, Thomas May, William Cartwright, Thomas Carew and Sir Lucius Cary [109], many of whom were to be both made and broken by the civil wars of the 1640s. Although Jonson's own sons were now long dead, in this substitute progeny his own authority as a father might be revivified.

However, problems were in evidence. In 1623 a large part of Jonson's library was destroyed in a catastrophic fire, lamented in a verse 'execration' listing the valuable and various works which had succumbed to the flames **[112]**. Moreover, the Jacobean peace assumed by such coterie pieces as *The Gypsies Metamorphosed* was itself in some peril. Since 1618 Europe had been descending rapidly into a conflict that would last three decades and occasion some of the most widespread brutality witnessed on the continent before the twentieth century. The beginning of the 'Thirty Years' War' had involved James's own daughter Elizabeth, married in 1613 to the middle European Elector Palatine, and now forced into exile with her ill-fated husband by the Catholic Hapsburg Emperor. In the early 1620s support for armed intervention in European troubles had gained more than a foothold in influential English circles, running directly in opposition to James's own unpopular policy of securing peace with Spain, still Europe's preeminent Catholic power, through the dynastic marriage of his own son and heir Prince Charles to the Spanish Infanta. When Charles and Buckingham (elevated to a Dukedom in May 1623) set off on a foolhardy mission to arrange the 'Spanish Match' themselves, only to meet with a distinctly cool reception from their Iberian hosts, James's policy lay in tatters; indeed, the Prince and the favourite returned to champion hostility to Spain through the proposal of a marriage to the French Princess Henrietta Maria, offering a clear challenge to the old King's direction of affairs. Royal entertainments needed to negotiate all these difficulties, a task that sometimes eluded even someone as used to mediating between differences as Jonson. His 1624 masque to celebrate Charles's return, *Neptune's Triumph for the Return of Albion*, was cancelled due to diplomatic problems with the Spanish ambassador. Such tasks were perhaps made harder by the increasing alienation of some of Jonson's old friends and patrons from James's rule. Pembroke, who had been instrumental in Buckingham's rise to power, was now his rival; outside the court, figures such as John Selden were becoming more clearly identified with an organised opposition to royal policy which was articulated in the occasional parliaments called by the King.

(k) RETURNING TO THE STAGE: 1625–1637

These problems did not die with James in 1625. The first years of his son's reign were marked by increasingly strident parliamentary opposition to his policies, in which not only Selden but the venerable Sir Robert Cotton were strongly involved. Charles's response was always to raise the stakes, seeking new ways such as 'forced loans' to escape the kinds of financial check placed on his rule by Parliament. In

1628, with the political tension already particularly high, Buckingham was assassinated. His death provoked a bout of repressive activity from the government in which even Jonson found himself under suspicion of sedition. Perhaps because of his contacts with oppositional figures he was identified as the author of verses in praise of the assassin and interrogated by the Attorney General, though he vehemently denied responsibility. Meanwhile Charles dissolved the Parliament of 1629 and resolved on a policy of 'personal rule', attempting reform of church and state that generated an increasingly bold, broad and populist opposition.

There were other reasons why these were not good years for Jonson. Now in his late fifties, with many years of corpulence behind him, he suffered a debilitating – though perhaps not his first – stroke in 1628, and it has long been thought that he was subsequently confined to his house in Westminster until his death. It seems, however, that he was still agile enough in 1632 to walk in the Lord Mayor's procession that year, so perhaps reports of his incapacitation – beginning with Jonson's own frequent complaints about his condition in his letters to various patrons – have been somewhat exaggerated (Bland 1998: 169). His masque commissions had dried up, with Charles marking the difference between his court and that of his father by economising on such Jacobean splendours. It seems, too, that his pension was not now being paid with anything like the regularity necessary to keep want at bay. Jonson's often repressed connection to the guilds and civic structures of London provided a route to some relief, with the offer in 1628 of the post of City Chronologer (a cross between hagiographer and historian, and the appointment which required his participation in the Lord Mayor's procession). Even this was not without its problems: between 1631 and 1634 Jonson's failure to perform the role resulted in his remuneration being withheld. In his relations with the court, though, matters improved in 1630, with Charles acknowledging the family debt to Jonson in increasing his pension to one hundred pounds a year. The following year also brought an involvement in two new masques for the Caroline court, deft contributions to the iconographic repertoire of the government of Charles and his queen. The respite was short-lived: Jonson quarrelled disastrously with his collaborator, Inigo Jones, and when the two men could no longer work together it was the poet who proved the more replaceable. His career as masque-writer by royal appointment was finally over.

The venom and persistence of his attacks on Jones **[98, 116]** indicate how keenly Jonson must have felt his exclusion. He was still capable of attracting the patronage of highly placed courtiers, however, and in the early 1630s we find him among the clients of Charles's deeply unpopular Lord Treasurer, Richard Weston (eventually Earl of Portland) and the accomplished William Cavendish, Earl of Newcastle, an amateur poet and dramatist who was to become tutor to Charles's eldest surviving son and a leader of the royalist armies during the civil war **[97]**. For Newcastle Jonson wrote his final masques, performed before the King during visits to the Cavendish properties at Welbeck and Bolsover in 1633 and 1634 respectively. Even here the feud with Jones intruded, *Love's Welcome to Bolsover* featuring a comic turn by one Coronell Vitruvius, a thinly disguised caricature of the architect.

Yet while his career as a laureate faltered, his involvement in the theatre – perhaps out of necessity – was startlingly renewed. Since *The Devil is an Ass* had been performed by the King's Men in 1616, only *The Staple of News* (for the same company) had been staged, a play which anyway made use of ideas and material originally crafted for inclusion in the masques *The News from the New World Discovered in the Moon* (1620) and *Neptune's Triumph*. In 1629 the sophisticated audience of the Caroline private theatre were treated to *The New Inn* **[93]**, but on Jonson's own account the play was far from a success. Despite his own declared renunciation of the stage **[93]** he returned in 1632 with another innovative drama, *The Magnetic Lady* **[96]**, and in 1633 *A Tale of a Tub* **[98]** was staged. This was a deliberately archaic comedy, which yet managed to incorporate more satiric attacks on Inigo Jones. Evidently too much for the licensing authorities, who required that this personal attack be removed from the play as performed, they were partially restored to the first printed edition and so persist in the inherited text.

Though Jonson began two other dramatic projects, neither was ever finished **[99]**. In his final years he was as concerned to order and publish his already completed texts, continuing the attention to such matters evidenced in the *Works* of 1616. His plans for a successor volume were not to be realised during his lifetime, however, and had to await the efforts of his literary executor, Sir Kenelm Digby, whose late wife had been immortalised by Jonson as his 'muse', and who ensured that Jonson's extant works were published posthumously. The poet himself died on 16 August 1637, and was buried – after being 'accompanied to his grave with all or the greatest part of the nobility and gentry then in the town', as the herald put it (Kay 1995: 183) – in the royal resting place of Westminster Abbey, under a stone inscribed 'O Rare Ben Jonson'. It was not far, of course, from where he had started: only yards away he had received his formative education at the hands of William Camden. But the journey he had travelled since then was a rare one indeed.

Further reading

All modern biographies are indebted to the account of Jonson's life given in *HSS*, I, and to the documentary sources also reproduced in that edition. There can be little doubt that this version is now showing its age, however, and some of its datings and assumptions are particularly questionable. The Oxford editors had the added burden of dealing with the extensive mythology surrounding Jonson, much of it built on hearsay, the gossipy accounts of Jonson's life given by seventeenth-century antiquarians and biographers, or the later extrapolations by critics for whom Jonson's only significant role is as a foil to the genius and humanity of Shakespeare **[125]**. But Jonson has been well served by more modern biographers, and it is to the following narratives that the reader should initially look. Miles (1986) is a readable and engaging account, while Riggs (1989) delves deeper if more speculatively into Jonson's psychological make-up, and has a keener eye for the particularly telling detail. Nonetheless, he is not always alive to the contrasting interpretations that might be placed on the evidence. Kay (1995) follows in the footsteps of Parfitt (1976) and Dutton (1983) in marrying biographical narrative to a critical account of the Jonsonian canon, and is extremely scrupulous in his handling of his sources.

PART II

WORK

(a) INTRODUCTION

This section provides a descriptive account of, and indicative commentary on, the body of Jonson's writing. It concentrates on the dramatic work that has been the major focus of critical attention over the years, giving at least a brief account of each of his extant and complete plays, while also providing a more selective outline of his important work as a non-dramatic poet, a writer of masques, and author of the strange, unique *Timber: or Discoveries*. Resisting the urge to reduce Jonson's career to a simple narrative of progressive development, the section nonetheless draws connections and suggests comparisons between works. As commentary, it constellates a series of overlapping Jonsonian tropes and topoi – rhetorical structures and thematic motifs – to ground the encounter with the vast and disparate body of Jonson criticism that makes up Part III. The word as deed or event, the ethical or political responsibility of writing and the importance of theatricality or the performance are all prominent elements in this constellation, and each element impacts on the others. This commentary is supported by an account of the literary-historical milieu of the texts: the circumstances of their production and circulation, their relation to other works of the time or of antiquity. Indeed, thematic commentary and this account often overlap, for Jonson's work often makes such circumstances its explicit concern. It can be described as insistently *self-reflexive*, a quirk which plays an important role in shaping the ways in which critics have read Jonson over the years.

(b) WORKS

At the turn of the seventeenth century, the notion that the plays of a mere English dramatist could be accounted 'works' was not widely entertained. Works were the province of classical writers, those figures enshrined at the heart of the humanist curriculum that laid the foundations of every Renaissance education [9, 10]. Authorship, too, was a status and an aura which attached itself to those classical figures rather than to the jobbing playwrights of the London theatres. In fact, the Jonsonian coinage 'playwright' said it all: this was one trade among the many pursued in the booming city, and one which despite its novelty existed within the corporate, guild-like structures of the theatre companies [12]. A classical authorship, subsisting in the monumental name that united a series of apparently autonomous, unchanging texts, seemingly unmarked by the economic processes of commodity production, could not be more different from this workaday product.

In 1616, however, the majority of Jonson's dramatic efforts were published in a folio edition, a high-quality and expensive format which positioned his book firmly in opposition to the pamphlet and chapbook literature dominating the cheaper end of the market. The format's grandeur was matched by the volume's title, 'The Works of Benjamin Jonson', and by the associations with classical literature which cluster together on the titlepage. Its motto from the Roman poet Horace – Jonson's foremost classical role model – ('Neque, me ut miretur turba, laboro: / Contentus paucis lectoribus' – 'I do not work so that the crowd may admire me: I am contented with a few readers') establishes that this is not only a volume for a highly educated minority, but also one which is about as far from a performance text – and in particular the context of commercial performance – as one could get. The plays included are set out according to the format found in early editions of classical drama (Riggs 1989: 221). The volume is also prefaced by a portrait of Jonson as author, not as playwright – he is crowned with the bays of the classical poet.

Such pretensions were an obvious target: one brief squib commented, in mock puzzlement, 'Pray tell me Ben, where doth the mystery lurk, / What others call a play you call a work' (HSS, IX, 13), while another critic thought it absurd that 'the very plays of a modern poet are called in print Works' (Miles 1986: 177). The novelty of Jonson's strategy, though, is perhaps more nuanced than such comments might suggest. The disgrace of vernacular drama, for a start, lay less in its modernity or its Englishness than in its incorporation into a new and unprecedented culture industry. In severing the connections between his own drama and that industry, removing it as far as possible from the context of its production and first circulation, Jonson's Folio helps its contents to get over their past (though it ought also to be noted that this strategy was one that Jonson's earlier quarto editions of his plays had been pursuing, right from the publication of Every Man Out of His Humour in 1600 [Barish 1981: 136–7]). It does so not simply by effacement, but also by recasting that past as a narrative of something other than disgrace. So the Folio's various dedications to the dominant institutions of Stuart England – the court, Oxford and Cambridge, the lawyers' Inns of Court [6] – and to aristocrats and figures prominent in and around those institutions, obscure any link to the commodity culture of the public theatres. Furthermore, they are printed in the company of Jonson's court masques, his *Epigrams*, and the collection of lyrics entitled *The Forest*, texts which might speak of other contexts and occasions.

It is not the case, however, that the printing of masques and poetry would necessarily have been entirely free from controversy. The printed text of a court masque might always be thought to miss the point somewhat – despite Jonson's assertions to the contrary – in its inability to represent the dancing around which the whole confection was assembled **[118]**. The kind of occasional verse which makes up the bulk of the Folio's non-dramatic poetry was more commonly and acceptably circulated in manuscript, copied or passed round among relatively homogenous circles (of which the author was usually a member) at the Inns, at court or in the church and universities, often finding its way into print only after its author's death or without an authorial imprimatur. The commitment of his plays and these texts to print, for open sale, constitutes two potentially indecorous breaches of context: either in making available to an undifferentiated public the private conversations of a delimited network, or in tearing playtexts from their origin in the playhouses of Blackfriars or Southwark and pasting them into the framework appropriate to a classical inheritance of which they can only fall short. In its use of an expensive and exclusive format Jonson's volume clearly aims to forestall the first breach, while its reconfiguration of his plays as reading texts for the very auditory with which he converses in his non-dramatic writing helps to proof him against the second.

This is the difficult terrain negotiated by the Folio, a terrain unfamiliar to those of us who read his work almost four hundred years after its first receptions, after four centuries in which the breaches of decorum broached by Jonson (though not just by Jonson) have become not only decorous but old-fashioned. But it is not something that we can easily ignore, because – as many critics have noted – the circumstances of production and circulation have a habit, in Jonson (though hardly just in Jonson), of figuring in the text itself in ways that inevitably question the comfortable separation of text and context. Their self-reflexivity, in other words, ensures that when we speak of 'work' in relation to Jonson we have to mean not only the monolithic 'book' but also a process, or processes – of writing and reading, making and distributing, performing and watching, and the process of reflecting on those processes. As we might imagine, such multiplying processes are not always easy to follow. But an awareness of their significance has long been the starting point for the critical engagement with Jonson.

Further reading

Brady and Herendeen (1991) offer a valuable collection of essays on the Folio of 1616, expanding effectively on the basis established in Newton (1982). Butler (1993a) locates Jonson's book squarely in the context of its patronage relationships, while Loewenstein (1985) and McLuskie (1991) couple this focus to an exploration of the commercial basis of dramatic and literary production. Helgerson (1983) addresses the significance of laureateship in Jonson directly, situating his occupation of the role in the context of his poetic contemporaries, predecessors and successors.

(c) LOOSE ENDS AND FALSE STARTS: *THE CASE IS ALTERED* AND *EVERY MAN IN HIS HUMOUR*

The author of the 'Works', crowned with bays, looms over the matter from which he draws his authority. 1616 was the year that Jonson received his royal pension, famously becoming the 'first poet laureate' in the process **[30]**, and 'Jonson's contemporaries', as Martin Butler has said, 'immediately recognized the claims for laureate status that were implied in the publication of such a corpus' (Butler 1999: 5). His book presented to the world a narrative of the singular and steady production of an authorial as well as textual corpus. Yet such a narrative necessarily ignores or effaces the traces of contingency or accident, the disruptions of the unforeseen and unintended that left their mark on Jonson's progress, just as it is unable to make sense of that which comes after the apotheosis it posits as its climax. So it is that Jonson's book leaves out all mention of those other voices which had contributed to the author's, in excluding all the collaboratively authored plays on which he had worked. *Sejanus* appeared, following the precedent of the 1605 quarto edition, purged of the 'good share' contributed by 'a second pen' (probably Chapman: see Corballis 1979), as the quarto's address 'To the Readers' put it (and the omission of this address in the Folio therefore suppressed even the memory of the collaboration). Similarly, Jonson omits tonalities of his own which are for whatever reason not felt to contribute to the laureate voice, his additions to Kyd's *Spanish Tragedy*, for example, a now lost play such as *Richard Crookback*, and early work like *The Case is Altered*. For the Folio, Jonson's career begins with *Every Man in His Humour*: in his dedication of that play to his old schoolmaster, William Camden, he declares that he is offering him 'the first' of his 'fruits' (11).

Yet it is hard to see why *The Case is Altered* should be written off as a loose end, destined not to feature in the roll of honour, for it shares important characteristics with the false start Jonson later made out of *Every Man in His Humour*. It is based heavily on the Roman comic drama of Plautus **[10]**, combining the plotlines of two of his plays in a dense mix typical of late Elizabethan comedy and familiar to modern readers in Shakespeare's *Comedy of Errors*. From the *Captivi* ('The Captives') Jonson takes the story of a long lost son captured and ill-treated by his unwitting father, while from *Aulularia* ('The Pot of Gold') he borrows the triangulation of a miser, his gold and his daughter, and the threats to this triangulation presented by a myriad of suitors. Both plots are welded together ingeniously enough: while Count Ferneze of Milan discovers that the foreign slave he has been persecuting is in fact Camillo, the son he lost in the chaos of war, Rachel, seeming daughter to the miser Jacques, is revealed as the sister of Camillo's French master, Lord Chamont, abducted in infancy by Jacques, who was in fact her father's disgruntled steward. The conditions are thus in place for the restoration of the gold to its rightful owner, and for Rachel's marriage to Ferneze's other son, her suitor Paulo. The case is altered; and its alteration is the banishment of all confusion and disturbance in the resolution appropriate to a romantic comedy. Even the desires of Rachel's other suitors are somehow purged, and they are left – as Christophero puts it – 'content' (V.xiii.36).

This resolution has not always convinced (Barton 1984: 41), and it seems that the play's fascination is primarily with the mechanics of narrative, despite the disparagement of plotting in the exchange between Antonio Balladino, Juniper and Onion in Act I scene ii. Which is not to say that it is without other interest, offering hints of future Jonsonian commonplaces or a neat counterpoint to later configurations. The character of Balladino, the bad poet, offers not only an early example of the kind of manoeuvre which was to constitute the 'war of the theatres' **[24]**, but also one of Jonson's first attempts at making a drama out of his writing, placing the processes and categories of composition into the very experience they animate. Around Jacques de Prie cluster fetishistic figurations of money which are to be revisited, most notably, in *Volpone*. And Ferneze's grief for his son Paulo, when he thinks him betrayed and mistreated at the hands of his enemy, forms an interesting counterpoint to Jacques's obsessive attachment to his gold. As the miser sees a plot to steal his gold at the heart of any attempt to woo his daughter, so Ferneze locates a 'complot to betray my son' (IV.xi.21) in the change of identity practised by Camillo and his master, Chamont. His grief for Paulo produces a form of madness: he denounces Maximilian, his ally, and prepares to seek revenge in the killing of Camillo, whose true identity is as yet unknown, despite the breach of all civilised behaviour that this action would constitute (as Maximilian points out: Act V, scene ix, 11–12). In fact, Ferneze seems to have become for the moment the protagonist of a revenge tragedy, echoing the example of the genre best known to and most beloved of the Elizabethan audience. *The Spanish Tragedy* tells the tale of Hieronymo, mad in pursuit of vengeance on his son's murderers. In 1601–2 Jonson was to receive two payments for writing 'new additions' to Thomas Kyd's old play, additions which were particularly concerned to elaborate the protagonist's grief for his son and his descent into madness (Foakes and Rickert 1961: 182, 203; Barton 1984: 13–28). They were additions he foreshadowed, if only in outline, in *The Case is Altered*.

More immediately, though, this brief engagement with the pathological distortion of personality presents a taste of the mechanistic psychology of *humours* which was to feature, in various ways and to differing degrees, throughout Jonson's dramatic career. According to a widespread account derived from the classical physiology of Galen, the health of the human body depended on the balance of its four constituent humours, or elemental fluids. Thus a healthy person was defined as someone in whom blood, bile (or black bile), phlegm and choler (or yellow bile) were in harmony, and therefore not in symptomatic evidence. Yet if the humours became unbalanced the symptoms which resulted were not simply bodily, because each humour was also responsible for generating particular behavioural effects.

The thinking is hard to summarise exactly, largely because there were sufficient variations and appropriations to render it somewhat amorphous. It was, for example, used to account for specific episodes of disease, events that befell a pre-existing psyche, but also deployed to account for the constitution of varieties of character, what we might call personality types. Furthermore, as its presence in Elizabethan drama demonstrates, it had long since ceased to be a rigidly medical discourse. In the drama of the late 1590s the language of the humours performs both an explanatory, classificatory function, and also features as a discourse whose particular application, if not general validity, might be contested. We might suppose as much from Jonson's classic account in the Induction to *Every Man Out of His Humour*, where it is given a literal definition first, and then also described as 'metaphor':

As when some one peculiar quality
Doth so possess a man that it doth draw
All his affects, his spirits, and his powers,
In their confluctions, all to run one way;
This may be truly said to be a humour.
                                        (Induction, 105–9)

Yet a third level of significance is also admitted, if contested, in this account: humour as affectation, rather than affect. This is described as an 'abuse of this word humour' (Induction, 80), but it is in fact one of the central forms in which the comedy of humours configures its object.

The precedent for Jonson's first explicit engagement with this discourse was provided by his friend and rival George Chapman, whose play *An Humourous Day's Mirth* was performed with particular success in 1597. Shakespeare's *Merry Wives of Windsor* incorporated extensive ridicule of 'humorous' characters the same year. So *Every Man in His Humour* emerged in dialogue with the works of Jonson's contemporaries as much as from his own earlier work. It is also a play that might be described as being in dialogue with itself: it exists in two, significantly different versions, the quarto text of 1601 and that of the 1616 Folio. The most striking difference between the texts is a change in location, the quarto being set – at least nominally – in Florence, a standard Italianate location for the 1590s stage, while the revised version is firmly located in contemporary London. The characters swap the glamour of names such as Lorenzo, Thorello, Giuliano, Prospero and Hesperida for the local colour of Knowell, Kitely, Downright, Wellbred and Bridget. Bobadilla appears as Captain Bobadil; Matheo and Stephano mutate gently into Matthew and Stephen. Yet this is not just a case of rebranding: the Folio text is awash with topical references. The social structure exhibited in the arrangement of such diverse types as Clement, the urban magistrate, Cob, the water-carrier, and Stephen, the 'country gull', is brought home to the reader of the revised text in a manner that the quarto avoids. The new location allows the employment of particularly contemporary locutions, too, and gives the language of the Folio text a colloquial robustness not found so strongly in the quarto.

For all this, both texts display the debt to the comedy of Plautus and Terence found in *The Case is Altered*. In both quarto and Folio the plot includes the efforts of an outraged father, Lorenzo Senior/Old Knowell, to frustrate his son's attempts to live an independent life, attempts which culminate in a marriage arranged without paternal sanction. Edward Knowell is assisted in his attempts to evade his father by the wit and ingenuity of the family servant, Musco/Brainworm, whose actions mark a wily transfer of allegiance from the waning powers of his old master to the ascendant authority of the son. This central plot is somewhat attenuated, though, as the play puts as much emphasis on displaying and ridiculing an array of 'humorous' characters. The Prologue to the Folio text announces its focus on:

> persons, such as Comedy would choose,
> When she would show an image of the times,
> And sport with human follies, not with crimes.
> (Prologue, 22–4)

These 'follies' include the pathological humours of Thorello/Kitely and Giuliano/Downright, jealousy and irascibility respectively, and perhaps also – shades of Ferneze and Hieronymo – the obsessive fatherhood of Old Knowell. Yet the play is more strikingly concerned to 'sport' with Stephen, Matthew and Bobadil. What these figures share is not a 'character' forged by bodily imbalance, but an altogether more complex psychology. Bobadil is determined to be thought a choleric soldier, and acts accordingly; Matthew would be an amorous poet, and plagiarises shamelessly to make himself so; Stephen's pretensions are less focused. In other words, these characters ought to be thought of as the *lack* of character, figures in whom character is only a character-shaped longing. Bobadil, Stephen and Matthew exemplify the quarto text's definition of a humour: 'a monster bred in a man by self love, and affectation, and fed by folly' (III.i.157–8). A monster in a man, the inhuman in the human, bred out of a self-love that would be best thought of as a *desire* for selfhood. It is this that splits the humorous self in two as an ongoing *misidentification* with an ideal, an identification that can never quite be completed.

These humours are prodded, goaded and encouraged to heights of absurdity in a chain of occurrences that suggests no easy purgation. The end, when it comes, is the first instance of a Jonsonian signature piece – the judicial intervention. Justice Clement dominates Act V, discovering, ordering and resolving the disputes of the preceding Acts, sanctioning the marriage of Edward Knowell and Bridget, exposing Bobadil and Matthew. While the former is finally silenced, the latter's books of stolen verse are seized and burnt. The play, though, is careful not to construe this as a kind of condemnation of poetry in the interests of political discourse, reminiscent of Plato's *Republic*. For in response to Old Knowell's expressed scorn for verse, the Folio's Clement responds:

> Nay, no speech, or act of mine be drawn against such, as profess it worthily. They are not born every year, as an alderman. There goes more to the making of a good poet, than a sheriff ...
>
> (V.v.33–5)

Clement's declaration replaces a much more fulsome defence of poetry mounted by Edward Knowell in the quarto text. In this context, though, a brief statement is all that is required, as long as it issues from a figure who embodies judgement. Clement speaks for authority, in the language of justice. His speech offers an intertextual hint of the esteem in which poetry is here being held – the claim that poets 'are not born every year' recalls one of Jonson's favourite observations, in which poet and ruler are likened to each other in their rarity **[104, 155]**. The execution of law and the work of poetry are thus briefly but deftly intertwined in Clement's defence, in a manner which would become crucial to the development of the Jonsonian poetic. It is perhaps less of a surprise than we might have thought to see a laureate Jonson finding in this play, rather than *The Case is Altered*, sufficient moments that spoke of his royal progress to stamp this as its beginning.

There are still what might seem to be some loose ends, however. Chief among them is Brainworm, the servant, whose career throughout the play presents an interesting comparison with the humorous gulls. Bobadil is not the only seeming soldier to be found around town, peddling fictions, nor Matthew the only figure claiming others' lines as his own. Brainworm, in taking on his first disguise, commits himself to 'creat[ing] an intolerable sort of lies' (II.iv.2–3), and later describes this as 'the day of my metamorphosis', during which he has 'run through' a number of different 'shape[s]' (V.iii.72–3). He has been a consummate actor, disguising his language (as Old Knowell comments, V.iii.70), a performance existing in recitation. In this he is necessarily a parasitic creature, like Matthew and Bobadil, living off the activity of others – as is indicated both by his name in the quarto, Musco, meaning 'tree-moss', and the Folio's more disturbing 'Brainworm'. This appellation not only locates the parasite deep inside the host but gives it too an intellectual aspect: he is an infection of mental faculties and structures of knowledge, a disease of reason. Yet a cure, it seems, is not needed, because Clement *allows* the parasitic mimicry of this figure even as he condemns the pretences of Matthew and Bobadil: 'Thou hast done, or assisted to nothing, in my judgement, but deserves to be pardoned for the wit o' the offence' (V.iii.96–8).

Brainworm may be, as Anne Barton puts it, the 'incarnation' of a 'kind of anti-classical poetry, irregular and wild' (Barton 1984: 55), but he is retroactively tamed by Clement's indulgence. In this he is like the Folio text itself, which in its last words declares its mimicry and shape-shifting performed 'With the allowance of the Master of Revels'. Such an admission to civility, like the concomitant expulsion of other kinds of irregularity, can only take place for as long as Clement's authority to pronounce sentence, his *capacity* to perform in language the work of judgement, is itself beyond question. That questioning does not necessarily happen here – but this is not to be the parasite's final word.

Further reading

The Case is Altered has not received much exclusive attention – Hannaford (1980) and Mack (1997) are significant exceptions. But Dutton (1983), Barton (1984) and Kay (1995) give good accounts of this play as a starting point for Jonson's subsequent work. The chapter on 'Character' in Womack (1986) is an invaluable aid to thinking about the juncture of psychology and fiction found in the comedy of humours. Holdsworth (1979) collects together essays on *Every Man in His Humour*, while Miola (2000) is an edition of the Quarto text of this play to set against the more broadly available editions based on the Folio revision. Barton (1984) again offers a soundly argued account of the play and its place in Jonson's development.

(d) THEATRES OF JUDGEMENT: *EVERY MAN OUT OF HIS HUMOUR*, *CYNTHIA'S REVELS*, *POETASTER*

The association of poetry and governance that we find in *Every Man In* establishes the stakes. Writing is shadowed as law, set in the context of the regulation of civil society. This, obviously, is both a political and an ethical context – it is precisely what ethics and politics denote. In the plays that follow, the question is taken rather further than the evocation of the figure of Justice Clement allows, both by exploring the work of judgement in greater detail and in making absolutely explicit the lines of authority in which poetry is actually to be situated. In passing, we might note that the Folio dedicated *Every Man Out of His Humour* to the Inns of Court, and *Cynthia's Revels* to the Court of the sovereign himself. And the fact that these plays also put satire on the stage shortly after the bishops had proscribed its appearance in print makes the juridical context even more pertinent **[22]**.

In some ways, then, *Every Man Out of His Humour* could be described as a sequel to Jonson's earlier play. As the title would suggest, it is once again the display of humour which is to allow judgement to be exemplified. So the audience is confronted with Sordido, the miserly farmer, who plans to profiteer from an anticipated grain shortage, and his brother, Sogliardo, a rustic with the desire to be an urbane gentleman. They are accompanied by Fungoso, Sordido's son, who wishes to be at the cutting edge of courtly fashion, and Fastidius Brisk, the not particularly successful courtier he mimics. Deliro, a citizen, is excessively uxorious, while his wife, Fallace – 'proud', 'perverse' and 'officious' in the words of the brief character Jonson prefixed to the printed text of the play – dotes on Brisk. Puntarvolo is something of a puzzle. Described as 'vainglorious' (Characters, 13), he is fond of amorous role-playing with his wife, courting her at their window as if he were a knight from Sidney's *Arcadia* and she an unknown damsel – the real problem may lie in his willingness to have the touching scene watched by the play's other characters. He is also a gambler, wagering on his ability to get himself, his wife and his pets safely to and from the court of the Great Turk. Carlo Buffone is a more straightforward case, 'a public, scurrilous and profane jester', a peddler of 'absurd similes' that 'will transform any person into deformity ... His religion his railing, and his discourse ribaldry' (Characters, 22, 29). Macilente, a malcontented scholar, is simply consumed by envy.

Here are pathological, metaphorical and affected humours. These layers of delusion are given form in a series of scenes taking up most of Act III and set in the middle aisle of St Paul's cathedral (a popular meeting place of Elizabethan London, a place to be seen, to trade, and to catch the latest news – despite their Italianate names, these characters are local). The characters enter in groups, meet others, are rearranged, and leave, all in the constant movement of a choreographed promenade (described in detail in Ostovich 1999: 82–90). Paul's Walk is the stage on which humours were meant to be performed.

It is interesting to note that the broad reach of this play brings women in under the umbrella of its pathology – or perhaps it does not, given the early modern association of the female body with a kind of incontinence which would make women, in this scheme, *normally* humorous. A humour is after all fundamentally *liquid*, 'fluxure and humidity, / ... wanting power to contain itself' as the authorial Asper puts it in the Induction (96–7). Humorous behaviour is the result of these liquids flowing beyond their proper bounds, and women's bodies were customarily 'leaky vessels' to Jonson's culture (Paster 1987 and 1998). Thus there is often something less than manly about the humorous character: in spending his time in attendance on court ladies the fashionable Fastidius Brisk displays one of the prime symptoms of effeminacy, while Fungoso, the would-be courtier, actually swoons at a point (for him, at any rate) of crisis. Fashion itself is described by Buffone as 'flux of apparel' (IV.viii.112), a liquidity in which the malaise of the humour and the imperfection of women meet and reinforce each other. In designating Deliro and Fallace as humorous, then, the play evokes the gendered language of a physiological imbalance in order to declare their marriage *sick*: his failure to contain and control her reproduces at an interpersonal level the overflowing of boundaries in the humorous body.

But this is *Every Man Out of His Humour*, and the action of the play ('plot' would be too strong a word) proceeds apace toward purgation. For one, the end comes quickly: Sordido is knocked out of his humour by the end of Act III, and takes no further part in the play. The rest, with the exception of Macilente, have a series of humiliations inflicted on them in the final act. Puntarvolo's dog is killed, Brisk is left to rot in a debtors' prison, Deliro is confronted with the sight of his wife in the courtier's arms. Most shockingly, Buffone has his scurrilous mouth sealed with hot wax. This generalised punishment, a particularly forceful exhibition of quasi-judicial violence, is instituted though not always executed by Macilente. In turn, his humour simply evaporates as soon as the undeserving rich – its object – have all received what was coming to them. It is thus figured almost as an *anti*-humour, making him into an instrument of a justice that stands behind him, primarily in the potent authorial figure of Asper. It is Asper who dominates the opening Induction, is identified there as playing Macilente in the forthcoming drama, and who reoccupies the personage of Macilente at the end, once his humour has evaporated. Asper (the name means 'rough') is primarily a satirist, who at the play's opening has declared his resolution – against the advice of his more temperate companions – to 'strip the ragged follies of the time / Naked, as at their birth ... and with a whip of steel, / Print wounding lashes in their iron ribs' (Induction, 17–20).

Asper/Macilente is also associated with another power, who dominates the end of the play as it was, it seems, first presented on the public stage, and who more easily dominated its performance at court. In this version, Macilente's humour is instead dispelled by the factual or represented presence of Queen Elizabeth herself, who thus takes over and redoubles his purgative function. In these ways, the play's aggressive judgement and silencing of humorous deviations from an ideal or norm is a figuring forth both of satire and of royal government, and assimilates the one to the other in this figuration. So the play – in line with Asper's declared intentions – becomes a theatre in which judgements happen, the place where a power both literary and legal can perform exemplary enactments of its authority.

But the play is also a theatre of judgement in another way. The action is punctuated at regular intervals, between and even within scenes, by the readerly conversation of Asper's two companions from the Induction, who thus act as a chorus (or, as Jonson terms it, 'Grex'). Cordatus, the author's friend, continually explains elements of the play's design – details of its construction and its purpose – to his slightly dim companion, and in doing so places the very activity of watching or reading – judging – a play firmly on the stage itself. In judging correctly, or in deferring before that judgement, they provide a model for the audience to follow. But they also make this a play which is about its own reception, concerned not just to present a 'comical satire', as Jonson termed it, but also to prescribe the ways in which such a satire ought to be received. The Grex seems to be there in order to stitch its audience to the play, to ensure that it is taken 'correctly' or 'understood' (to use a crucial Jonsonian term) – certainly the placement of Cordatus and Mitis on the stage puts them simultaneously in the view of the audience and actually among it [13]. But it is arguable that in intervening between the audience in the Globe, or at court, or the reader at home, and the exemplary if improvised justice dispensed by Macilente, the inclusion of the Grex serves to open up the space between the differing acts of writing and reading which are hopefully elided in these two characters. Such a breach is implicit in the differentiation the play makes between Asper and Macilente, even if their speaking together, as it were, in the Epilogue, works towards concealing it. It is then replicated in the fact that Cordatus and Mitis are characters within the play, not members of its audience; and presumably what led to the amendment of the ending at the Globe was a persistent sense of the dubiousness involved in presenting the Queen on the stage, a stubborn awareness that such an act would be the impersonation of the monarch in a play rather than a means of dissolving the boundary between playing and the context within which it happens. The play's attention to that boundary and to its crossing constitutes an attention to the activity of reading as an *animation* of the text, an animation that makes the text itself into a *process* as much as a book.

Jonson's next play was also a 'comical satire'. *Cynthia's Revels, or the Fountain of Self-Love*, was produced by the Children of the Chapel Royal, in the indoor theatre at Blackfriars **[14]**; perhaps its formal departures from the precedents of his earlier work were the result of Jonson writing for the somewhat different audience assembled at this venue. The play also situates itself in relation to the work of contemporaries or predecessors: its allegorical Cynthia looks back to John Lyly's representation of Elizabeth in his *Endimion* of 1588 (Barton 1984: 79) and its evocation of Echo resembles Thomas Dekker's *Old Fortunatus* of 1599 (Kay 1995: 52). But it is distinctively Jonson's work, certainly distinctive enough to spur Marston and Dekker on to personal ridicule **[24, 128]**. It paints a satiric portrait of court life, delineating in familiarly humorous characters the vices of affectation, folly, luxury and prodigality which infest the very centre of the political realm. Such humours are again aligned with self-love, here represented on the stage at the play's outset in a scene in which Narcissus's admirer, Echo, bemoans his demise. That this is the *fountain* of self-love, its *source*, makes of Narcissus's experience both a kind of original sin and a paradigm, a structure that can account for the humours or vices that beset the court. So the kind of divided and dysfunctional self represented by Narcissus is provided to underwrite the failings displayed in the rest of the play.

Their placement in the court, as its characteristic flaws, establishes a clear institutional focus for their examination. The site of governance is the 'Special Fountain of Manners', as the Folio dedication puts it:

> Thou art a bountiful and brave spring: and waterest all the noble plants of this island. In thee, the whole kingdom dresseth itself, and is ambitious to use thee as her glass. Beware, then, thou render men's figures truly, and teach them no less to hate their deformities than to love their forms ...

The danger, in other words, is that the court might function like a poisoned water supply, bearing its own evils out into the nation as a whole: the ethical moment in the psychology of self-love has allowed its extrapolation into an account of political function and an ideal of representation, with the court able to choose between the confounded and confounding vision of Narcissus or the clear sight of a Cynthia. In the play itself the wrong choice has long since been made, and Cynthia's court languishes in folly and misrepresentation. Its reformation comes ultimately from Cynthia herself, who arrives in Act V to resolve matters, but it is enacted primarily through the figure of the Jonsonian poet, Crites. Though he is slighted for four Acts by the courtiers among whom he dwells, the play blossoms into a fantasy of his apotheosis. In a sign of divine favour, the gods are able to see the merit to which the foppish courtiers are blind – Mercury describes him as:

> A creature of a most perfect and divine temper. One in whom the humours and elements are peaceably met, without emulation of precedency ... His discourse is like his behaviour, uncommon, but not unpleasing; he is prodigal of neither. He strives rather to be that which men call judicious than to be thought so: and is so truly learned that he affects not to show it.
>
> (II.iii.109–118)

His unblemished character allows him to take on the authorial and readerly function of the Grex in *Every Man Out*, pronouncing authoritatively on his milieu and demonstrating his suitability for the purgative responsibility with which Cynthia will invest him.

Given that the poet is entrusted with such tasks, it should come as no surprise to learn that the play works out its contrast between Crites and the degenerate court in the characterisation of their language. In the passage quoted above, Crites's 'discourse' is the first of his many specific qualities to be isolated as a mark of his virtue. His courtly antagonists, given to idle chatter, are similarly marked, if with opposing implications. And judicial intervention, when it comes, happens through the medium of poetry. Crites, by Cynthia's command, pens a masque; while the courtiers are performing it their disguises are removed, revealing them to be impersonating allegorically the very virtues from which their vices need to be carefully distinguished. The revelation stages a masque within the masque, where a theatre of praise becomes a theatre of judgement. Thus begins their chastisement: and the sentences which Crites imposes on all of them include another performance, this time of a 'palinode' or song of recantation, in which the shamed characters formally renounce their humours.

Such is indeed an apotheosis of poetry. But the play, in its condemnation of the courtiers, also seems to encode some contrary notes which sit somewhat uneasily alongside this enthronement. Judgement, in *Cynthia's Revels*, proceeds primarily by revelation: it takes the form of an unmasking, seeing through the image to check whether it accurately imitates – and thus shows – what lies beneath. Anything that is not what it appears to be is judged not merely false but also transgressive. Cynthia's revels themselves, as played fictions, are therefore dangerously close to being caught up in the very condemnation they stage – after all, it is 'those clouds of masque' which '[make] you not yourselves', as Cynthia herself declares (V.xi.48). The masque's revelations showed how closely vice could resemble virtue; in its association of representation with falsehood, and its insistence on the propriety of a poetry which also proceeds by representation, the play bears out its own contention.

This tension becomes a central organising principle of his subsequent 'comical satire' for the Blackfriars boys, a work which also constitutes Jonson's first attempt at staging classical Rome. This was not necessarily a singularly Jonsonian project, but in *Poetaster, or His Arraignment* critics have found his particular determination to make a drama out of poetry itself underpinning the enterprise. The play puts three of the classical poets who were most widely read and celebrated in the Renaissance – Ovid, Horace and Virgil – on stage. Their poetry is imitated and translated; the first three scenes of Act III actually dramatise one of Horace's *Satires* (Book I, ix). The play serves to contrast them not only with the blustering liar Captain Tucca and Lupus, an informer, but also with the feeble poetasters Crispinus and Demetrius. But the three great poets are not considered equals: Ovid's sensuous, erotic poetry is lived out through his affair with Caesar's daughter, Julia, and he eventually falls foul of her father. At the end of Act IV he is banished from Rome and takes no part in the denouement. Horace and Virgil, by contrast, are very much present at the climax: Horace successfully fends off false accusations of treason and he and Virgil are installed as Caesar's trusted and respected counsellors.

It has always been recognised, however, that *Poetaster* is not simply or even mainly 'about' Ovid, Horace and Virgil. The play is one of the loudest salvoes in the 'war of the theatres' fought out among the competing playwrights and companies around the turn of the century. Horace is clearly a cover for Jonson, while Crispinus and Demetrius are caricatures of his rivals Marston and Dekker respectively. Ovid is made to speak his own poetry at least partly through the translations of Marlowe, heightening the sense that this character too is a representation of an English equivalent. Even so, we should resist the temptation – all too easily indulged by past critics – to reduce the play simply to its participation in a dispute among rival dramatists **[128]**. Its most recent editor has pointed to another, broader, engagement with its moment, an evident concern with the Essex rebellion of 1601 (Cain 1995: 40–44) **[182]**.

Once again, a Jonsonian text welds political and literary concerns together, finding each to be a metaphor for the other. It is part of Ovid's problem in the play that he refuses to make that connection, to perceive the public responsibilities with which poetry is necessarily invested. His refusal to study law, as his father wishes, is thus both a gesture of youthful vitality against the crabbed incomprehension of the old – the play certainly does not stint from satirising the debased practice of the law – and a mark of his own unhealthy lack of interest in the ethico-political realm in which poetry's proper function is discharged. His verse is not only amorous and lustful but also idle, trivial, enabling a slippage into vice rather than supporting its rigorous exclusion. This reaches its height in Act IV scene v, when Ovid, Julia and others enact a 'banquet of the gods', playing the heavenly parts themselves. This masque-like performance is interrupted by Augustus, and his condemnation of what he finds echoes the severe aesthetic at the heart of *Cynthia's Revels*. It is no more than a 'pageant' (IV.vi.16), a blasphemy against the gods, the actions of those 'that live in worship of that idol, vice' (IV.vi.66), and thus a kind of idolatry itself. Augustus's intervention here elaborates on the subtle but absolute distinction between the 'sacred poesy, thou spirit of the arts' that Ovid hymns (I.ii.203) and the idol he foolishly takes for it.

The last Act of *Poetaster*, though, is concerned to define poetry against other adversaries. Crispinus and Demetrius are accused, tried, found guilty and punished; Crispinus is forced to take pills that cause him to vomit into a waiting basin all the peculiar and awkward words that characterise his discourse. Their crime, though, is more than writing badly, as the trial scene makes clear at a number of crucial points. They are formally charged with having 'most ignorantly, foolishly and (more like yourselves) maliciously, gone about to deprave and calumniate the person and writing of Quintus Horacius Flaccus' (V.iii.194–6); at the play's end, they are required to swear that they will never 'offer, or dare … to malign, traduce, or detract the person or writings of Quintus Horatius Flaccus' (V.iii.540–3). In other words, their offence is *slander*.

Thomas Cain has written of 'the centrality of calumny to *Poetaster*' (Cain 1995: 41), and slander played a crucial part in the events surrounding the Essex rebellion. As Cain points out, contemporaries were willing to think the Earl 'a man who, though rash, was condemned by gossip, malicious innuendo and conspiracy' (ibid.). Such malice is a central part of the world of Augustan Rome. Horace is confronted not only with the libels of Crispinus and Demetrius but with the far more insidious (if ultimately absurd) calumnies of Lupus, who steals an emblem on which Horace has been working for his patron, Maecenas, and egregiously misreads it as evidence of treason against the state. Slander, in other words, is doubly potent: it exists both in the lies that can be fabricated, and in the construction that can be placed by the malicious on innocent phrases. This latter is more insidious because it offers to condemn a speaker out of his own mouth, to find a text which confesses to its author's crimes. To make its accusations stick, it needs to insist that speakers should be fundamentally responsible for their utterance, that the meaning produced by this interpretation corresponds to the intentions of the author. But the assumption of transparent communication is not just the basis for this kind of accusation. It is also the basis for a civic language that could be *responsible*, forming the ethico-political bond between individuals, negotiating, prescribing and confirming their obligations to each other and their commonwealth. Slander by interpretation, the kind attempted by Lupus, turns such responsible language against itself or its proper ends. Little wonder, then, that the judgement exemplified by the constellation of Augustus and Maecenas, as patrons, and Virgil and Horace, as writers, involves the accurate assessment of the world *and* of the world in writing, the policing both of the state and of the commonwealth of letters. But since the *possibility* of slander is not dispelled with the punishment of each instance, the price of civilisation is eternal vigilance.

Within the narrative framework of *Poetaster*, the utopian fantasy of an arraignment that results in definitive and final banishment can be entertained, as the denouement enthrones a healthy language in a healthy state. For readers of the play, though, the limits of this narrative framework are made dramatically clear by the 'Apologetical Dialogue' which Jonson appended to the play in his Folio, or by the account of its censorship with which the quarto edition of 1602 concludes. In this brief epilogue the Author takes to the stage to give a very different account of the polity he inhabits and the language it speaks. Slander here is the order of the day, particularly slander through misreading, and this Author has been its enduring victim. Not for him the trust and respect of an Augustus or a Cynthia, the friendship and support of a Maecenas; instead his civil poetry is relentlessly calumniated. It is an abrupt and unsettling last word, but it serves also to indicate a coming change of direction:

> And, since the Comic Muse
> Hath proved so ominous to me, I will try
> If Tragedy have a more kind aspect.
> (Apologetical Dialogue, 220–2)

Dutton (1983), Barton (1984) and Kay (1995) again offer useful readings of all these plays in context. Ostovich (1999) provides an important account of the interaction of seeing and judging in *Every Man Out*, while Clare (1998) considers the comical satires in the context of courtliness. Wiltenburg (1991) roots much of Jonson's work in a preoccupation with self-love established paradigmatically in *Cynthia's Revels*. Cain (1995 and 1998) locates *Poetaster* within the framework of slander, a focus shared and elaborated by Kaplan (1997).

(e) WORDS AS DEEDS: *SEJANUS* AND *CATILINE*

As his conclusion to *Poetaster* had promised, Jonson's next play was a tragedy, which, while not his first, is the earliest (of only two) to survive. The text we have is by no means the text that was first performed, possibly at court, in 1603 (Ayres 1990: 9). It was extensively rewritten before its publication in a quarto edition of 1605, removing all traces of co-authorship with Chapman, and the apparatus included in that edition – extensive notes and annotations, giving sources and references for the events re-enacted in the play – make it clear that this is a reading rather than a performance text. Such bookishness may not have prevented Jonson from getting into trouble again – something in the play, either as performed or as printed, brought its author the wrong kind of close attention from the authorities **[25]** (Dutton 1991: 11–12).

There has been plenty of speculation regarding the nature of the offence. The play's possible reference to the Essex rebellion has been suggested; more recently it has been claimed that the arraignment of Silius in Act III glances provocatively at the 1603 trial for treason of Sir Walter Ralegh (Ayres 1990: 16–22). It is certainly a few steps deeper into a consideration of 'matters of state' than the anti-courtly satire of his preceding works. In this, it follows its main source, the *Annals* of the Roman historian Tacitus, both a popular and a contentious read in the early modern period. As W. David Kay has noted, Tacitus's accounts of Roman political intrigue at the height of empire were read 'in the early seventeenth century either as a manual of state intrigue or as a warning against tyrannical rule' (Kay 1995: 71). Both possibilities offered an engagement with contemporary politics, though the latter would be the more obviously oppositional in the climate of incipient absolutism fostered in many of the European monarchies at the time. To dramatise Tacitus was to participate in a Tacitism that was clearly identified as 'a vehicle for discontent' (Kay 1995: 69). In painting a picture of a realm riven by rumour and fear, bedevilled by spies and *agents provocateurs*, where plotting and conspiracy are the order of the day, Jonson produced a work that might give the discontented matter off which to feed. Perhaps no more explicit reference to contemporary events was needed for the arousal of suspicion.

Jonson's play does not rigidly follow Tacitus, but selects and simplifies in places. His Sejanus is a self-seeking villain who rises by the favour of the emperor, Tiberius, and is then deserted by his master when his ambition destroys the trust between them – in Sejanus's request to marry Livia, the widow of the emperor's son Drusus (himself a victim of Sejanus), Tiberius finally locates a threat to his own security and position. In Act III the Senate is the site of one of Sejanus's triumphs, the denunciation and destruction of Silius, a follower of the late prince Germanicus; in Act V it becomes the stage for his public downfall, after which he is executed – off stage – and torn to pieces by the mob. So Sejanus is the protagonist of this tragedy, but he could hardly be described as its 'hero' in the manner of an Othello, or even a Macbeth. In dramatising his fall, Jonson focuses less on any psychological crisis than on the convulsions of a dystopian political realm which is the very antithesis of the Rome of *Poetaster*.

In the earlier play, the slander with which Horace is confronted is comically ineffective: it does not *work*. The words of Crispinus, Demetrius and Lupus are dead matter, obstructions to proper human functioning that must be voided, whereas the speech of Horace, of Virgil and most obviously of Augustus is stunningly potent – these figures are able to order the world through their utterance, to perform actions in opening their mouths. This emphasis on the *force* of language is a Jonsonian commonplace, but only because it is a commonplace of the humanist culture in which he and his contemporaries were educated **[9]**. An education which gave a large place to the study of rhetoric could hardly be blind to the power of the word, particularly when attention was paid both to the ways in which language might be able to persuade people to action, to *move* them, and to the suggestion (familiar particularly from works by or attributed to the Roman rhetoricians Cicero and Quintilian) that questions of definition, of what might count as the true or the good and how it might be known, were themselves bound up with the art of rhetorical construction. According to such writers, ideas were not to be considered separable from their expression, somehow capable of utterance or inscription in an unelaborated, 'pre-rhetorical' form. Rhetoric was precisely the way in which propositions, and the arguments supportive of them, might be formulated, and not just the matter of choosing a set of clothes in which they could be dressed. If the language of the rhetorically competent man could be described as *ornatus*, this did not mean (simply) 'ornate'. It was to be translated more precisely as 'armed' (Skinner 1996: 49).

This classical rhetoric understands language most frequently in its political capacities. The skills of invention, organisation and elocution were the very substance of political endeavour, in that political debate was precisely the arena for which such skills were developed. The sixteenth century witnessed a number of attempts, following the early example of Machiavelli, to adapt Roman rhetorical theory to the differing forms of government of contemporary Europe. Rhetoric was the language of power: it was thus the very model of a powerful language. As the language of politics, it was closely connected to the making of law – rhetoric encompassed all the acts of praising and blaming, declaring and pronouncing, that were undeniably linguistic but also the actual exercise of authority. Tudor and Stuart monarchs, it should not be forgotten, sometimes made their laws by *proclamation* (Hughes and Larkin 1973; Larkin 1983); as they did so, they took for their model the 'effectivity' of the divine 'Word' itself. This was a power to move which exceeded the terms of the classical rhetoricians, adding its own account of linguistic force to theirs.

The influence of Machiavelli's concern with political discourse is detectable in the language of *Sejanus*; Tacitus's focus on the same issue has obviously also left its mark. But the forcefulness of language is everywhere apparent in Jonson's plays, from their concern with law, their dramatised accusations, confessions, trials, judgements and sentences, to the accounts they give of their juridical power. In *Poetaster*'s 'Apological Dialogue', for example, the Author declares that he could 'stamp [his enemies'] foreheads with those deep and public brands / That the whole company of barber-surgeons / Should not take off, with all their art, and plasters' (162–5). Indeed forcefulness, the word as *deed*, is a necessary assumption for the Jonsonian model of political or ethical language. Such activity is apparent in the language of Cynthia and Augustus in the comical satires. Both Augustus and Cynthia embody a divinely authorised position which makes their word law. Both are therefore in the position to judge *in* their speaking, to order their worlds into the good and the bad, the true and the false. What the comical satires dramatise is the process whereby such an ordering word is seen to correspond to what the narrative has already presented as the truth. Prescription is made to follow description.

The crucial innovation of *Sejanus*, the basis of the shift from comedy to tragedy, is the abandonment of this alignment. Suddenly, the power of the word is made to work *against* the ethical distinctions the play makes elsewhere. Sejanus and Tiberius are hardly embodiments of a divinely aligned good, whatever the pretensions to divinity they both entertain, yet their speech has the force of law. It does so, the play suggests, because they occupy the positions from which judgement can be pronounced, the places in the civil structure which determine that their words will be effective and those of others will not. This, of course, is power: it is power explicitly thematised as a power *in* language that becomes a power *over* language. In other words, in this imperial Rome, rhetorical force makes things happen: it fixes identities, responsibilities, vice and virtue. As Sejanus says to Eudemus, the physician, in response to the latter's scruple over the 'honour' he might lose in acting for the former:

> Sir, you can lose no honour,
> By trusting aught to me. The coarsest act
> Done to my service, I can so requite,
> As all the world shall style it honourable ...
> (I.326–9)

The play stages a dark descent into a language that parodies the naming capacity of the divinely authorised word. A succession of figures – Silius, Sabinus, Gallus, Cordus – is *pronounced* guilty in a series of denunciations and condemnations. Furthermore, the play flags up the fact that this guilt is the effect of its pronunciation in the preparations made by both Sejanus and Tiberius for their crucial orations, preparations to which the reader is privy. In Act II, before they have made any move against their Germanican opponents, Tiberius asks Sejanus, 'Have we the means to make these guilty, first?' (II.317). The play's nightmare subsists in the difference between *finding* and *making* that is highlighted here, visible to the audience but capable of making no difference in the Rome we see on stage.

Such ungrounded rhetorical force, though, does not dissolve the network of political responsibilities and liabilities in which the characters are held – far from it. The judicial Senate is the scene of the play's most significant instances, the condemnations of Silius and Cordus in Act III, and the reading in Act V of the letter by Tiberius proclaiming Sejanus's fall. All these acts are ones to which their addressees are fatefully subject. Furthermore, the mechanism of slander by interpretation that was ridiculed in *Poetaster* is given free rein here. Silius and Cordus are held responsible for the construction that can be placed on their words, forced to own the treason their accusers locate in their utterances (as Lorna Hutson has suggested: Hutson 1998: xxv). The horror is that this network is now self-validating, an absolutism in the purest sense. It is, as Silius argues at the outset of his trial, a law which is unconnected with justice (III.221), not answerable to anything beyond itself – certainly not to the gods or the good.

To this enactment of political discourse the play opposes the Germanicans. They are the object of Sejanus's murderous attentions, but they are also the embodiment of a different model of language and action. Despite their place in Sejanus's schemes, figures such as Silius and Arruntius often play a choric role, describing events both off stage and on. They do not act: there is no counter-plotting, no resistance. They simply oppose to Sejanus, Tiberius and the rhetorician Afer a language that is seemingly forceless, no matter how virtuous they are or how true their statements. Perhaps, though, this is enough: their words provide the standard of discrimination which enables the audience to recognise the vice of Sejanus and his master as vice, even as it recoils from their rhetorical power. In this we are helped by the unexpected intervention of the goddess Fortune at the opening of Act V, offering non-verbal signs of Sejanus's lack of worth and his true, serpentine nature. Although he strives to label this merely 'superstition', the intervention of the divine provides a transcendent validation of everything the Germanicans have so ineffectively said. Even this, though, is a double edged matter: Fortune may reinforce a sense of the difference between true and false, but she does not offer the prospect of an end to tyranny. As Tiberius still reigns, and the devious Macro has simply stepped into Sejanus's sandals, it looks likely that the Rome Jonson paints here is not easily to find itself another Augustus.

Sejanus's concern with the potency of language threatens to make a demon of rhetoric itself. It is notable that Afer, the orator, is one of Sejanus's chief instruments in his intrigues, a figure whose skills are symbolically contrasted with the plain speaking of Silius's wounds and the truthfulness of Cordus's writing in Act III. In *Catiline*, Jonson changed tack: this time, an orator is its hero. Performed in 1611, it marked a return both to Rome and to tragedy after the comic achievements of *Volpone*, *Epicene* and *The Alchemist*. Unsurprisingly, considering its genre and its topic, there are many similarities between this play and its predecessor. It too draws on the work of a Roman historian for its narrative, this time Sallust's *Bellum Catilinarium*. It is set entirely in the enclosed world of the Roman state, the violence of events or deeds outside Rome always off stage. It too features a struggle for power fought out in the political institutions of the state. The same questions regarding the contemporary applicability of historical writing which the earlier tragedy had both raised thematically in the treatment of Cordus and endured itself are suggested by the later play. Where Sejanus looked perhaps to Ralegh's trial, or perhaps to the Essex rebellion, *Catiline* offers parallels to the role of Jonson's patron Salisbury in the foiling of the Gunpowder Plot in 1605 (Kay 1995: 121–4), and although it is republican rather than imperial Rome that offers the setting, it 'is as little republican as it need be and as nearly imperial as it can be' (Worden 1999: 153). Nevertheless, the threat here emerges not from an established ruler and his favourite but from a would-be tyrant. To this extent, then, it is a portrait of a possible rather than a realised dictatorship, and a narrative which works through the prevention of that realisation. Where Sejanus's Rome was much the same at the play's conclusion as at its outset, the same cannot be said necessarily for that of *Catiline* – the removal of its nominal protagonist at least appears to be the kind of judicial purgation familiar from the comical satires.

Catiline's conspiracy to subvert the republic forms the basis of the play; but as much as it dramatises the conspirators (and its opening scenes, full of supernatural portents and the grim rituals of Catiline's murderous gang, offer a dark initial focus) it also dramatises the exposure of their plot. Here, the focus is on the statesman and orator Cicero, whose rise to prominence and battle to save Rome offers a counterpoint to his opponent's fall. It is Cicero who is able to infiltrate the conspiracy and expose it in the Senate, forcing his opponents to increasingly desperate and violent measures which result eventually in their destruction. It is Cicero who holds the republic together during the period following Catiline's resort to open warfare, keeping potential threats such as the barbarian Allobroges on side and healing the breaches left by the conspiracy in the body of the state itself. He is as active in its defence as the Germanicans of *Sejanus* are passive.

The play works hard to draw out the differences between its two poles of attraction. Catiline is a member of the nobility; Cicero, by contrast, is a self-made man. At crucial moments this difference breaks out into the open to govern their relationship, as when Catiline responds to the claim that Cicero has preserved Rome with a patrician sneer:

> He save the state? A burgess' son of Arpinum.
> The gods would rather twenty Romes should perish,
> Than have that contumely stuck upon 'em,
> That he should share with them in the preserving
> A shed, or signpost.
>
> (IV. 480–4)

His contempt is that of a man whose own relationship to the state is predicated upon oligarchic rather than meritocratic principles. His disdain latches onto the artisanal qualities of his opponent, the oratorical skills that have underpinned Cicero's rise to prominence and prevented his birth from governing his destiny:

> Remember who I am, and of what place,
> What petty fellow this is, that opposes;
> One, that hath exercised his eloquence,
> Still to the bane of the nobility:
> A boasting, insolent tongue-man
>
> (IV. 157–61)

Catiline's complaint, on behalf of everyone born with a silver spoon in his mouth, is that 'exercise' of any sort should never result in eminence – not for him an appreciation of the dignity of labour. But that Cicero's work should have been verbal, his skills rhetorical, is a particular affront. The 'tongue-man' is an apt characterisation of the kind of vice Catiline wants to impute to his enemy, a puffed-up peddler of hot air who embodies an unwarranted violation of the natural order.

Here, then, is the patrician demonisation of rhetoric again – but coming, now, from the source of vice itself rather than the representatives of virtue. It finds an easy echo in the fringe conspirators Caesar and Crassus, whose asides puncture Cicero's oration at the beginning of Act III in a manner reminiscent of Germanican commentary on their opponents' speeches. Caesar dismisses reports of conspiracy against the state as the ruses of a self-seeking upstart:

> Reports? Do you believe 'em Catulus,
> Why, he does make and breed 'em for the people;
> To endear his service to 'em. Do you not taste
> An art, that is so common? Popular men,
> They must create strange monsters, and then quell 'em;
> To make their arts seem something.
>
> (III.93–8)

Rhetoric is thus aligned with ambition, self-aggrandisement and the kind of fearful political climate exemplified in *Sejanus*. Oratory is telling stories, peddling fictions, the means by which an unsanctified power performs the judgmental function it has usurped. As Crassus comments, 'Treasons and guilty men are *made* in states / Too oft, to dignify the magistrates' (III. 102–3; emphasis JL).

That such criticism should come from those implicated in a hellish conspiracy obviously colours it somewhat, and demonstrates amply the difference between this text and the earlier play. Yet criticism of rhetoric emerges elsewhere in the play. The Chorus at the end of Act IV condemns the slander of Cicero that has followed his exposure of Catiline's plot, his 'virtue' taken for 'vice', his actions described as 'deceit' rather than 'diligence' (IV.884, 886):

> Oh, let us pluck this evil seed
>   Out of our spirits;
> And give to every noble deed
>   The name it merits.
>   (IV. 888–91)

The historian Quentin Skinner has suggested that this passage draws on a classical and humanist anxiety regarding the ethical dangers of rhetoric (Skinner 1996: 178–9). It also clearly recalls the renaming or redescribing that characterised the potent but ungrounded rhetoric of *Sejanus*. The concentration on the figure of Cicero has not entirely banished such concerns from the later play.

Although the orator is the heroic centre of the play, he is not uncomplicatedly so. He seems to be a figure whose power depends upon his orientation towards a general good, the health and survival of the virtuous state. His orations, crucially, align force, truth and virtue, yet we find him fulsomely praising his spy, Fulvia, in public, whilst condemning her in private as a 'common strumpet' (III.451). More seriously, the play allows us to catch him in the act of exactly the kind of redescription that the Chorus unequivocally condemns. In a departure from Sallust's account (yet following a Renaissance source – see Kay 1995: 121–2), Jonson has Caesar and Crassus participate in the conspiracy; they also have the sense to extricate themselves at the point of its exposure, and are opportunistically positioning themselves to achieve best advantage thereafter. This Cicero knows. Indeed, he discusses what should be done about them with his associate Cato in Act IV:

> They shall be watched, and looked to. Till they do
> Declare themselves, I will not put 'em out
> By any question. There they stand. I'll make
> Myself no enemies, nor the state no traitors.
>   (IV. 534–7)

Thus, when later confronted with proof of their treason Cicero refuses to admit it into consideration. He denounces one of the informants as a 'lying varlet' (V. 340), writing the accusation off as 'slander' (V. 344) and 'some men's malice' (V. 354). He simply *declares* that 'Crassus is noble, just and loves his country' (V. 350). Those who assert otherwise are to be repressed or expelled. In short, he refuses to call vice by the name it merits but uses his consular powers to effect a redescription: he revisits, in other words, the capacity to 'style' or name people and deeds shared by Sejanus and Tiberius, living down to the estimation offered by Caesar earlier in the play. Even in Cicero's polity, here, judgement emerges as a rhetorical effect – with all the possible ethical consequences that might entail.

Such a moment shapes the critical unease surrounding Cicero. His is not the stoic virtue and merely choric language of the Germanicans; but in his rhetorical activism there persists the ethical danger that now seems ineradicable from the model of forceful language staged in these plays. Cicero's speeches are the deeds of a statesman, clearly, one who had good political reasons for not tackling Caesar and Crassus (though a reader's knowledge that Caesar would one day succeed in subverting the republic Cicero strove to defend might undercut even this justification). But to the extent that he is a statesman, his words circulate in an apparently malleable earthly language, where the names of 'virtue' and 'vice' can be apportioned in accordance with state interests and might not necessarily connect with any fixed framework of ethical standards. Yet in dramatising the breach between such realms the play insists on its importance. Rome is invoked by Jonson, twice, as the site of a peculiar drama, the enactment of a theatre in which the capacity to judge is the ruse of power rather than its source.

Further reading

Maus (1984) gives an account of the debt to classical thought evident in both the Roman plays and Jonson's other work, while Sweeney (1985) and Ayres (1990) offer thought-provoking and comprehensive accounts respectively of *Sejanus*. Hutson (1998) presents briefer but illuminating comments on the same play, while De Luna (1969) gives a strongly argued if somewhat contentious topical reading of *Catiline*. The discussions of both plays in Barton (1984) and Cave (1991) are thorough and accessible. Sanders (1998a) includes discussion of the plays in the context of a 'republicanism' partially derived from classical sources. Worden (1994) and (1999) discuss both in the context of their debts to and differences from the histories of Tacitus and Sallust.

(f) OBJECTS OF DESIRE: *EASTWARD HO!*, *VOLPONE* AND *EPICENE*

Eight years separate *Sejanus* and *Catiline*. The line which stretches from *Cynthia's Revels* to the later tragedy needs to be seen alongside a different trajectory pursued in parallel, a route taking in the great comedies of Jonson's middle years and cementing his place in popular estimation in a way that the political drama of his two extant tragedies could not manage. This route includes a detour to the Venice evoked in *Volpone*; but otherwise it navigates a path through the various interlocking social and symbolic circuits in which Jonson and his audience lived, the restless buzz and hum of early modern London.

The play that provides the most striking evidence of the difference between these two narratives was not included in the 1616 Folio. *Eastward Ho!* is the result of a collaboration between Jonson, Chapman and Marston, a peace treaty between two of the participants in the 'war of the theatres' evidently having been concluded (*HSS*, I, 192). Although it too landed its authors in hot water **[26]**, its differences from the wordy tragedy of *Sejanus* are particularly striking. In some ways it looks back to the humour plays, but it eschews the orchestrated parade of pathologised characters in favour of an emphasis on plotting not seen in Jonson's works since *Every Man in His Humour*. In telling the story of two apprentices, the industrious Golding and the flighty Quicksilver, and their intertwined paths to the rewards befitting each, *Eastward Ho!* appropriates the structure of the prodigal son play. But it wears its didactic burden lightly, burlesquing the form with vigour in its concluding scenes (see Barton 1984: 244–7; it is the latter portion of the play that has been ascribed most firmly to Jonson – Van Fossen 1979: 1–12). It is more clearly concerned to trace the outlines of the city they inhabit, a city to which the prologue dedicates the play and could hardly be more distant from the imperial or republican state of Jonson's Rome. This is not the site of statecraft but the place of production and exchange, its morality already an economy. Thus Touchstone's shop (the place both for making and trading) provides the space in which the moral dichotomy embodied in his two apprentices is to be made apparent. Quicksilver's prodigality is his vice, while Golding's virtue consists in his adherence to the traditional artisanal values of hard work, thrift and the accumulation of symbolic and material resources, virtues celebrated in the craft-based civic structure of London government and its cultural manifestations. Golding has heeded their employer's catchphrase, the exhortation to

'Work upon that now', to labour for advancement, while Quicksilver maintains cheerily that 'the curse of man is labour' (I.i.105–6). The contrast between them finds a parallel in the opposition between Touchstone's two daughters. Where Mildred commits herself to a sensible marriage to Golding, Gertrude's union with Sir Petronel Flash – a title in want of substance – exemplifies her headlong, libidinal pursuit of status and position. Gertrude, Flash and Quicksilver offer the spectacle of an unbridled expenditure, a pursuit of goods that are both intangible and extravagant. Quicksilver and Flash plan an escape to riches in America – it is ruined before they have even put the Thames behind them. Gertrude is left by Act V in an alehouse, furiously spinning far-fetched strategies for her escape from poverty into gentility. As her companion Sindefy comments, 'They are pretty waking dreams, these' (V.i.79). The elaborate scenes of repentance at the play's climax serve to reintegrate the wastrels into the industrious city they had been seeking to escape. On this basis Touchstone, the goldsmith, can conclude by offering a pat formulation of the entirely predictable 'moral' that the London audience ought to learn from this fiction (V.v.188).

Though some critical readings have settled for this moral dichotomy, most have suggested that the play exceeds this neat framework. In the figure of Security we have an usurer whose suffering and repentance seem to locate him easily in the general redemption. When we first encounter him, however, he has a somewhat Mephistophelian air, offering a justification for his activities that borrows directly from the discourse of prudence with which Golding and Touchstone are associated:

> The merchant, he complains, and says traffic is subject to much uncertainty and loss: let 'em keep their goods on dry land with a vengeance, and not expose other men's substances to the mercy of the winds, ... and all for greedy desire to enrich themselves with unconscionable gain, two for one, or so: where I and such other honest men as live by lending money are content with moderate profit ...
>
> (II.ii.83–90)

The usurer, that is to say, is not utterly to be opposed to the respectable tradesman: rather, he is the logical extension of the rational calculation that underpins that accumulative respectability, risk and effort measured against potential profit. While Quicksilver is condemned for his gambling, Security is damned for his refusal to venture enough. Furthermore, the play's own distinction between usurer and productive craftsman itself might not hold: goldsmiths offered basic banking and money-lending facilities to their fellow Londoners.

Similarly, the sober citizen/riotous gentleman dichotomy figured in the two apprentices is never quite as impermeable a division as the simplistic moral requires. As Quicksilver points out in the first scene, 'by God's lid, 'tis for your worship and for your commodity that I keep company':

> Well, I am a good member of the city if I were well considered.
> How would merchants thrive if gentlemen would not be unthrifts?
> How could gentlemen be unthrifts if their humours were not fed?
> (I.i.23–5, 29–32)

Consumption is the necessary corollary of production and accumulation, an integral moment in the economic processes represented by Golding and Touchstone and not their excluded opposite. As much is apparent from the very business in which these figures are engaged: as well as a banker, the goldsmith is also a figure central to the production of fashionable luxury goods rather than necessities, pandering not to need but to desire (Knowles 2001: xxxii). The moral economy of the play is not quite in tune with this network, however much the prodigal narrative assumes and attempts to enforce their correspondence.

The position in which *Eastward Ho!* places the institution of the theatre itself serves to complicate the picture further. The drama is associated with the prodigality of Quicksilver, as one of the recreations on which he wastes his time and money – he is given to quoting lines from that old favourite, *The Spanish Tragedy*. Theatre, furthermore, was in the business of ministering to the accelerating desires of the developing city's new consumers [7]. As such, it shares the ambivalence associated with Quicksilver himself. It is that which the city seeks to suppress as an enervating force but which is simultaneously a means of its growth and health, an inadmissible condition of its development. In the epilogue's references to the pageantry of the Lord Mayor's Show the play compares its own practices with the self-representation of the civic authorities, the city's 'official' self-image:

> Oh, may you find in this our pageant, here,
> The same contentment which you came to seek;
> And, as that show but draws you once a year,
> May this attract you, hither, once a week.
> (Epilogus, 5–8)

This is an attempt at reconciliation, certainly, but it also reads as a possible challenge. *Eastward Ho!* ends by declaring itself a product in a consumerist economy, offering the satisfaction of intensified desires that neither civic pageantry nor its moral economy of thrift *versus* prodigality can ever hope to address. As such a product, it claims to speak for its city as authoritatively as the institutions of urban government themselves.

Such complications emerge again in perhaps the most familiar of all Jonson's plays, *Volpone, or The Fox*. A resounding success on the public stage when played by the King's Men – Shakespeare's company – in 1606, it was also performed before the universities at Oxford and Cambridge, and dedicated to these 'most noble and equal sisters' on its publication in 1607/8 (Kay 1995: 87). Prefacing the text of the play is a Dedicatory Epistle which has long been read as Jonson's definitive elaboration of his theatrical principles, particularly helpful for situating the ethical work that his satirical endeavours are understood to be performing. Here he denies ever launching *ad hominem* attacks, clears himself of 'ribaldry, profanation, blasphemy, all licence of offence to God and man' (Dedicatory Epistle, 34–5), and sets out the public function of his writing as being to 'inform men in the best reason of living' (100–1). The epistle concludes with an reinvocation of the kind of judicial inscription threatened in *Poetaster*'s Apologetical Dialogue:

> [Poetry] shall out of just rage incite her servants (who are *genus irritabile*) to spout ink in their faces, that shall eat, farther than their marrow, into their fames; and not Cinnamus the barber, with his art, shall be able to take out the brands, but they shall live, and be read, till the wretches die ...
>
> (127–32)

This purpose underpins the narrative drive of the play. A patrician Venetian, Volpone (the name means 'fox'), is childless and apparently sick; in hope of becoming his heir a succession of citizens visit and leave gifts, guided in their actions by the seemingly friendly advice of Volpone's servant, Mosca. They are of course being conned, as their desire for wealth paradoxically leads them into giving it away. Volpone's project is put at risk by his determination to acquire not simply the wealth but also the wife of one of his victims, the merchant Corvino. Celia's resistance to his advances leads them all towards a courtroom showdown, from which the tricksters emerge unscathed at the end of Act IV. There is a hiatus at this point: the play could, it seems, end here. But the restless energy of its two protagonists takes them on beyond this apparent ending, tumbling them into a disaster of their own making: Mosca turns on his master and attempts to force him into parting with a share of his wealth, and to prevent such an outcome Volpone reveals the extent of their deceits to a reconvened court. Across this narrative, almost at right angles to it, wanders the figure of Sir Politic Would-be, an English visitor given to pretending intimacy with affairs of state. He is accompanied by his wife, keen to be accepted among the cosmopolitan sophisticates of Venice; the inevitable purgation of their humours concludes their stories.

Clearly, then, this is a satire on greed, the vice in which Volpone, Mosca, their three victims and other characters are implicated. Like *Eastward Ho!*, though, it exceeds the framework its didactic purpose imposes, opening the text up to the possibility of a burlesque of its own moralising. Its Venetian setting, for example, is very carefully evoked – in ensuring that the details are precisely fashioned, Jonson makes clear that this Venice is not just London in disguise. Thus the setting comes to take on all the connotations which Venice held for early modern English culture. It was understood to be the archetypal mercantile city, the site of the kind of exchange in which London had only recently begun to specialise. In particular, it was the acknowledged centre for the trade in luxury goods that Jonson and his collaborators had treated with such ambivalence in 1605. But Venice was also, as recent commentators have noticed, held up as an ideal city-*state*, 'the most perfect modern example of the "mixed" constitution that was supposed to have accounted for Rome's republican liberty and greatness' **[156, 186]** (Hutson 1998: xxvii; see also Goldberg 1983: 74, Sanders 1998a: 35). Just as democracy and the free market are assumed to be somehow necessarily interdependent today, so Venice's commercial freedom and its political liberty were deemed to be mutually constitutive.

Volpone clearly notes the ethical dimensions of the transactions it documents and the avarice it condemns: the bond between husband and wife is destroyed in Corvino's pursuit of wealth, and Corbaccio willingly breaks the ties between father and son in chasing the same goal. Beyond that, the Avocatori or judges are clearly not as impartial and rational a group of arbiters as champions of the city's constitution might wish to claim. Not only are they comprehensively hoodwinked in Act IV, but their subsequent attempts to settle matters are tainted: in his stately disguise the parasite Mosca is courted by one of their number as a possible son-in-law. Only Volpone's self-destructive unmasking permits them to reassert the fitness for exercising judgement which has earlier been so little in evidence. The economic and the political are connected in this Venice, but not necessarily in a way that guarantees the integrity of both.

Money is at the root of this. And that is because money in this play is so much more than the facilitating token of exchange. Money, that is to say, does not work here to establish the standard by which all differences can be calibrated and quantified, a means by which a quantity of shoes, for example, can be said to be 'worth' seven hours of my unskilled manual labour or the benefit of your specialist advice. It appears instead as the inverse of this, a strange principle of transgression and transformation to which no limits can be put, twisting and warping the world into ever-shifting shapes. It is a social *force*, and is celebrated as such in the blasphemous speech with which Volpone opens the play:

> Such are thy beauties, and our loves! Dear saint,
> Riches, the dumb god, that giv'st all men tongues:
> That canst do naught, and yet mak'st men do all things;
> The price of souls; even hell, with thee to boot,
> Is made worth heaven! Thou art virtue, fame,
> Honour, and all things else! Who can get thee,
> He shall be noble, valiant, honest, wise –
>
> (I.i.21–7)

Critics have often noted the play's preoccupation with the disruption of stable entities produced by such a potent force. It is apparent in the transformation of Sir Pol, the parrot, into the form of a tortoise, or that of the crow Corvino, for example, into 'a chimera of wittol, fool and knave' (V.xii.91) – the very emblem of such disruption. It underpins the strange indeterminacy of Volpone's supposed children, the three characters who perform an entertainment in Act I detailing the transmigration of Pythagoras's soul through a potentially infinite number of bodies and forms. It is most strongly felt perhaps in the extraordinary attempt at seduction that Volpone addresses to the trapped Celia, an articulation of the erotic promise held in the transgressive possibility of mutation that takes more than its cue from Ovid's *Metamorphoses*:

> my dwarf shall dance,
> My eunuch sing, my fool take up the antic.
> Whilst we, in changed shapes, act Ovid's tales,
> Thou, like Europa now, and I like Jove,
> Then I like Mars, and thou like Erycine,

So, of the rest, till we have quite run through
And wearied all the fables of the gods.
Then will I have thee in more modern forms,
Attired like some sprightly dame of France,
Brave Tuscan lady, or proud Spanish beauty;
Sometimes, unto the Persian Sophy's wife;
Or the Grand Signior's mistress; and, for change,
To one of our most artful courtesans,
Or some quick Negro, or cold Russian;
And I will meet thee in as many shapes:
Where we may, so, transfuse our wandering souls,
Out at our lips, and score up sums of pleasures ...

(III.vii.220–34)

The fusion of luxurious abundance and eroticism in this passage identifies wealth with the cultivation of desire (Hutson 1998: 461), a restless hunger for sensual pleasure strongly at odds with the miser's joy in his inert pile of metal. Jacques de Prie buried his wealth under a pile of manure **[43]**; Volpone keeps his in his boudoir. Such a passage cannot help but invoke theatre here as well. It is not just that theatre is the archetypal site of dressing up and role-playing, though that could hardly be ignored. Volpone himself correlates his arousal in this situation with a remembered theatrical triumph:

I am now as fresh,
As hot, as high, and in as jovial plight,
As when, in that so celebrated scene,
At recitation of our comedy,
For entertainment of the great Valois,
I acted young Antinous; and attracted
The eyes and ears of all the ladies present,
To admire each graceful gesture, note, and footing.

(III.vii.157–64)

Theatre, in this characterisation of an aristocratic entertainment, is clearly the scene of desire, a mode of its articulation. But it is also among the commodified promises of 'contentment' – objects of desire – available to early modern consumers with some time on their hands and a bit of money in their purses. The theatre does not just address the link between desire and money in the experience of consumption – it enacts it.

The insertion of Sir Politic Would-be into this libidinal landscape makes him seem very much the Englishman abroad. While his wife seeks to learn the arts of the Venetian courtesan, his preoccupation with spurious affairs of state grates carefully against the concerns of the main plot. He deals in rumour and report, the fantastical tale and the spurious inference, in a manner familiar from Jonson's earlier comedies. Such a commentary certainly serves to keep issues of state at the surface of the play's concerns, in contrast to the neglect of such topics in the central narrative (Hutson 1998: xxvii). But he is inscribed into the triangulation of money, theatricality and desire with the revelation that his humour has theatre at its centre. Accused of plotting 'to sell the state of Venice to the Turk', he is forced to confess that he has no suspect papers, 'but notes / Drawn out of play-books' (V.iv.38, 41–2).

In Celia and Bonario we have two other figures who seem at odds with Volpone's Venice. It has often been suggested that it is their virtue which makes these figures seem so estranged from the drama in which they play a full part. Certainly the absence of desire from these characters counts against them – but Celia's crucial presence as an object of the desires of others affirms the play's ready association of all this transgressive play with a certain violence. Volpone's seductive speeches are the prelude to an attempted rape, after all, while the Ovidian exemplars he deploys are also laced with compulsion. Jupiter (Jove) tricked and abducted Europa; Mars and Venus ('Erycine') were themselves entrapped by Venus's husband, and exposed to the scorn of their fellow gods. Such violence is worked out on the body again in the emblematic deformation of the hermaphrodite, the dwarf and – especially – the eunuch. An undercurrent of bodily damage inheres too in the characterisation of Mosca. Where the cunning fox feigns an infirmity that screens and channels his desires, Mosca – meaning 'fly', but specified as 'flesh-fly' by Voltore (V.ix.1) – lives off the desires of others. He is another 'brainworm' **[47]**, an opportunistic infection, a parasitic disease that also works by feigning and playing, 'chang[ing] a visor [i.e. a mask] swifter than a thought' (III.i.29).

It is against these forces that the judicial pronouncements of the Avocatori direct their own violence, echoing the punitive satiric aspirations with which Jonson's Dedicatory Epistle concludes. In the play's final scene the word of the law is effectively mobilised, the theatre of judgement bearing down on the theatricality of desire; but since this amounts to a theatrical condemnation of theatre it is perhaps understandable that critics have disputed its justice and sincerity since the play's earliest performances.

If Venice is the nexus of commodities and desires in *Volpone*, London fulfils that role in Jonson's next play, *Epicene, or the Silent Woman*, first performed in 1609 by the Children of the Queen's Revels at the private, indoor Whitefriars theatre. Early in the work we are confronted by the figure of Sir Amorous La-Foole, a model consumer of the luxury goods that excited Volpone and a typical inhabitant of the leisured, moneyed society that is sustained by such consumption. His appearance is prefaced by a brief introductory 'character' provided by one of the play's crucial trio of wits, Clerimont:

> He does give plays and suppers, and invites his guests to 'em aloud, out of his window, as they ride by in coaches. He has a lodging in the Strand for the purpose. Or to watch when ladies are gone to the China houses or the Exchange, that he may meet 'em by chance, and give 'em presents, some two or three hundred pounds-worth of toys, to be laughed at. He is never without a spare banquet, or sweetmeats in his chamber, for their women to alight at and come up to for a bait.
>
> (I.iii.30–37)

The focus on London has moved westwards since *Eastward Ho!*, alighting on the newly fashionable districts between the court at Whitehall and the city itself. In the Strand was now to be found the New Exchange, or 'Britain's Burse', a kind of luxury shopping mall – Jonson himself had written an entertainment in praise of trade performed at its opening in April 1609 (Knowles 1999) **[106]**. 'China houses' were premises in which the expensive commodities obtained through the developing trade with the Far East were on display. Fashionable coaches and lodgings on the Strand itself were the preserve of the wealthy gentry and nobility who made up this high society, abandoning their obligations in their home districts to flock together in the capital. Official anxiety generated by this social whirl resulted in proclamations commanding the gentry to return to their estates, and something of the ethical concern that underpinned government action finds its way into the play. La-Foole and his counterpart Sir John Daw are made twin targets for the ridicule of Clerimont and his friends Dauphine and Truewit, their pretensions eventually exposed before the very society ladies whose attentions they court so assiduously. Those ladies are themselves rendered absurd – in the play's terms – both through their obsession with make-up, clothing and other trivialities and through the shared pretension to *gravitas* they display in styling themselves a 'College'.

Yet the wits are themselves thoroughly implicated in the practices of the world they, La-Foole, Daw and the Collegiates all inhabit. The play's opening scenes at Clerimont's lodgings reveal a man at home in the leisured world of the London gentry, wasting his time with no thought of being productive. Truewit begins by making a half-hearted attempt to mount an ethical critique, only to meet with a dismissive response:

> *Cler.* Foh, thou hast read Plutarch's morals, now, or some such tedious
> fellow; and it shows so vilely with thee: 'fore God, 'twill spoil
> thy wit utterly. Talk me of pins and feathers, and ladies, and
> rushes, and such things: and leave this Stoicity alone, till thou
> mak'st sermons.
>
> (I.i.54–8)

From then on, the play is happy to leave 'Stoicity' alone. It develops a comedy in which the ethical function of wit is explored on a terrain more commonly associated with the drama of the later seventeenth century, where morals blur into manners and the pursuit of the good becomes the maintenance of good form.

The real object of scorn is not a courtier or gallant but Dauphine's uncle. Morose is the character of the old man familiar from Jonson's classical exemplars, attempting to deprive the young wit of his inheritance, but he is equipped here with an overriding and absurdly pathological humour. He is unable to tolerate noise, requiring his servants to communicate with him by gestures, seeking out a 'silent woman' to marry and provide him with an heir to displace Dauphine. He cannot abide the pleasantries of conversation, the noise of a wedding feast, the reverberations to be found in 'a belfry, at Westminster Hall, i' the cock-pit, ... the Tower Wharf, ... London Bridge, Paris Garden, Billingsgate, ... a play that were nothing but fights at sea, drum, trumpet, and target' (IV.iv.12–17). His humour sets him against all the features of the urban and urbane world he has the misfortune to inhabit, a society figured in the utterances that connect its participants, the cries of trade and the babble of pleasure (see Smith 1999: 49–71). Prey to the torments unleashed on him by the young gallants, he finds his refuge from this world – a soundproofed house – made instead a more fitting epitome than a restless royal curiosity of its defining characteristics:

> You do not know in what a misery I have been exercised this day,
> what a torrent of evil! My very house turns round with the tumult!

I dwell in a windmill! The perpetual motion is here and not at
Eltham.

(V.iii.52–5)

That it should be this figure who is dismissed from the play by his
nephew with the words, 'I'll not trouble you, till you trouble me with
your funeral, which I care not how soon it come' (V.iv.184–5), reveals
the bounds of its tolerance. Those who hold out against the new city
are far from being credited with wisdom – the play cannot with ease
be read as a jeremiad against conspicuous consumption. Instead, it is
perhaps more helpful to locate its primary concerns elsewhere.

The centre of the narrative is Morose's marriage to Mistress Epicene,
the woman whose demure silence is for Morose her most appealing
characteristic. Once married, of course, she turns out to be as talkative
as any of the Collegiates who make up the play's quota of female
characters. Desperate to seek a route out of the contract into which he
has so rashly entered, Morose promises all his wealth in return for
Dauphine's assistance. Instantly, the joke is redoubled, in a revelatory
moment of which the audience has the forewarning only of Epicene's
name. Her peruke, or wig, is removed – she has been a he all along. The
revelation crystallises the play's persistent interrogation of the
significance of gender, a focus which has proved particularly interesting
to recent critics **[143, 175]**. The hierarchical opposition of male and
female, masculine and feminine, that has underpinned modern
ideologies of gender is perhaps left looking rather less unchanging and
inevitable in the light of these strange goings on, particularly as this is
a play which from a different angle depends so firmly on the adequate
specification of both sides and of the divide.

The monstrosity of the city's 'Collegiates' provides a negative
definition of the feminine norm: Madam Centaur, for example, partakes
of peculiarity in her name, a fusion of the human and the beastly. These
women are unnatural in their much-discussed use of cosmetics, an
application of art that seeks to hide the defects of their nature. They
are similarly grotesque in their parody of the institution of the college,
an inappropriate usurpation of judgement characterised by Truewit as
'most masculine, or rather hermaphroditical authority' (I.i.71), and in
Mistress Otter's exertion of her power over her husband. Their loqua-
city, like their fondness for consumption, speaks of the kind of libidinal
transgression that is the mark of the humour in earlier plays. In all,
they form a strong contrast to the modesty and restraint exemplified
by the silent Mistress Epicene when she first meets Morose. She is a
proper woman, the ideal wife. But on hearing her speak out once the

marriage ceremony is past, Morose declares in horror: 'Oh, immodesty! A manifest woman!' (III.iv.36). The 'proper' woman does not exist (she is, after all, a boy), and yet the proper identity of 'woman' seems simultaneously to be 'manifest' as the horrifying deviation from this ideal. It is as if 'woman' were simply the name of monstrosity, the naturally unnatural – the negation of its own proper meaning. No wonder, then, that so many critics have found in *Epicene* an element of misogyny, even if they are not agreed as to its place or role **[175, 179]**.

The play couples this unstable misogyny to an evocation of a masculine world in which the unsettling influence of the homoerotic plays a significant part, as the sexual bonds between younger and older men are acknowledged from the very start. The opening scene between Clerimont and his page reveals a close relationship, coloured by Truewit's characterisation of his friend as one whose time is expended on 'his mistress abroad, and his ingle [i.e. catamite] at home' (I.i.22). The admission of same-sex desire that is so casually effected here finds its expression in the play's apparent demonstration that the ideal woman – the ideal object of male desire – is actually a boy (one of Jonson's sources establishes the precedent, the Italian satirist Pietro Aretino's tale of a stable master aghast at the prospect of marriage who cheers up on discovering that the bride is in fact his page in drag – see Campbell 1931; Hutson 1998: xxxi, 474). Even if it could not be argued that such a demonstration is left unqualified, *Epicene* does more than mobilise the comfortable opposition of masculine to feminine and the articulation of their difference through a universal heterosexuality. The ambiguity of which the word 'epicene' itself speaks is at least allowed a complicating role in the invocation of that opposition.

Epicene is centred on a wedding, a crucial and powerful affirmation of gender differentiation and heterosexuality, the union of one man with one woman. Though the actual wedding takes place offstage, most of the last Act is taken up with an extended interrogation of its validity. Dauphine masterminds a quasi-judicial investigation, running through all the circumstances which would make the marriage void. All are considered, all are discounted, until Dauphine's removal of Epicene's wig provides the incontrovertible evidence that the wedding can now be said never to have taken place, whatever any of the other characters or the audience may have thought.

The latter's position is the tricky one here. On the early modern stage, with boys playing all the female parts, the audience would have known from the start that 'Mistress Epicene' was in fact a boy **[13, 143]**. The fact would have been registered, and then forgotten, in order to allow the play to take place. Failure to forget means taking the play too literally – or, rather, not taking it literally, as 'a play' at all. By turning her hair into a wig Dauphine punishes us for our forgetfulness, forcing an immediate re-examination of the basis on which we entered into this experience in the first place. That wig, which ought to be an insignificant element of the conditions within which the play happens, turns out to be necessary, a crucial part of its happening. The conventions which govern this performance are casually, brutally shifted, and the meaning of the performance is retrospectively revised. Because this is a process of retrospection, however, a rereading that must proceed from an initial reading, the revision itself features as a narrative. The play narrates, as its last act, the annulment of a marriage: but it also tells the story of its *own* annulment, inscribing and reinscribing dramatic experience in a manner that makes it neither singular nor certain. Within this experience, Mistress Epicene remains both male *and* female, as his name suggests. The cost imposed by narrative on that ambiguity is that she is never allowed to settle into the happy simultaneity, the paradoxical self-identity, of either indeterminacy or union.

Further reading

Barton (1984) provides a generally solid account of all three of these plays, sketchier on *Eastward Ho!* perhaps because of its collaborative nature. Barton's account can be complemented with the introductions to this work offered in the editions of Knowles (2001) and Van Fossen (1979). *Volpone* is the subject of a volume of essays in the Casebook series (Barish 1993) and has been a persistent focus of critical attention over the years. Knights (1937) and Partridge (1958) are classic readings, while Creaser (1978) offers a good introductory essay. Greenblatt (1976) is an authoritative interrogation of the narrative structure of the play, complemented by the chapter on *Volpone* in Donaldson (1997). Womack (1986) reads the play through a concern with the politics of theatricality and festivity, while Cave (1991) offers a reading of this and *Volpone* organised around their manipulation of early modern theatrical conventions. The introductions to *Volpone* and *Epicene* found in Hutson (1998) are similarly engaged with such questions. The later play has been the focus of much criticism informed by feminism, the thinking of gender, sexuality and society: Rose (1988), Newman (1991), Levine (1994) and Swann (1998) offer contrasting but related interrogations of the play in this light.

(g) UNREAL CITY: *THE ALCHEMIST* AND *BARTHOLOMEW FAIR*

The first scene of *The Alchemist* is one of the most explosive openings in early modern drama. Face bursts onto the stage with a sword in his hand; Subtle follows, clutching a phial and throwing insults. Dol vainly attempts to mediate, before opting for the more successful strategy of matching their violence with her own. Within the space of two hundred lines their confederacy has been torn apart and stitched back together, their tripartite – but not entirely stable – agreement marking out the space that all the other characters in the play will have to negotiate. Face has memorably sketched a portrait of his collaborator, Subtle, as he first found him:

> at Pie Corner,
> Taking your meal of steam in, from cooks' stalls,
> Where, like the father of hunger, you did walk
> Piteously costive, with your pinched-horn-nose ...
> (I.i.25–8)

Subtle has countered by reminding Face of his own circumstances prior to their encounter, alone 'in your master's house' where 'you, and the rats, here, kept possession' (I.i.49–50). Both, it seems, feel that the other owes them a huge debt – it is Dol's function to reassert their shared purposes, the need to 'leave your factions, sir. / And labour, kindly, in the common work' (I.i.155–6).

So this is an opening which quickly establishes the social network which will underlie all the action to come. Dol's language, her talk of their 'republic' (I.i.110), their 'venture tripartite' founded on the principle of 'all things in common' (I.i.135) provides a strong characterisation of its basis, just as her fear that Subtle and Face will 'undo yourselves, with civil war' (I.i.82) specifies the threat they pose to each other. We need to be clear, though, as the scene itself is, what this network amounts to. This is not Rome; Dol is not Cicero; neither Subtle or Face is a Caesar or a Catiline. We are instead watching the internecine disputes of a trio of tricksters, clinging together in a joint endeavour to squeeze some cash out of the dimmer inhabitants of their city. Dol is a prostitute, Captain Face is in fact a servant named Jeremy, and Subtle is a con artist of no fixed abode. Somehow, though, their association has become dignified with the language of radical political thought, characterised as a free state. Dol Common's surname marks

79

her clearly as a whore, but it also resonantly evokes here the community of property she herself asserts as the founding principle of their *commonwealth* **[186]**.

How has this happened? Two related reasons suggest themselves. First, their co-operation takes its place as a developed institution of the Jacobean underworld, a subcultural formation which is not a series of fragments on the outside of legitimate society, but an alternative to that society, its image and its opposite (with all the tensions that paradoxical formulation implies) **[174]**. Second, it is growing out of all control in London's ruins, in the space abandoned by the city's natural rulers. An outbreak of the plague has driven the gentry from the city: the house in which Jeremy serves has become, for as long as the sickness persists, Face's domain. When Subtle is subsequently disguised in Act III as a 'priest of faery', and Dol as the Faery Queen herself, the device seems highly appropriate. Their world too is a shadowy, night-time realm, coexisting with – but not in the full sight of – the quotidian daylight world of early modern London. It is just that the prolongation of the night by plague allows that realm an extended spell in which to articulate its form and its promise.

This world, then, is the realm of fantasies, a dream space in which desires unfold freely. In Dapper and Drugger we find two characters seduced by the promise of wish-fulfilment, by the hope of prosperity in gambling and in trade. Once brought to trust their desires, there appears no limit to their reach into absurdity. Thus Dapper's initial request for a 'familiar' leads him on into an encounter with the Queen of Faery, while Drugger's desires expand to encompass the rich widow Dame Pliant. Most noticeably, though, it is the dreamworld of Sir Epicure Mammon which finds its sustenance in the environment of Face's house. His desires are famously articulated in a passage which has an obvious kinship with the voluptuous fantasies of Volpone:

> I'll have all my beds blown up; not stuffed:
> Down is too hard. And then, mine oval room,
> Filled with such pictures, as Tiberius took
> From Elephantis: and dull Aretine
> But coldly imitated. Then, my glasses,
> Cut in more subtle angles, to disperse
> And multiply the figures, as I walk
> Naked between my *succubae*. My mists
> I'll have of perfume, vapoured 'bout the room,
> To loose ourselves in; and my baths, like pits

To fall into: from whence we will come forth,
And roll us dry in gossamer and roses.
                                                    (II.ii.41–52)

Encompassing the full range of the senses and thoroughly sexual,
Sir Epicure's litany of bodily pleasures is thoroughly appropriate to a
man of that name. The mention, too, of obscene pictures and of 'suc-
cubae' – demonic entities who take human form for sexual purposes –
marks this as a transgressive longing beyond the limits even of mere
luxury. Equally significant, though, is the *global* quality of Sir Epicure's
desires, their formal similitude to the structure of the tricksters'
republic. Mammon himself describes arrival at their house as effectively
setting foot 'on shore / In *novo orbe* [the new world]' (II.i.1–2), and this
Eldorado is the occasion for the production of his own. The space of
his desires is a monarchy in which his initial plans to do good, as a
benevolent despot, are soon displaced by its organisation around the
satisfaction of his corporeal appetite. When Dol objects that his
forthcoming riches will lead him into trouble with authority, 'it being
a wealth unfit / For any private subject' (IV.i.149–50), Mammon
concedes the difficulty:

                          'Tis no idle fear!
We'll therefore go with all, my girl, and live
In a free state.
                                                    (IV.i.154–6)

A free state is also the goal of the Anabaptists, Ananias and Tribu-
lation, the figures in the play who most obviously represent a community – 'we of the Separation' (III.i.2) – at odds with the governmental
structures of the city. The offstage Brethren to whom they report figure
a world apart, underpinning the radicalism of their claim that 'we know
no magistrate' (III.ii.150). The accusations of hypocrisy that are
customarily levelled against them are perhaps less appropriate here than
an attention to the contradictions presented by their attempt to live
separate, and the political dimensions of their creed. They anticipate
that the wealth that they will gain from their dealings with alchemy
will enable them to destroy the Catholic church and thus herald the
rule of the true believers. Dol's portrayal of a gentlewoman driven mad
by the writings of a puritan theologian, her fit triggered by Mammon's
mention of 'a fifth monarchy' (IV.v.34 – this was the hope of a saintly
government on earth entertained by some of the more radical puritans),

only serves to emphasise their politics, and the clear structural similarities between the desires of Mammon and the Anabaptists.

Alchemy is the means through which these desires are to be made real, the link between the insubstantiality of longing and the actuality of any 'free state'. In early modern England the possibility of alchemy was both widely entertained and as widely dismissed (Abraham 1998: xv–xxii). The idea that all metals might be transformable into gold could be inferred from inherited 'scientific' assumptions, as Subtle demonstrates in his dispute with Mammon's sceptical companion Surly, and increasing experiment in 'natural philosophy' offered the prospect of paradigm-shifting breakthroughs in the future. Crucially, alchemy also offered a metaphor for the perfectibility of the world itself, a way of configuring the promise of a future and an elsewhere different from the here and now. As a means of thinking change it was, to some extent, a guarantee of the possibility of revolution – in the modern sense of that word. The house where Face, Subtle and Dol ply their trade is thus a threshold between the world as it is and the world as it could be: to step inside is to step into the experience of the promise. Since the truth or falsity of a promise can only be judged retrospectively, in a future that is yet to come, it always faces its audience with a decision. Necessarily a gamble on the future, it can either be believed or dismissed. In this play, only Surly decides not to believe in alchemy as practice or as promise – but his choice does not save him from the humiliation suffered by those who choose differently.

This is not to say that the play has not made its own choice. In this text alchemy is an impossible promise, an entrapment rather than an intimation of freedom. The complex of *technical* jargon that gives alchemy its credibility, that anchors its seductive promise in a set of operations on the present, is marked emphatically as the cant of a fraud. All transformation, in other words, is mere pretence. The pace of the play is unrelenting, the repeated knock on the door heralding the arrival of a new victim before the old has been thoroughly fleeced. Face, Dol and Subtle are continually shepherding their clients upstairs, inside, out through another exit, before dashing off to change themselves into other shapes – Face plays Lungs, the alchemist's assistant, while Dol gets the parts both of the Faery Queen and of the mad gentlewoman. Even Surly, disguised as a Spanish nobleman, gets caught up in this contagious transmutation. This, though, is never an alchemical transmutation: a tawdry series of illusions has been substituted for any proclaimed transformation. The pretence displayed is the polar opposite of alchemy's promise, but unerringly true to its failure to deliver.

The return of Lovewit at the beginning of Act V heralds a change in the fortunes of all the characters. The offstage explosion of Subtle's 'equipment' has already rendered his victims' hopes vain. With this *coup de théâtre*, though, the scandalous multiplicity of performances in which the confederates were engaged begins to be exhausted. The duplicity of the stage-space is itself revealed to the gaze: on the one hand, the noise and bustle reported by his neighbours, the cry of the imprisoned Dapper, all the evidence of men at work; on the other the bald shabbiness shown by Lovewit to the disappointed and vengeful gulls who have gathered outside:

> The empty walls, worse than I left 'em, smoked,
> A few cracked pots, and glasses, and a furnace,
> The ceiling filled with posies of the candle:
> And Madam, with a dildo, writ o' the walls.
>
> (V.v.39–42)

Furthermore, with Subtle and Dol having fled over the back wall and Face restored to his identity as Jeremy, the republic is itself by now in dissolution: Jeremy has already been labouring in the service of his master to effect Lovewit's marriage to Dame Pliant, stitching up his ex-comrades. For all its structural similarities to the utopian projects of Mammon and the Brethren, though, their commonwealth has had an existence in the present as more than a promise – but it has existed only to the extent that it, like the play, never believed in that promise. Its substance is stashed in the cellar, goods that are now the property of Lovewit rather than the collectively held wealth of the tripartite venture. The returning master has sanctioned the expropriation enacted by his erring servant, but not the form in which it occurred: 'all things' are no longer to be held 'in common'. The pretensions of the commonwealth have solidified into the assets stripped from a short-lived theatre company.

Like many of his earlier comedies, *The Alchemist* demonstrates the Jonsonian engagement with the culture industry of his city, the commerce in pastimes in which both the outdoor and indoor theatres played their parts. While their comic possibilities never escaped him, his plays are themselves too deeply rooted in such pastimes ever to be at a safely dismissive distance from them. *The Alchemist*'s topical debt to the popular currency of 'coney-catching' pamphlets – cheaply printed, morally ambivalent accounts of urban villainy – sufficiently indicates its own implication in this end of the leisure industry as firmly as *Epicene*'s comedy of manners roots it in the consumerism of high society. It is not possible simply to correlate the social distinction between classes with a differentiation between minority culture and mass civilisation – the dividing line of commodification cuts across all other boundaries, and is itself never a stable partition. Similarly, the political questions which simmer throughout the play are persistent, sustained as they are by its thematic concern with utopian possibilities. But since the play also characterises such possibilities both as delusory and as the form of an existing underworld, settling it into a single interpretation has been a trickier matter. The relationship in these plays between theatricality and political promise, on the one hand, and theatricality and delusion, on the other, has been a particular point of critical concern [142, 170]. And the third of Jonson's most celebrated comedies, *Bartholomew Fair*, has proved an equally troublesome or fertile object of speculation [172].

First performed at the Hope theatre on Bankside – a regular venue for bear-baiting as well as plays – in the autumn of 1614, the play is set largely in London's annual Bartholomew Fair. This was an important event in the urban calendar, taking over a site in Smithfield at the north of the city and filling it with both the commerce of a cloth market (its original basis) and that of popular festivity. It was a place for Londoners to go to eat, drink, see puppet plays and curiosities, or buy gifts and trinkets. The fair was inhabited by merchants, by those who serviced the demand for diversion and entertainment and by those who profited illicitly from this congregation of pleasure-seekers. In Jonson's play the interactions of the inhabitants and the visitors are traced through the trickery to which the latter are subjected after their appetites have drawn them into the world of the former.

The Alchemist, like *Volpone* among the major comedies, is written in verse (in these two plays, only Volpone's speeches as Scoto the mountebank are in prose). *Bartholomew Fair*, like *Epicene*, is by contrast a prose work. But *Bartholomew Fair* resembles *The Alchemist* to the extent that it locates a space of fantasy that promises the gratification of desires. Win Littlewit's feigned longing for pig brings her party to Smithfield: at the booth of Ursula, the 'pig-woman', the symbolic centre of the fair, their longings are satisfied. The fair offers, like Lovewit's house, a space apart from the restrictions and limitations of the quotidian world they inhabit, the very negation of Zeal-of-the-Land Busy's Puritan prohibitions on sensuous pleasure (a pleasure of which he nonetheless avails himself). It is to that extent a *carnivalesque* space, in the European medieval tradition traced through the work of the sixteenth century French writer Francois Rabelais by the Russian cultural theorist Mikhail Bakhtin and more broadly by recent scholars such as Peter Burke (1978). The Rabelaisian writing of carnival drew on a medieval and early modern popular festivity that set itself against all the structures and strictures of an authoritative, 'official' culture. The world was turned upside down in carnival, hierarchies inverted and boundaries crossed, the earthly and transient exalted in place of the spiritual and eternal. Celebrated for its mutability and openness to the world – its involvement in generation, regeneration and degeneration – the human body itself was identified as one of the most important emblems of carnival, while its language was the language of the marketplace, colloquial and irreverent:

> Abuses, curses, profanities, and improprieties are the unofficial elements of speech. They were and are still conceived as a breach of the established norms of verbal address; they refuse to conform to conventions, to etiquette, civility, respectability.
>
> (Bakhtin 1968: 187)

As many critics have noted, Jonson's Fair clearly shares some of these characteristics **[168]**. Through its organisation around the activities of eating and drinking, the figure of the 'pig-woman', its repeated invocations of urination and the onstage vomiting of Mistress Overdo in its closing moments, it establishes itself as the site of an impeccably carnivalesque corporeality. These bodies find their linguistic counterpart in the game of 'vapours' played by both inhabitants of and visitors to the fair, the meaningless exchange of insults and abuse accompanied by serious drinking. The pig, whose image hangs over Ursula's booth and dominates the setting, gathers together all these elements into a single emblematic focus (Stallybrass and White 1986: 44–59; Womack 1986: 145–6).

What Jonson brings to this feast is the institution of theatre. There are of course some similarities, often noted, between the coming together of carnival and the festivity of theatre, particularly the emphasis on collective experience, the performance of shows and diversions, the emphasis on mutability and the promise of gratification or 'contentment', as the final lines of *Eastward Ho!* put it. *Bartholomew Fair*, however, is also organised around a theatrical performance, a puppet show written by John Littlewit and put on by Lantern Leatherhead in Act V. It serves as the climax of the action, bringing together the visitors in time to witness the humiliation of Busy and offering Justice Overdo – who has stalked the fair in disguise, observing the goings on of both inhabitants and visitors – a stage on which to perform his own denunciation of the 'enormities' he has witnessed.

The show the puppets actually perform itself seems a carnivalesque inversion of 'proper' theatre, since Littlewit has adapted the classical story of Hero and Leander from Marlowe's poem of the same name into a tale of a drunken fumble down by the Thames, awash with crude innuendo and abuse. The puppets themselves seem a literal and figurative diminution of the theatre's dignity, and yet a diminution that simultaneously presents itself as the essence of the theatrical process. This is a parody of theatre; but then, theatre here simply *is* parody. It already embodies a playful evasion of positive content that serves to confute Busy when he interrupts the performance to parrot a series of Puritan objections to the stage. His problem is that he fails to appreciate the impossibility of engaging a puppet in debate, even though a puppet is precisely the right spokes-non-person for this construction of theatricality. In the end, Busy's attack on the cross-dressing practised on the English stage is evaded by the puppet hoisting up its skirt to reveal the spectacular absence of an underlying sex that could determine the propriety or impropriety of its apparel. Like the audience of *Epicene*, Busy has taken theatre too seriously – and has therefore missed the point completely, or failed to take it seriously enough. On both occasions – and this is surely significant – it is the issue of gender differentiation that has opened up such possibilities.

This suspension of the question of propriety appears elsewhere in the play. When both Win Littlewit and Mistress Overdo are inveigled into becoming whores by Whit and Knockem, two of the Fair's shady denizens, it is not only drink that enables the shift. Whit announces that 'dey shal all both be ladies, and write [i.e. style themselves] Madam' (IV.v.80), and it is the ambiguity of that word 'madam' that holds together the proper and the improper – as indeed it still does today. More dramatically, we are confronted with the performance of Justice Overdo in the play's final scene. He has throughout been distinguished from the other characters, pursuing his plan – declared to the audience at the opening of Act II – to detect and then proclaim the 'enormities' occurring in the fair. In other words, he announces a plan to implement the kind of judicial intervention familiar from all Jonson's earlier comedies. His preparation for such an intervention by disguising himself, so that ill deeds will be the more evident to him, inevitably recalls both Shakespeare's *Measure for Measure* and the long tradition of 'disguised duke' narratives in which similar plans have been executed. One of the major problems of interpretation offered by *Bartholomew Fair* is its parody both of this tradition and of Jonson's own theatres of judgement. Overdo's judgements, expressed in choric asides during the action, are eminently hopeless – most obviously, his identification of the cutpurse Edgworth as an innocent youth. His real achievement, though, comes at the end of the play, in a spectacular denouement of his own devising. Throwing off his disguise he declares that 'it is time, to take enormity by the forehead, and brand it' (V.v.108), deploying the motif of judicial inscription that Jonson had claimed for his poetry in *Poetaster*'s Apologetical Dialogue and *Volpone*'s Dedicatory Epistle. He follows up with resort to the formulaic invocations with which Touchstone had asserted the didactic thrust of *Eastward Ho!* in the strained conclusion to that play [68]:

> Now, to my enormities: look upon me, O London! And see me, O Smithfield; the example of Justice, and Mirror of Magistrates: the true top of formality, and scourge of enormity.
>
> (V.vi.28–31)

Here it is not only the 'disguised duke' narrative that has stumbled into parody – Overdo's speeches are also a comic reworking of the Ciceronian oratory Jonson had rendered so faithfully in *Catiline* [63, 183]. Unlike those of his Roman exemplar, though, Overdo's denunciations don't get very far: his characterisation of Edgworth as 'this easy and honest young man' (V.vi.39) is a mere prelude to his own wife's liquid intervention. 'Her husband is silenced', reads the stage direction: the theatre of judgement is abruptly suspended, possible brandings postponed, and what actually ensues is a prolongation both of the fair and its attendant theatricals. Overdo, reminded by Quarlous that he is 'but Adam, flesh and blood' (V.vi.89), invites the assembled company to his house for supper; the young gull Bartholomew Cokes agrees, declaring, 'yes, and bring the actors along, we'll ha' the rest o' the play at home' (V.vi.104–5).

It has been argued that such an ending represents the triumph of the carnivalesque, an extension beyond its boundaries of Smithfield's festivity [171]. But we ought to note features of the play that might militate against such a conclusion. First, as in *The Alchemist*, theatricality is never separated from the commercial basis on which it takes place. This fair is, after all, a market, its noise precisely a mélange of street cries and the general bustle of trade, as the first scene to feature its inhabitants (II.ii) makes abundantly clear. Its shows and diversions are often the cover for robbery, such activities enforcing the distinction between the people of the fair and their visitors rather than fusing them into a single incarnation of 'the people'. Ursula is not just Rabelaisian corporeality – she is also a bawd, furthering the commodification of the female body, while the play itself has flagged its own status as a commodity in the Induction which began its first performance at the Hope. There, a scrivener takes the stage to publish 'Articles of Agreement, indented, between the Spectators or Hearers, at the Hope on the Bankside, in the County of Surrey on the one party; and the Author of Bartholomew Fair in the said place, and County on the other party' (57–60). This is a commercial contract between the audience and the author, Jonson, governing the supply and consumption of the service he is contracted to provide. It is manifestly absurd in some of its particulars, but in making explicit the commercial nature of the interaction between the producers of a play and its consumers in the early modern theatre it is far from absurd. If the theatre is an enterprise, it is perhaps no more unproblematically carnivalesque than the fair it dramatises.

Second, its suspension of judgement is placed within similar limits. The play's next performance took place only a day later, but this time at the court in Whitehall. Instead of the Induction it began with a Prologue to the King, making of the play a 'fairing' (12), a gift, and ended with an Epilogue that contrasts perhaps with the failures of judgement exemplified by Overdo. There the King is described as the man who 'can best allow' the play (2), and 'can tell / if we have used that leave you gave us well' (5–6). Such questions of 'allowance' also emerge in Busy's intervention during the puppet play, Leatherhead countering his complaints with the assertions that 'I present nothing but what is licensed by authority', and 'I have the Master of the Revels' hand for 't' (V.v.12, 14). It might be argued that the corrosions of parody are circumscribed by this framework of allowance, leaving it with a delimited space in which to operate but denying its capacity to break out of those limits. Such perhaps is what the boundary between the play and its framing devices amounts to: the definition of theatre within the frameworks of both royal authority and the market. That these are alternative ways of determining the play's context, and ones that are not perhaps easily assimilated to each other, begins to explain the sheer variety of critical interpretations *Bartholomew Fair* continues to provoke.

Further reading

Knights (1937) deals at some length with *The Alchemist*; consideration of *Bartholomew Fair*, on the other hand, is omitted from his exploration of the social resonance of Jonsonian comedy. Partridge (1958) and Barish (1960) are also classic accounts, the latter dealing particularly thoroughly with Jonson's prose style and its significance for the reading of his texts. Donaldson (1970) examines the place of comic inversion in Jonson, while the topic of carnivalesque festivity has been taken up more recently – often in the light of Bakhtin's work, but not always in agreement with its larger claims regarding the political valency of carnival – by McCanles (1977), Rhodes (1980), Bristol (1985), Womack (1986), Stallybrass and White (1986), Marcus (1986), Haynes (1992), Burt (1993) and Miller (1996), to mention only a selection of the available literature. Holdsworth (1979) contains a number of essays on *The Alchemist* from other perspectives, and Haynes's chapter on the play complements both the essay in Donaldson (1997) and the discussions of both plays in Barton (1984) and Cave (1991), which proceed other than via the dominant concerns of the bulk of recent criticism.

(h) THE SHOCK OF THE NEW: *THE DEVIL IS AN ASS* AND *THE STAPLE OF NEWS*

In the years after *Bartholomew Fair* Jonson's dramatic output dropped sharply. In 1616 *The Devil is an Ass* was performed; a full decade later, in the different climate of a post-Jacobean England, *The Staple of News* followed it onto the stage. Yet both plays share and recast some of the characteristics that distinguish Jonson's earlier work, even as they grapple with distinctive problems of their own. In *The Devil* we can find collegiate ladies reminiscent of *Epicene*, a cross-dressed man in Wittipol's disguise as a Spanish lady and in Merecraft a conman whose bizarre 'projects' or get-rich-quick schemes recall the promises of Face and Subtle. In the central figure of Fitzdottrel the play presents us with a gull to rival any of the alchemist's victims, and one whose idiocy and unpleasantness is thrown into sharp relief by its contrast to the evident virtues of his wife. Her eventual refusal of the seductive attentions of the gallant Wittipol not only enhances her standing in the play, it also allows Wittipol and his friend Manly to become something more than the urban gentlemen of *Epicene* in their behaviour too. Wittipol's plotting in the latter half of the play has a goal beyond the exposure or exploitation of folly, seeking to secure the title to Fitzdottrel's property in order to prevent him from surrendering it into the clutches of Merecraft and thereby exposing his wife to ruin. Her seducer becomes her champion and protector, in a narrative that brings Jonson closer to romance than his work has ever been before.

It would be unwise, however, to over-emphasise this aspect of the play. Too many other features militate against it, not least of course the sweeping evocation of the urban world inhabited by these figures.

In the opening scenes Fitzdottrel is on his way to the Blackfriars theatre to see a play, Newgate prison provides an important setting, a crucial role is played by the emblematic commercial figure of Gilthead, a goldsmith (and therefore banker [68]). The play also repeatedly and explicitly raises the question of its own borders, and therefore of its own possible status as an act or a performance. In Act I, Wittipol gives Fitzdottrel a cloak in return for the opportunity to address his wife for fifteen minutes; Fitzdottrel is tempted by the offer because it will give him something to show off at the theatre later in the day, sat among other spectators on the stage. In its Prologue, the play has already called attention to this practice and the constricting limits it places on the playing space – now the mutual implication of text and context is made even more apparent in the revelation that the play that Fitzdottrel intends to see is called 'The Devil is an Ass' (I.iv.21). Later on, when Merecraft needs someone to dress up as the Spanish lady to prise more money out of Fitzdottrel, he and the middleman Engine hit upon the idea of obtaining the services of Dick Robinson, a one-time boy actor, used to playing women, who had in fact performed in *Catiline* in 1611. But Engine instead returns with Wittipol, a change of plan which produces a narrative supplementary to that pursued within the space of the play itself. In the 1616 production Wittipol was in all probability played by the now mature Dick Robinson (Happé 1994: 128). Robinson, as Wittipol, is called on to stand in for Robinson: contingent details of performance come to infiltrate the narrative as performed. Indeed, Wittipol has been framed as player in Act I scene vi, making his address to Mistress Fitzdottrel (using 'all the tropes / And schemes, that Prince Quintilian can afford you', as Fitzdottrel says [I.iv.100–1]) from within a bounded playing space marked out by the rushes that covered the stage itself (Happé 1994: 83). Speaking her lines as well as his own (the bargain with her husband stipulates her silence), Wittipol not only prefigures his own cross-dressing but also recalls Robinson's youthful occupation as a player of the woman's part.

Such details not only focus attention on the context of production, they also make the act of representation into a thematic concern of the play. This is a function they share with the whole diabolic apparatus in which the narrative is wrapped. The devil of the title is Pug, a mere junior demon, who petitions Satan in the opening scene to be allowed to visit some hellish mischief on London. This he proposes to do in the company of Iniquity, a stock character from mid-sixteenth century dramatic interludes. Iniquity speaks in the metre familiar from this genre, promising a whole series of tricks that can be played in the city. But Iniquity is, as Satan makes clear, thoroughly outmoded (at I.i.56

he is seemingly unaware that the steeple of St Paul's no longer exists –
it had been struck by lightning in 1561). As Pug finds out, London's
vice is not to be compassed within the representational forms symbolised by characters such as Iniquity or himself. His attempts to
generate a narrative of diabolic intervention into the lives of the citizens
result only in his progressive marginalisation from the narrative they
generate themselves. In the end, after he has been imprisoned in
Newgate, he is summoned away by the Devil – his departure from the
city, frightening Fitzdottrel out of his schemes to win back his rights
to his property, has a much greater effect than his arrival. In short,
Pug's trip to London is untimely. Or, rather, 'Pug', as trope, and the
kind of narrative mode for which he stands, are untimely. The structure
of Jonson's play thus identifies this form of representation as past, as
the past itself, and separates itself from that past. It formulates an
awareness of the breach between past and present that cultural historians have described as the archetypal experience of 'modernity'. When
The Devil is an Ass correlates the date of its action with the date of its
own performance it insists on its own contemporaneity, uniting audience and action in the simultaneity of an event that is happening *now*.

Despite the ten years separating their composition, this insistent
modernity is also an oft-remarked component of *The Staple of News*.
Here too Jonson looks back to the devices of the old morality plays,
and in particular a late example entitled *The Contention between Liberality
and Prodigality* (see Parr 1988: 16). The central figure is Peniboy Junior,
a young prodigal. His father, Peniboy Canter, puts into effect a scheme
to test his son's prudence by faking his own death and observing, in
disguise, Peniboy Junior's use of his newly inherited wealth. The play
contrasts the young man with his miserly usurer of an uncle, Peniboy
Senior, and their very different treatment of Pecunia, an allegorical
personification of wealth attended by her maidservants Mortgage,
Statute, Wax and Band. While Peniboy Senior's loss of Pecunia drives
him mad, Peniboy Junior's wastefulness is only stopped by his father's
revelation of himself at the end of Act IV. Father and son are reconciled
by the latter's assistance in dispelling threats to the former's property,
allowing a closing emphasis on the right use of wealth to be delivered
by Pecunia herself:

> And so Pecunia herself doth wish,
> That she may still be aid unto their uses,
> Not slave unto their pleasures, or a tyrant
> Over their fair desires; but teach them all
> The golden mean ...
>
> (V.vi.60–5)

The play is not simply a reproduction of such familiar representational modes, though. Giving it its title, and the centre of recent critical attention, is an office or 'staple' for the production and retail of news, a monopolistic enterprise which recalls not only the projects of Merecraft but also the alchemical hopes fostered by Subtle – at the end of Act IV it effects an offstage disappearance reminiscent of his laboratory's dissolution. It is thus linked to the kind of hopes and desires familiar from Jonson's earlier comedies, both for new worlds and new things – indeed, it is first outlined by Thomas Barber as the new fashionable resort for urban gallants like Peniboy, a commercial centre appropriate to the developing metropolis:

> Where all the news of all sorts shall be brought,
> And there be examined, and then registered,
> And so be issued under the seal of the office,
> As staple news; no other news be current.
> (I.ii.34–7)

On the one hand, the Staple signifies the constraint of the free circulation of gossip (itself dramatised and gendered in the play's exchanges between four female gossips who occupy the place of the chorus) within the bounds of a particular enterprise; on the other, it frees that circulation from multiple, narrow social networks and makes it available to all via the single means of the market. It also, crucially, makes of conversation itself a primarily commercial interchange. Its major significance lies in the act of exchange, not in what is exchanged: language is called away from the work either of description or prescription and surrendered to other processes and valuations. As one of the Staple's early customers puts it, 'I would have, sir, / A groatsworth of news, I care not what' (I.iv.10–11).

This, of course, is something of a scandal. For these reasons, the play aligns news thematically with the language games of 'canting' (the dialect of the criminal underworld) and jeering it also dramatises, recalling the litany of linguistic abuses that have marked Jonson's texts from the slanders of *Poetaster* to the vapours of *Bartholomew Fair*. News is a particular kind of commodity; as language it has a necessary signifying capacity (indeed, it needs to be capable of signifying to be this kind of commodity: this is, to an irreducible extent, a trade in meanings). The scandal of news is that it puts into circulation a series of meanings that are incidental to, but nevertheless inseparable from, the linguistic artefacts in which they abide. The play claims that the consumerist logic of fashion or *novelty*, the incitement of desire through commercial exchange, instead determines their dissemination and their value, a value which is now only commercial. This logic is necessarily temporal, forever producing the new only by simultaneously differentiating it from the old, living by their separation: it is the logic of modernity once again. As Jonson's play amply demonstrates, the word 'news' itself implies both a meaningful story and this emphasis on the value of novelty. Newspapers were only just beginning to be developed in the England of the 1620s, and the business was still extremely rudimentary (Frank 1961). In his portrait of the Staple, Jonson gives us a compelling hyperbolic image of the emergent trade's institutional or technological framework, and of the ethical difficulties it appeared to raise.

Further reading

Neither *The Devil is an Ass* nor *The Staple of News* have commanded anything like the critical attention devoted to their predecessors in the Jonsonian canon. Nonetheless, significant work has been done, most notably in the last twenty years, though the reading of *The Staple* advanced in McKenzie (1973) is a slightly earlier example of such work. The editions of Happé (1994) and Parr (1988) offer comprehensive general introductions. Again, Barton (1984) provides close readings of both plays, particularly through the Jonsonian creation of character and his negotiation of generic boundaries; her accounts, and those of Cave (1991) can profitably be read alongside the more recent and detailed historicist analyses of Sanders (1998a and 1998b). The romantic comedy of the earlier play is effectively explored in Ostovich (1998), while Lanier (1983) develops a detailed account of *The Staple*. Wayne (1995 and 1999) attends more specifically, like Sanders and following McKenzie, to the later play's engagement with modes of cultural exchange and circulation.

(i) LAST PLAYS: *THE NEW INN, THE MAGNETIC LADY* AND *A TALE OF A TUB*

Critics have always struggled to take *The New Inn* seriously. Staged in 1629, it appears to have met with the scorn of its original audience, famously provoking its author to pen an 'Ode to Himself' in which he urged his own departure from 'the loathèd stage / And the more loathsome age' (1–2). In a verse riposte to this 'Ode', Jonson's contemporary Owen Felltham complained of the play's 'jests so nominal' and its 'unlikely plot', suggesting that it was as absurd as

Shakespeare's romance *Pericles* (*HSS*, XI, 339). Certainly, the conclusion of *The New Inn* is one which resembles those of Shakespeare's later works. The play is set in the Light Heart Inn in Barnet, north of London, an establishment presided over by the genial host Goodstock, and temporary home to the melancholy gentleman Lovel. He is hopelessly in love with the young Lady Frampul, an exuberant if spoilt young woman who descends on the inn for the purposes of merriment. Her maidservant Prudence is established as 'sovereign' for the occasion, convening a court or parliament of love in which Lovel's passionate orations win over the previously dismissive Lady Frampul. Meanwhile, in a reprise of *Epicene*, the host's son Frank, attended by an old Irish nurse, is dressed up as a fine lady and married off to the aristocrat Lord Beaufort. Such would appear to be material sufficient for establishing the basis for a comedy – but in the hundred and fifty six lines of the closing scene it is revealed that Goodstock is in fact the lost Lord Frampul, father of the young Lady; that the old nurse is his long lost wife, and Frank his younger daughter Laetitia. No wonder Felltham described the plot as 'unlikely'.

Perhaps such complaints miss the point. This is after all the Light Heart, and in the play's first Act the similitude between inn and play-house is asserted by the Host himself. It is a place where he can 'imagine all the world's a play':

> The state and men's affairs all passages
> Of life, to spring new scenes, come in, go out,
> And shift, and vanish; and if I have got
> A seat to sit at ease here i' mine inn,
> To see the comedy; and laugh, and chuck
> At the variety and throng of humours
> And dispositions that come jostling in
> And out still, as they one drove hence another:
> Why, will you envy me my happiness?
>
> (I.iii.128–37)

A lightness of approach would seem to be appropriate here, and in the context of Lady Frampul's revelry. That a maidservant might take the place of the sovereign for a short while indicates that this is a time apart from the world, a festive space in which some licence might be permitted to absurdity. Yet Jonson's own Dedication, 'To the Reader', insists that the play should be taken seriously, that reading, in fact, is no other than taking it seriously. And the question of seriousness is one that the play raises itself at thematic and rhetorical levels. The carnivalesque rule of Prudence might be permitted; but the inversions of social order practised by Nick Stuffe and his wife meet with ridicule and punishment. Stuffe, a tailor, likes nothing more on completing a dress for a wealthy client than dressing his wife in it, driving out to the country with her, and playing out his favourite fantasy of sex with great ladies. Their practice discovered, the pair are subjected to a quasi-judicial shaming ritual. This playfulness cannot be tolerated: it is a serious infringement, and it provokes a serious response.

The parliament of love enables a further interrogation of this question, not least perhaps because 'parliament' is a particularly fraught concept in the context of the late 1620s **[185, 186]**. Here, Lovel speaks according to the rules of the game; Lady Frampul's responses too are part of this game. Yet he is also serious – he means what he says – and so, in her declarations of love, is she. The problem is that this seriousness is hard to distinguish from mere play, and at the crucial conclusion to Act Four, Pru and her Lady fall out over just this uncertainty. Lady Frampul insists that she was only sporting a 'visor' or 'mask' (IV.iv.294, 295) of mockery to start with, and rebukes Pru for letting Lovel go – the latter has done so because 'I thought you had dissembled, madam' (IV.iv.310), and asks regarding the 'mask':

> But how do I know, when her ladyship is pleased
> To leave it off, except she tell me so?
>
> (IV.iv.296–7)

A reasonable question, it would seem – but Lady Frampul insists that Pru should have been able to tell what she really meant, and her anger at not being 'understood' (IV.iv.309) leads her into an outburst against her maidservant. Pru's hurt at this is met with the Lady's insistence that she now does *not* mean what she says, that 'it was a word fell from me, Pru, by chance' (IV.iv.325). Pru herself responds by claiming that it was this retraction that was in fact not meant, even if – to add a whole new layer of complication – her mistress did not know that she did not mean it, and that she – Pru – *can* in fact tell the meant from the accidental:

> Good madam, please to undeceive yourself,
> I know when words do slip and when they are darted
> With all their bitterness ...
>
> (IV.iv.326–8)

Lady Frampul is likewise adamant that 'one woman reads another's character, / Without the tedious trouble of deciphering, / If she but give her mind to't' (IV.iv.300–2). What is remarkable, given both their mutual and acknowledged incomprehension and Pru's suggestion that Lady Frampul does not know her own mind, is the accompanying and apparently contradictory insistence that utterances either *could* not or *should* not be misunderstood. Here, the problem of seriousness emerges as the whole business of reading, the determination of what is meant in what is said. It is asserted that this is a distinction that an utterance makes for the attentive reader, despite the circumstances which have called forth such an assertion. Language, they claim, ultimately reveals the intentions it embodies – only contingent factors such as ignorance, weakness or deliberate fault can in the last analysis impede such communication.

The play's trope of revelation provides rhetorical support to this contention. In its last scene all the playing and dissembling that has characterised the Light Heart is brought to an end. Disguises are thrown off, identities revealed; characters speak as they are. Goodstock, now Lord Frampul, declares that during his time away, 'All my family, / Indeed, were gipsies, tapsters, ostlers, chamberlains, / Reduced vessels of civility' (V.v.127–9). Now, his shadowy, 'gypsy' existence is traded for the fullness of his proper name and his proper place within the social or 'civil' body. For Lovel, this process of revelation has been 'a dream, ... fantasies made i' the Light Heart' (V.v.120–1), and such it has seemed to many other readers; but this is actually the *end* of fantasy, the point at which things get serious and the play-space of the inn is left behind. *The New Inn*, in other words, insists that it speaks most seriously at precisely the point where its playfulness seems least in doubt. Such a disjunction marks out the space of Pru's disavowed uncertainties. Her 'but how do I know ...?' is a question which prefigures much of the critical puzzlement and exasperation that the play as a whole has occasioned.

Despite the exhortations he addressed to himself, Jonson returned to the 'loathèd stage' in 1632 with *The Magnetic Lady*, or *Humours Reconciled*. The play's title suggests an explicit return to the humour theory of his early works, a move elucidated in the Induction:

> The author, beginning his studies of this kind with 'Every Man in his Humour', and after 'Every Man out of his Humour', and since, continuing in all his plays, especially those of the comic thread, whereof 'The New Inn' was the last, some recent humours still or manners of men, that went along with the times, finding himself

now near the close or shutting up of his circle, hath fancied to
himself in idea this magnetic mistress.

(Induction, 83–90)

This, then, is a Jonsonian retrospective, looking back over his whole
career to find the consistent concern with 'manners' defining and
uniting all his works. It also happens to coincide with the critical
narrative of Jonson's work propounded by one of his last patrons, the
Earl of Newcastle [35] (Rowe 1994: 206). In describing the last stages
of the circle this play reconciles the Jonsonian corpus to itself: as much
is clear from its redeployment of the 'Grex' frame familiar from *Every
Man Out*, the roles of Mitis, Cordatus and Asper here taken by Mr
Damplay, Mr Probee and a boy of the company.

This figure of reconciliation marks the action too. The narrative is
organised around Lady Loadstone, the 'magnetic lady' of the title,
whose attraction is in fact her marriageable niece Placentia. The plot
concerns itself with the attentions paid by a number of suitors, while
also leading towards the revelation that Placentia is actually the
daughter of Loadstone's 'she-parasite', Polish. Polish substituted her
infant child for the real heiress, Pleasance, who has grown up as the
impostor's waiting woman – here, the inversions and convolutions of
romance plotting are strongly in evidence. Despite these revelations
Polish is not subjected to a judicial punishment, as all the characters
are reconciled to each other and – crucially – 'to truth' (V.x.126) at the
play's resolution. Nonetheless, the spectre of a disorderly, female
household must be exorcised for any restitution of proper order to take
place [178]. The restored Pleasance is married off to a character called
Compass, a force for order who is identified with the author himself
(in Act I scene ii, 33–4, he explicitly attributes his own epigrammatic
comments on a fellow character to Jonson; a broken compass, moreover,
was Jonson's own *impresa* or emblem). The authorial judgement
exemplified in Asper's playing of Macilente is relatively muted here,
both in the reconciliatory moves of Compass and in the counsel of
passivity urged by the boy on Damplay and Probee; indeed, the chorus
finds itself at the end 'changed into an epilogue to the King', abstracting
judgement from itself and from the action, postponing it in ceding it
to a monarch who is definitely not to be brought on stage. Such gestures
notwithstanding, the play attracted less than favourable attention from
the church authorities for its topical references to the doctrinal disputes
which were beginning to strain the fabric of the established church
(Butler 1991/2: 75–81).

Despite this narrative of closure, Jonson's work did not cease with *The Magnetic Lady*. Indeed, his last complete play is as relentlessly loose an end as any of the works omitted from the autobiographical story told in the first Folio and updated in 1632. Jonson's twentieth-century editors, following earlier suggestions, declared *A Tale of a Tub* an early play dusted down and cobbled together with topical matter in 1633 (*HSS*, I, 275–81). This view was convincingly challenged by Anne Barton (Barton 1984: 321–37), though the matter is still not definitively settled (Craig 1999). Furthermore, a satirical representation of Inigo Jones **[28]** as 'Vitruvius Hoop' was excised by order of the Lord Chamberlain, along with 'the motion of the tub' which concludes the play (*HSS*, III, 3). The printed text contains the latter, but the former has been recast as the character of In-and-In Medlay, leaving us with a text which bears the marks of censorship in ways that are not quite knowable.

The suggestion that *A Tale of a Tub* is substantially an early work draws sustenance from its setting in an Elizabethan world and the archaism (for 1633) of much of its verse. The play evokes a rural community near London, but not in its orbit – this is the country as a world apart. Its plot is concerned with the wooing of Audrey Turf by a number of suitors, a series of comic intrigues which leave the Tub family servant Pol-Martin victorious. The play concludes with a wedding feast and entertainment provided by the cooper Medlay, a bathetic shadow play which offers a mock-heroic recapitulation of the action. In a duality of function with which the play seems quite happy, Medlay is both inhabitant of the locale and, in relation to Inigo Jones, a satiric impersonation. His show brings the courtly art form of the masque, central to Jonson's career, into some disrepute; or else the aspirations of these yokels to such an elevated representational mode as the masque is itself held up to ridicule; or else it is the whole play which is reduced to its essential absurdity in this concluding 'motion of the tub'. Whatever, we might say, and with a degree of textual authority, our nonchalance underpinned by the play on the word 'Tub'. Read as the squire's proper name it makes this his tale, and the concluding show – originally commissioned by Tub from Medlay – a *précis* of the whole narrative. Tub's plans are derailed, and in the entertainment he is pushed to the side of his own tale. But 'a tale of a tub' is also a cock and bull story, an inconsequential noise, and the play anchors its own proceedings in such inconsequentiality with its reference to the 'virst Tale of a Tub' in the apparently digressive – self-confessedly discontinuous, at any rate – 'Scene Interloping' in Act IV. Here, the writer Scriben recalls his godfather:

A mighty learned man, but pest'lence poor.
Vor, he'd no house, save an old tub, to dwell in,
(I vind that in records) and still he turned it
I' the wind's teeth, as't blew on his backside,
And there they would lie rowting one at other,
A week, sometimes.

(Scene Interloping, 29–34)

This first tale roots the play in the windy noise of a 'rowting' – belching, snoring, farting – scholar. Furthermore, the absurdity of Medlay's concluding 'motion', during which the solemnity of a marriage masque disappears into travesty, reinforces the sense of mockery established in the Scene Interloping. While recent critical work has managed to establish contemporary political resonances for the play **[184, 185]**, the note of flippancy perhaps also requires some attention.

At his death Jonson left two dramatic fragments, one much more substantial than the other. *The Sad Shepherd* is a version of the Robin Hood story, carefully located in a Sherwood forest that is yet the habitat of pastoral shepherds familiar from classical and Renaissance precedent. *Mortimer His Fall* exists only as the outline of a play in which English history would have furnished the matter for the tragic treatment given years earlier to Rome. Both enterprises look back, like *A Tale*, to the dramatic genres and conventions of his early years, recalling precedents from which he had learnt. But they also constitute departures for Jonson, the intrusion of the unexpected or unprecedented into the Jonsonian canon in a move that undermines his claim to have been always labouring on the single grand project. Such fragments, for different reasons, share the openness of all tub-tales. They dispute the feasibility of the closure claimed for *The Magnetic Lady*, the endpoint that orders preceding elements and fixes their relation to each other in a syntax of the *oeuvre*, that defines the meaning of the *work as a whole*. Jonson's work, at this late stage, cannot settle back into monolithic completion. The effort is still visible; and as his readers have often found, much work remains to be done.

Further reading

Written off as 'dotages' by Dryden, the late plays have been the focus of much critical debate in the last two decades in particular. Barton (1984), Butler (1984) and Marcus (1986) helped to foster an exploration of the peculiar features of these works which didn't assume their 'failure' as its starting point, paying particular attention to their political meanings. This is a project continued in relation to particular plays in Butler (1990) and (1991/2), while his historicist argument is made more generally in Butler (1992a). Rowe (1994) and Sanders (1998a) offer important augmentation and qualification of Butler's claims, while Harp (2000) presents brief but helpful commentary on the 'late plays' as a whole. Womack (1989) and Cave (1991) explore *The New Inn* in the light of its revival by the RSC in 1987, the latter paying particular attention to its reflexive inspection of theatricality, while Ostovich (1994) and (1997) explore *The Magnetic Lady* and *The New Inn* respectively from a feminist perspective. Hattaway (1984) and Happé (2000) are currently the standard editions of these two works. Craig (1999) presents the most recent attempt to resolve the issue of the dating of *A Tale of a Tub*, and a good account of the history of the debate, while Hayes (1992) is among the few commentators to deal at length with *The Sad Shepherd* and its use of the Robin Hood narrative.

(j) THE NEXT DEED: NON-DRAMATIC VERSE AND PROSE

In his 1616 Folio, Jonson estimated his non-dramatic verse above his writing for the stage. There can be no doubt that he was a prolific, accomplished and extremely versatile poet. His verse straddles the genres – epigrams of praise and blame, scatological satire, elegies, odes, pastoral – and yet, despite the fame of 'A Celebration of Charis in Ten Lyric Pieces' – his *oeuvre* is remarkable for its lack of amatory poetry. That other preoccupation of English Renaissance poetry, religious devotion, is equally under-represented. Jonson, in other words, is no John Donne. But he wrote in the same contexts as Donne, the relatively enclosed social networks of the court and the Inns of Court, the coteries in which poetry was written and circulated among people bound together by the ties of friendship and patronage. While Donne's public reputation came to rest on his standing as a preacher, however, and his poetry circulated – albeit ultimately quite widely – in manuscript, Jonson committed his coterie verse to the press. It is just possible that an edition of his *Epigrams* was published separately in 1612 (*HSS*, VIII, 16), but they were certainly in print four years later, when they appeared with the sequence *The Forest* in the 1616 *Works*. The posthumous second Folio featured a further collection, *The Underwood*, which the poet himself had (to an unknown extent) prepared for publication as a sequence. Many others went uncollected, and have been drawn together only gradually over the centuries since their author's death. The woody metaphor found in the titles of two of these collections is explained in Jonson's introductory note to *The Underwood*. *The Forest* was 'that kind of body ... in which there were works of diverse nature and matter congested, as the multitude call timber-trees, promiscuously growing, a wood or forest'; by analogy, then, the title of the latter collection derived from its status as 'lesser poems of later growth'.

While the 'diverse nature and matter' of the fifteen poems which make up *The Forest* illustrate the formal range of coterie verse, the sequence as a whole offers a glass in which an idealised image of aristocratic life might be contemplated. Here, despite an opening disclaimer, we do find love poetry, including the sensual address 'To Celia' from *Volpone* and a translation from the Roman poet Catullus. There is even a devotional lyric. What we also find are a number of poems addressed to prominent patrons: two 'Epistles' to the kind of aristocratic women whose patronage and involvement sustained such circles, one of whom – Elizabeth, Countess of Rutland – was a poet, the daughter of Sir Philip Sidney, and therefore a member of the family whose praise occupies a large part of the sequence. It underlies the praise of 'To Sir Robert Wroth' (*The Forest* 3), in which the son-in-law of the aristocratic poet's brother, Sir Robert Sidney, is presented as a country gentleman, his rural life identified against the twin corruptions of court and city. The countryside is evoked in a familiar pastoral fashion, but its idealisation is associated with the estate of Wroth himself. This gentleman can 'at home in thy securer rest / Live with unbought provision blest':

> Free from proud porches or their gilded roofs,
>   'Mongst lowing herds and solid hoofs;
> Alongst the curlèd woods and painted meads,
>   Through which a serpent river leads
> To some cool, courteous shade, which he calls his,
>   And makes sleep softer than it is!
>
> (15–120)

Wroth's estate, in other words (and perhaps that tell-tale adjective 'serpent' both confirms and qualifies this), is a new paradise: a place of leisure, peace and above all safety. It is a festive paradise too, where the 'rout of rural folk come thronging in' (53) to be entertained by the lord and his lady:

And the great heroes of her race
Sit mixed with loss of state or reverence:
Freedom doth with degree dispence.
(56–8)

Urban and court life, on the other hand, share the characteristics of
a war of all against all, the evocation of soldier, lawyer, miser and
courtier serving to emphasise the external world's demarcation as the
site of struggle, flux and danger. Here, no one has the security of
'dwelling' which is Wroth's privilege and reward, a mark either of his
fortune or his virtue.

'To Sir Robert Wroth' is preceded in *The Forest* by one of Jonson's
most celebrated works, a similar identification of rural safety with the
estate of an aristocratic patron – in this case, Sir Robert Sidney himself.
Sir Henry Sidney, his father, had acquired the family seat at Penshurst
in Kent only in 1552, so it was hardly the kind of ancestral dwelling
that the poem (written by 1612 at the latest) at times suggests; furthermore, the house was not exactly an architecturally distinguished building, a detail that Jonson's poem effortlessly accommodates in its praise.
'To Penshurst' begins with a brief characterisation of the house itself,
its difference from the kind of elaborate 'prodigy houses' built by those
who had grown rich quickly through their elevation to important offices
of state identified as the sign of its integrity and virtue. The poem
then takes its readers on a tour of the estate instead, the 'marks, of
soil, of air, / Of wood, of water' which ensure that 'thou art fair' (7–
8). So the poem describes in pastoral terms a grove marked with familial
connotations, including an oak planted to mark the birth of Philip
Sidney. A crucial subsequent section describes the woods, 'the lower
land' (22), 'the middle grounds' (24), the river and ponds of the estate
in terms of the livestock they hold and yield up to the requirements of
the family:

Fat, agèd carps, that run into thy net;
    And pikes, now weary of their own kind to eat,
As loath the second draught or cast to stay,
    Officiously, at first, themselves betray;
Bright eels, that emulate them, and leap on land
    Before the fisher, or into his hand.
(33–8)

In similar fashion, the garden is described in terms of the fruit and
the flowers that it produces, as if the whole estate were paying rent or

'tribute' (32) to the Sidneys. Such anthropomorphic possibilities are enhanced by the poem's subsequent move back into the house, following a procession of loyal tenants who 'all come in' (48), bearing gifts, 'to salute / Thy lord and lady, though they have no suit [i.e. request]' (49–50). At this, the centre point of the poem, the direction of gift-giving is suddenly and tellingly reversed, with a new emphasis on the unmatched hospitality provided by the Sidneys to their guests. Here, as a consumer of their 'free provisions' (58), the poet himself enters into the work, closely followed by King James and Prince Henry themselves, who stop off unexpectedly when out hunting. The Sidneys' open house policy enables them to offer the King a hospitality that is a mark both of their loyalty and of their virtue, and it is on the family's virtues that the poem concentrates in its concluding lines. Contrasting Penshurst once again with other aristocratic estates, the poem articulates the virtue of 'dwelling' that also marks 'To Sir Robert Wroth':

> Now, Penshurst, they that will proportion thee
>   With other edifices, when they see
> Those proud, ambitious heaps, and nothing else,
>   May say, their lords have built, but thy lord dwells.
>   (99–102)

'To Penshurst' is a remarkable poem for a number of reasons. Its determination of the Sidney family through a characterisation of their landscape makes it one of the first examples of the 'estate poem' (alongside Aemilia Lanyer's 'A Description of Cooke-ham', critically neglected until recent years). Its idealisation of rural aristocratic life is also significant, particularly for its attempt to locate virtue in the gift-giving which marks the Sidneys' relationships both to their land and tenantry and to the world of monarch and guest beyond it. Many critics have agreed that what we find in 'To Penshurst' is a drawing together of ethics and economics in an evocation of the domestic – there has been less agreement on the nature and significance of that conjunction **[189, 190, 193]**.

While the poems of *The Forest* are held together in their engagement with aristocratic ideals and preoccupations, the *Epigrams* are somewhat different. They are, for a start, more clearly structured by genre and content, imitating the classical precedent of Martial in particular. Poems naming and praising Jonson's patrons and friends – from the King downwards – are interspersed with satirical attacks on unnamed figures of vice, 'My Mere English Censurer', 'My Lord Ignorant', 'Sir Luckless Woo-All', and so on, often following the satiric examples of the Roman poets Juvenal and Horace as well as that of Martial. In both these collections, if in different ways, Jonson's verse is dominated by – and indeed arranged so as to display – its sociality. This voice reproduces the sound of a community as the sum of its relationships, tracing the interactions which not only bind these people together but more fundamentally serve to forge their identities as patron, client, friend, rival, courtier, monarch. As importantly, it functions as a means of making the kind of discriminations which ground its attempt to police this community, to seek out the forms of interaction that depart from the implied norm of a just, transparent, harmonious commonwealth. This, of course, is a juridical function – Jonson's poetry, like his drama, arrogates to itself the faculty of judgement. Its praise of King James (*Epigrams* 4) as 'best of kings' and 'best of poets' (1,2) is an instance of the crucial elision that animates the 'comical satires'; elsewhere, the *Panegyre* written to mark the opening of James's first English parliament finds an emblem for the reciprocity of monarch and poet in the figure of Themis, the goddess of divine law accessible to them both (see Butler 1996: 74). As a poetry of judgement, Jonson's poems perform the job of recognising virtue in the community they survey. But it could not really be argued that the *Epigrams* go to great lengths to outline what might constitute the virtue they are concerned to identify. Their activity might better be described as *nomination*, a process akin to the kingly function of rewarding merit with titles. Thus friends and patrons are praised as examples of a virtue that needs no elaboration, such poems resembling the few epitaphs among the collection in pronouncing the subject's character with the sureness and finality of commemoration. In the same vein, the poems attacking nameless figures for their vices obscure their personal identities with the 'crimes' they have committed, branding them in a quasi-judicial manner.

A paradigmatic example is a poem (*Epigrams* 102) addressed to William, Earl of Pembroke, the Folio dedicatee of the *Epigrams* and of *Catiline* [24]. Jonson begins with 'I do but name thee, Pembroke' and it almost appears that Pembroke is here, like a ship, in the process of being named. Yet while no bottle of champagne breaks across the noble lord's bow, we do find that the word 'Pembroke' is identified as a name by which virtue might be known in the midst of the ethical shiftiness of others that threatens the clear apprehension of such qualities:

> They follow virtue for reward today,
> Tomorrow vice, if she give better pay;
> And are so good and bad, just at a price,
> As nothing else discerns the virtue or vice.
> (9–12)

The name of Pembroke becomes the sure mark of virtue, its constant 'face' in a society where identities are otherwise not so certain. It is a process similar to that enacted in the following epigram, 'To Mary, Lady Wroth'. Here, the wife of Sir Robert is praised simply, the poem says, by the utterance of her name. Anything more would be superfluous:

> And, being named, how little doth that name
> Need any muse's praise to give it fame?
> Which is itself the imprese [i.e. emblem] of the great,
> And glory of them all, but to repeat!
> Forgive me, then, if mine but say you are
> A Sidney ...
>
> (5–10)

Where the poem to Pembroke makes his the name of virtue, here the name of Sidney is similarly the mark of greatness. All Jonson's verse has to do, in order to praise these worthy objects, is to point them out in repeating their names back to them. While this is something of a *reductio ad absurdam* of his verse practice, it is nonetheless the common basis of such poems to patrons and those he addresses to figures as diverse as John Donne (96), the soldier Sir Horace Vere (91) and the actor Edward Alleyn (89). Since, as the poems to Pembroke and Wroth show, this act of nomination self-reflexively becomes the topic of these poems of nomination, it is apparent that Jonson's *Epigrams* are concerned to explore the ways in which such a social poetry might function – and, by implication, the dangers to which it might be subject.

This concern is noticeable in *Epigram 95*, 'To Sir Henry Savile', in praise of the English translator of Tacitus's *Histories* **[74]**. It is as a writer that Savile is praised, but specifically for the active quality of his work:

> Although to write be lesser than to do,
> It is the next deed, and a great one too
>
> (25–6)

And the poem goes on to elaborate the kind of writing that counts as 'the next deed':

> We need a man can speak of the intents,
> The counsels, actions, orders and events

Of state, and censure them; we need his pen
Can write the things, the causes and the men.
But most we need his faith (and all have you)
That dares not write things false, nor hide things true.

(31–6)

If this reminds us at all of the exploration in *Sejanus* of the political work done by the word **[58]**, their common root in Tacitism should go some way towards accounting for the resemblance. Yet in positing the active, social role of writing the poem is at the very least associating its own practice with the work here ascribed to writers of history.

That there are perils attendant on such work is apparent from a number of other poems in the collection. The first three *Epigrams* address, respectively, the reader, the book itself, and 'My Bookseller', and all three also address the issue of the poems' contexts, the ways in which their acts of praise and blame will be circulated and received. *Epigrams* 1, 'To the Reader' urges the person picking up Jonson's book 'to read it well; that is, to understand' (2), while 'To My Book' worries that potential readers will misunderstand the title, and think this a work 'bold, licentious, full of gall, / Wormwood and sulphur, sharp and toothed withal' (4–5) when it is not at all 'lewd, profane and beastly' (11). *Epigrams* 3 imagines the book at its point of sale, and hopes that its method of circulation – being bought and sold – will not compromise the dignity of its contents, or in some way negate the seriousness of the deed it is attempting to accomplish. Such anxieties emerge again, and most forcefully, from the juxtaposition of *Epigrams* 63, 64 and 65, the first two addressed to Robert Cecil, Earl of Salisbury **[22, 27]**, and the third titled 'To My Muse'. In 63 and 64 Cecil is identified as another name of virtue, calling out to be uttered in praise by a poetry alive to its proper function of recognising such virtue. Yet in the second of these poems – written, as its subtitle declares, 'Upon the accession of the Treasurership to him [i.e. Cecil]' – Jonson's description of his own act of homage proceeds negatively, distinguishing itself from those of flatterers, opportunists, and seekers after personal gain who might also be addressing congratulations to the newly promoted courtier. Nonetheless, the poem works its way round to the crucial utterance of the words 'noblest Cecil' (15), a name which it finds has made its praise of an individual into a wider commendation of 'the greater fortunes of our state' (18).

So far, so good. 'To My Muse', however, puts the validity of this process of nomination into question. It begins, abruptly:

Away, and leave me, thou thing most abhorred,
  Thou hast betrayed me to a worthless lord,
Made me commit most fierce idolatry
  To a great image through thy luxury.
                                                    (1–4)

In these lines Jonson's own verse stands accused of the vice ascribed in
the preceding poem and in some of the satirical *Epigrams* to other
writers. His praise of 'a worthless lord' is declared to be the false flattery
of a seeker after preferment, not the disinterested recognition of virtue
it claimed to be, while the poem's placement in the sequence makes it
seem a comment on the fulsome celebration of Cecil it follows. The
rest of the poem condemns the muse that has somehow betrayed the
poet into such 'idolatry' (a term with crucial resonance for a Protestant
readership – the use of religious imagery was identified as a defining
mark of the Catholic church's collapse into decadence and error),
welcoming instead another muse. Poverty, it transpires,

    shall instruct my after-thoughts to write
  Things manly, and not smelling parasite.
                                                    (13–14)

But then, in a final turn, the poem recants its banishment in rescuing
itself from the wreckage of this idol-worship:

    Whoe'er is raised
  For worth he has not, he is taxed, not praised.
                                                    (15–16)

As a collector of moral revenue, making demands of those it
addresses, a poetry of judgement retains the social force that its nominative function also assumes. Nonetheless, if the possibility of flattery
is here so compellingly admitted, it might be hard to argue that it is
simply and finally dispelled in the poem's final lines. Could it not remain
to affect the reading of even those poems to Pembroke, Wroth and
others which are found elsewhere in the collection?

In these poems, and in those which open the collection, the anxieties
around a juridical verse – the word as deed – actually concern the *contexts*
in which such a verse might be written and read. Neither sale on the
market, nor the dependency of patronage relations, offer the guarantee
of disinterested writing and 'understanding' reading which might be
thought to be required. Friendship, however, does offer just such an appropriate context. *Epigrams* 101, 'Inviting a Friend to Supper', is indebted

to classical models: not only is the genre of the invitation poem a common one among the Roman poets Jonson admired, but three specific examples by Martial are here drawn on extensively. The poem attempts to entice its addressee to attend with an extensive menu of delicacies, but also with the prospect of literary entertainment: 'my man / Shall read a piece of Virgil, Tacitus, Livy, or of some better book ...' (20–2). There will be drink, too, 'a pure cup of rich Canary wine' (29), not as a sign of debauchery but as a mark of something of greater moment. The occasion will be notable for its exclusion of 'Poley or Parrot' (36), notorious government spies whose duplicitous talk and breaches of confidence are the antithesis of the friendship the poem eulogises. It will be a space of trust, of understanding, and of honesty – in short, as the poem puts it in its closing line, a moment of 'liberty' (42).

In hymning such a space, 'Inviting a Friend to Supper' offers an alternative to the corrupting contexts dwelt on in other poems, a way to envisage a safe, undistorting space for the assured plain-speaking. Yet the *Epigrams* do not go so far as to produce such an offer as their endpoint. They remain to some degree a miscellaneous collection of poems, even if we can trace characteristic patterns and themes, and therefore faithful to the classical precedents on which the collection was modelled. Included, for example, are elegies on Jonson's daughter (22), and the boy actor Salomon Pavy (120), as well as the celebrated 'On My First Son' (45). Indebted for some of its sentiments to the classical example of Martial in particular, the elegy is nonetheless a mapping of grief which traces the complexities of a psychological state claimed, unequivocally, for the poet himself. Guilt and shame mingle with the attempts at self-consolation. Finally, the collection concludes with the extraordinary 'On the Famous Voyage' (133), a narrative work which rewrites the visit to hell familiar from classical models as a mock-epic journey through the London sewers. Written in rhyming couplets and drawing parodically on Virgil's account of his hero's visit to the underworld in the *Aeneid*, it sketches in scatological fascination the intestinal workings of a budding metropolis, a city already generating – on so many levels – vast quantities of *waste*. Its exuberant ride down the alimentary canal not only brings to the fore a particularly significant resource in Jonson's *corpus* (Boehrer 1997), it also combines the grotesques of Rabelaisian writing and the burlesque of epic that is typical of later, Augustan satire.

The inventiveness that distinguishes a poem such as 'On the Famous Voyage' is a mark too of the poems gathered together as *The Underwood*. Though the bulk of these date from later in Jonson's career, they – like the later plays – cannot be written off as the work of a fading talent.

The handling of grief we find in 'On My First Son', for example, is revisited in 'To the Immortal Memory and Friendship of That Noble Pair, Sir Lucius Cary and Sir H. Morison' (70), but to very different effect. Sir Henry Morison died in 1629 around his twenty first birthday – the poem was written for his best friend, as a work of consolation. It is perhaps the earliest attempt in English at imitating the complex verse patterns of the Greek poet Pindar, whose own works were intended for choral, public performance. Jonson's division of the poem into tripartite sections featuring a 'Turn' a 'Counter-Turn' and a 'Stand' is a rendering of the pattern derived from that choric origin. The sentiments of the poem are derived in large part from an epistle (CXIII) written by the Roman writer Seneca, offering stoic consolation to the bereaved; it is also the opportunity for Jonson to celebrate the strength of feeling between the pair as a model of friendship which exceeds even the impact of death, 'Two names of friendship, but one star: / Of hearts the union' (98–99). Their mutual respect and admiration is envisaged as their recognition of their own virtues in each other – the 'simple love of greatness, and of good' (105) which drew them to each other is a form of self-love that escapes the solipsistic errors of Narcissism:

> This made you first to know the why
> You liked; then after to apply
> That liking; and approach so one the t'other,
> Till either grew a portion of the other:
> Each stylèd, by his end,
> The copy of his friend.
>   (107–12)

And since this ability to recognise virtue when you see it is also the capacity claimed by Jonson for his own poetry of praise, it is perhaps no surprise to find him too caught up in this apotheosis, his name famously stretched across a stanza division in an anticipation of his own elegy or epitaph:

> And there he lives with memory, and Ben

> *The Stand*

> Jonson, who sung this of him, ere he went
> Himself to rest ...
>   (84–6).

Elsewhere, *The Underwood* returns repeatedly to the discourse of friendship. 'An Epistle to Master John Selden' (14) presents itself as exactly the kind of free speech among trusted intimates that was envisaged in 'Inviting a Friend to Supper', praising the jurist Selden's 1614 work *Titles of Honour* by conferring the appellation 'Monarch in letters' (65) on him. The context of interaction between friends ensures, as Jonson puts it, 'that my reader is assured / I now mean what I speak' (27–8). Similarly commended for its truthfulness, in a poem explicating its frontispiece, is Walter Ralegh's *History of the World* (1614) (*The Underwood* 24, 'The Mind of the Frontispiece to a Book'), while 'An Epistle Answering to One that Asked to be Sealed of the Tribe of Ben' (47) enacts the induction of a new member into a free association which fosters the qualities exemplified in the writings of Selden and, of course, Jonson himself. Here, though, is not the poet as guest, seated at someone else's table – Jonson is now the host or proprietor, the legislator for this amicable space in which the like-minded may come together in safety and freedom.

This reiterated engagement with the matter of friendship, though, should not be allowed to obscure the variety of short or occasional works which the collection contains. Bitter personal satire on Inigo Jones **[28]** is matched by a misogynistic attack on Cecilia Bulstrode, friend of Jonson's patron Lady Bedford (Jonson was later to elegise Bulstrode, in contrasting but not unrelated terms, as 'a virgin; and then one / That durst be that in court' in his 'Epitaph on Cecilia Bulstrode', 3–4). This 'Epigram on the Court Pucelle [i.e. whore]' (49) identifies its object as one of the poet's 'censurers' before vituperating effusively in return. Her ability to write and speak, her possession of the masculine quality of wit, leads to a grotesque image of her as a lesbian rapist, 'with tribade lust ... forc[ing] a muse' (7). Alongside the collegiates of *Epicene*, and the tributes to literate women elsewhere in Jonson's oeuvre, this characterisation of female authorship and autonomy is a striking articulation of the varying ways in which gender and other forms of identity might intersect. As, indeed, are the tributes to Lady Venetia Digby, wife of Jonson's patron Sir Kenelm Digby, which make up 'Eupheme' (84). Though only fragments of this sequence remained to make it into the collection, they are a eulogy of Lady Venetia as the poet's muse that approaches a religious intensity, and echoes the adoration of the Virgin Mary familiar from Catholic devotional writing. This was something with which Jonson was not averse to playing, despite (perhaps because of) his own erstwhile Catholicism. *Epigrams* 22, 'On My First Daughter' **[17]**, commends the deceased child to the care of her heavenly namesake, while 'An Epigram to the Queen, then

Lying In [i.e. after giving birth], 1630' (*The Underwood* 66) actually addresses a 'Hail Mary' to the Catholic Queen Henrietta Maria [33]. In fact, poems in praise of King Charles and his consort are a regular occurrence in this later collection. Set alongside addresses to such patrons of Jonson's later years as the highly influential Richard Weston, Earl of Portland and Lord High Treasurer [34], they commemorate the royal birthdays, are sent as new year gifts, or celebrate the birth of royal offspring. While they eulogise a 'royal family' precisely as such, and as a microcosm of the virtue expected from the nation as a whole, they also manage to acknowledge the existence of opposition to royal authority in a manner which has not gone unremarked. 'To the King, on His Birthday' (*The Underwood* 72) demands public celebration of the royal anniversary from the guns and bells of London and the wider realm. But in *demanding* this 'poetry of steeples' (10) – a popular equivalent of its own effusive greeting to Charles – the poem might be thought to be highlighting its absence, as happens explicitly in the two opening stanzas of 'An Ode, or Song, by all the Muses, in Celebration of Her Majesty's Birthday, 1630' (*The Underwood* 67). When the poem to Charles ends with the interrogative 'but where the prince is such, / What prayers, people, can you think too much?' it is not at all certain that the question, as we might put it, is merely rhetorical. It is just such intimations of openness as this which have fuelled the critical disagreements of recent years over the political weight and direction of Jonson's poetry for the Caroline court [191, 193].

Not all the non-dramatic verse is organised into the three extant collections. Indeed, a substantial body of work was simply brought together as 'ungathered verse' by Herford and the Simpsons. It consists largely of commendatory poems prefaced to the works of others, but also features a number of verses which Jonson perhaps deliberately marked for exclusion from his own compilations. Perhaps the most celebrated of these 'ungathered' works are Jonson's two tributes to Shakespeare included in the 1623 posthumous Folio edition of the latter's plays. The shorter of the two, typically, urges readers to 'look / Not on his picture, but on his book' (10), and thus to locate in Shakespeare precisely the kind of monumental authorship which Jonson regarded as the apotheosis of the dramatic poet's career [146], while the lengthier tribute pursues the theme more eloquently. The fact that this poem is so indecorous as to note Shakespeare's possession of only 'small Latin, and less Greek' (31) has been enough to convict Jonson of unbecoming jealousy for many of the former's impassioned defenders, yet the poem's imposition of its own criteria for artistic worth on the products of its author's friend – its contention that

Shakespeare exemplifies the kind of poetic labour that marked Jonson's own claim to laureate authority – is actually a much more subtle and wary negotiation. This relationship is not the comfortable one between ancient and modern but something far less easily settled: for Jonson to praise on his own terms is an act of simultaneous aggression and concession.

That the canon of Jonson's works, huge though it is, was once yet much larger is demonstrated by the poet's response to the fire which consumed his library in November 1623. 'An Execration upon Vulcan' is an extended address from the distraught laureate to the Roman god associated most strongly with fire, who is berated for allowing the destruction of Jonson's books. Culminating in the reiterated curse, 'Pox on your flameship, Vulcan' (191), the poem places the fire in Jonson's house in the company of other notable fires of early modern London, including those which consumed the Globe in 1613 and the Whitehall Banqueting House in 1618, thus prompting Inigo Jones's innovative reconstruction **[28]**. It also spells out at length exactly which books would have deserved the sentence executed upon his own by Vulcan, notably the romances, 'weekly *Courants* [i.e. newsbooks]' (81), pamphlet prophecies and alchemical treatises that stand as a synecdoche for the popular literature of an early modern urban readership. Such works deserve only to be consumed by fire, because they are themselves only commodities for consumption. What has been lost, though, is work of different mettle – books by other authors, some borrowed, even, from friends such as Cotton and Selden **[33]**, but more importantly works by Jonson himself. Burnt are a translation of Horace's treatise on poetry, the *Ars Poetica*, with commentary informed by Aristotle's *Poetics*; a translation of the contemporary Latin romance *Argenis*, by John Barclay:

> a Grammar too,
> To teach some that their nurses could [not] do,
> The purity of language; and among
> The rest, my journey to Scotland sung,
> With all the adventures ...
> ... and in story there
> Of our fifth Henry, eight of his nine year...
> And twice twelve years stored-up humanity,
> With humble gleanings of divinity,
> After the fathers, and those wiser guides
> Whom faction had not drawn to study sides.
> (91–5, 97–8, 101–4)

In fact, two attempts at a translation of Horace's *Ars Poetica* survive, both eventually published after their translator's death. Similarly, Jonson's *English Grammar* was rewritten (though not finished), because it too was published posthumously. The 'humble gleanings' don't appear to have made it, but a work which might very well be described as 'stored-up humanity' did appear in print in the second Folio of 1641. Beneath the title of *Timber, or Discoveries* it gathered a miscellaneous collection of observations on and ideas regarding matters literary and philosophical. It is unlikely that this edition stems from another copy of the store that disappeared in the fire – these 'discoveries' were most likely made after that event. And although *Discoveries* amounts almost to a literary-critical testament, it can only problematically be described as Jonson's. The selection and arrangement of its contents are undoubtedly his doing, but the contents themselves are in large part taken – translated, often directly quoted – from a wide array of classical and modern authorities.

This, in other words, is Jonson's commonplace book, a technology of humanist education in which all grammar school boys were trained and which many continued to practise throughout their intellectual lives **[10]**. In commonplace books we find significant observations taken down, extracts from books and manuscripts copied, notes made. This is obviously not plagiarism, in the modern sense, because it presumes a different model of one's own authorship and the authorships of others on which our concept of plagiarism cannot easily be brought to bear. Here, for example, is Jonson on precisely this topic:

> I know nothing can conduce more to letters than to examine the writings of the ancients, and not to rest in their sole authority, or take all upon trust from them; provided the plagues of judging and pronouncing against them be away: such as are envy, bitterness, precipitation, impudence and scurrile scoffing. For to all the observations of the ancients, we have our own experience; which, if we will use and apply, we have better means to pronounce. It is true they opened the gates and made the ways, that went before us; but as guides, not commanders.
>
> (131–40)

Here, then, Jonson steps outside and speaks of his borrowing, in a kind of prefatory remark which underpins and justifies the rest of the work. Here, too, he puts such borrowing in its place, relegating the ancients from commanders to guides, placing their observations within the wider field of our own experience. They are the objects of our activity, what we read, not we ourselves. In fact, though, even this passage is 'stored-up humanity', for here Jonson is paraphrasing Seneca. Even his claim to autonomy, to a distinctive voice, speaks in the words of another, or has that other speak through him. There is, then, a kind of haunting, a shifting experience almost of possession, at work in this way of configuring authorship. In what sense might this author be said to be autonomous? Does such a haunting undermine even the *concept* of the autonomous, self-identical author **[146]**, a concept of which Ben Jonson – whose signature, after all, is to be found metaphorically scrawled all over his texts – has sometimes been considered the author? For modern critics, the problem of speaking of *Discoveries* as 'Jonson's work' shows that such configurations are not all traceable to the monolithic authority of the 1616 Folio. The fact that they are to be found happening differently elsewhere ensures that such authority cannot simply dominate or pre-empt our reading.

Further reading

Good, book length studies of the non-dramatic verse are not rare. Trimpi (1962) was influential in its time, though his claims for 'the plain style' ought to be set alongside the rather different characterisations provided by Peterson (1981), van den Berg (1987), Evans (1989), Lee (1989) and McCanles (1992). Of the shorter pieces dealing with a wide range of the poetry, Helgerson (1993) and Donaldson (2000) might be the most helpful starting point, while Marotti (1972) remains useful. Greene (1970), Newton (1977) and Helgerson (1983) consider the authorial self-presentation which characterises the poetry, while Fish (1984) explores the ways in which the poetry seeks to marshal a community of virtue and ensure its own role as its arbiter. Norbrook (1984) presents an important account of the political context inhabited by the poems, one which can profitably be read alongside Butler (1996). Wayne (1979) gives a compelling politicised reading of the *Epigrams*, while Wayne (1984) provides a similarly engaged but much more detailed reading of 'To Penshurst'. Wayne (1990) extends the focus to the rest of the poems in *The Forest*. Patterson (1984 and 1985) explores the structure of *The Underwood* as a collection in the context of literary censorship, arguing that it is not as loose a miscellany as it might at first appear. *Discoveries* is the subject of a fine introduction and notes in Donaldson (1985), and a primary focus of the important investigation into Jonson's literary-critical writing undertaken in Dutton (1996).

(k) PRESENT OCCASIONS: JONSON'S
MASQUES

It was not his plays for the public or private theatres that Jonson placed at the climax of his 1616 Folio. That position was taken by the masques that he had written for performance before the court of his royal patron, King James, since 1605. These, rather than his other dramatic work, might be thought to cement his poetic authority – along with the royal pension he was granted that year they provided the strongest evidence of Jonson actually living the ideal of poetry and power commingled that we find in so many of his earlier plays. Though by no means the only masque writer, he was certainly the most prolific and the best favoured: he composed masques for the Stuart courts over the course of twenty five years, and was still capable of producing entertainments for performance before King Charles in 1634, only three years before his death. In this field, beyond dispute, he outshone his fellow poets.

This was a dominance of an inherited or borrowed tradition. The masque form had a recent royal history on the mainland of Europe and in Tudor England (see Orgel 1965: 19–36) as a central component in courtly self-representation. While Jonson's contributions involved the elaboration, refinement and ultimately transformation of the conventions governing the production of the masque, such work presupposed a clear sense of what a masque should or could be. Fundamentally, it was a social occasion. Masques were performed as part of Christmas festivities and in celebration of other important events, marriages or royal visits, for example. The fact that these were court occasions ensured that they had crucial political meanings that have been the focus of fruitful critical work in the last few decades **[197]**. The contrasting strengths of court factions could find themselves acted out in masques, as could the differing priorities of the various royal households themselves. As the ambassadors of major European powers were customary guests at these events, and visits by international royalty also rare occasions of such revels, international politics could also leave its mark.

The masquers at these social occasions were not entertainers performing for an audience, but members themselves of the elite community. Generally of noble birth, they included both men and women, and their function was not to speak, but to dance. This point was not forgotten by James, who apparently interrupted the perform-ance of *Pleasure Reconciled to Virtue* – Jonson's carefully composed edifice for the Christmas season of 1617–18 – with the cry, 'Why don't they dance? What did they make me come here for? Devil take you all, dance!' (*HSS*, X, 583, trans.). James's intemperance aside, the point remains that the dance of the masquers was the crucial moment in the whole event, and also served to link the performance of the masque to its context, as the masquers would at its conclusion take partners from their audience to join them in dancing. The masque would thus take its place at the heart of a broader moment of revelry – it had to register the weight of political meanings and their dispersal into the pleasures of festivity. Jonson's contention that the masque might be more than a frivolous entertainment thus represents a none too tacit acknowledgement of the complexities and tensions of its occasion.

This contention underlies Jonson's willingness to make of his masques the apotheosis of his art. Yet while this lifts him free of the throng of lesser poets, it does so only at the cost of pitching him into conflict with his collaborator, Inigo Jones **[28]**. The architect designed the costumes and settings of the masques, a role that – apparently to Jonson's chagrin – was clearly much more than merely artisanal. Their personal rivalry was thus articulated also as the rivalry between the differing arts of poetry and architecture, Jones's compositional practice contesting Jonson's claim that the essence of the masque lay in its poetry (see in particular Gordon 1975: 77–101) **[197]**. In the final years of their collaboration and the aftermath of their falling out Jonson not only satirised his rival personally but also criticised his masques explicitly in plays, entertainments and verse. In 'An Expostulation with Inigo Jones' he denounces the architect and his 'shows, shows, mighty shows':

> The eloquence of masques! What need of prose,
> Or verse, or sense to express immortal you!
> You are the spectacles of state! 'Tis true
> Court hieroglyphics, and all arts afford
> In the mere perspective of an inch board!
> You ask no more than certain politic eyes,
> Eyes that can pierce into the mysteries
> Of many colours, read them, and reveal
> Mythology there painted on slit deal!
> O, to make boards speak! There is a task!
> Painting and carpentry are the soul of masque!
> (39–50)

Jonson's heavy sarcasm underscores a claim he had made for the published texts of his earliest masques many years before. In a preface to his edition of *Hymenaei*, a masque performed in 1606 to mark the marriage of the Earl of Essex to Lady Frances Howard, he articulated a position directly opposed to that with which he credits Jones in 'An Expostulation':

> It is a noble and just advantage that the things subjected to understanding have of those which are objected to sense that the one sort are but momentary and merely taking, the other impressing and lasting. Else the glory of all these solemnities had perished like a blaze and gone out in the beholders' eyes. So short lived are the bodies of all things in comparison of their souls. And, though bodies ofttimes have the ill luck to be sensually preferred, they find afterwards the good fortune, when souls live, to be utterly forgotten. This it is hath made the most royal princes and greatest persons, who are commonly the personators of these actions, not only studious of riches and magnificence in the outward celebration or show, which rightly becomes them, but curious after the most high and hearty inventions to furnish the inward parts, and those grounded upon antiquity and solid learnings; which, though their voice be taught to sound to present occasions, their sense or doth or should always lay hold on more removed mysteries.
>
> (*Hymenaei*, 1–17)

In other words, it is the *writing* which is the soul of masque, its essence or 'inward' part, and Jones's contribution amounts really to no more than appearance, an outer and contingent component of the whole thing. This metaphysics of the masque is supported by Jonson's claim that the costumes, setting and so on belong to the senses – particularly that of vision – which are bodily, temporal ('present occasions') and therefore inferior, while the words are properly correlated with the soul or understanding ('removed mysteries'). When Jonson writes of his own contribution as the provision of 'invention', he reinforces this case with an appeal to a classical schema of rhetoric that identifies *inventio* as the formulation of the idea, and accords it a creative priority over *dispositio* and *elocutio*, the expression of that idea.

There are, as we might imagine, a number of difficulties attendant on Jonson's metaphysics, not least the existence of classical precedent for the identification of something like *inventio* as the starting point of artistic and architectural creation (Gordon 1975: 85–96). Such a precedent offered an equally strong counter-argument to Jonson's declared exclusion of the pictorial from the level of the idea. More troubled, however, is his attempt to separate the word from the senses and all connotations of temporality, corporeality, and so on. For a start, the merging of word and image in the hieroglyphic devices deployed in masques (sometimes explicitly, but equally generalised to account for the symbolic language of masque as such) threatens the integrity of the contrast at the heart of Jonson's arrangement of binary conceptual oppositions.

As crucially, the written texts themselves – particularly of the earlier masques – struggle to maintain their faith in themselves as the verbal soul of the performances, persisting after the body of costume and setting has long since been 'defaced' (as Jonson put it in his prefatory comments to his first court entertainment, *The Masque of Blackness*). These texts, for example, include a lot of writing descriptive of the scene, the persons, the allegory, the action: not the masque as words, but words *about* the masque. However comprehensive the account given, its structure *as an account* maintains a disjunction between the description and what is described. The word, here, is on the wrong side of that disjunction, not at all where Jonson would seek to put it. And it gets worse: at certain points, the dance intrudes its social priority into the conceptual ordering attempted by the texts. As the centre of the masque, and a centre that at best can only be described in words, the dance threatens to place the mere secondary word at a greater distance from the essence or soul of the masque. In *The Masque of Beauty*, the masquers' 'most elegant and curious dance' is figured only negatively as that which is 'not to be described again by any art but that of their own footing' (313–14). The word now is not only a description but one confessing its own estrangement from what it describes.

Jonson's masques are also structurally dependent on the senses, and on the sense of sight in particular, for their engagement with royal power. If they are spectacles, the visual order they articulate is organised around the figure of the king – as recent critics have noted [198]. For one thing, they were occasions in which the visibility of the monarch was a crucial element – he was as keenly watched by the spectators as the performance itself, as the accounts of masques preserved in contemporary correspondence often confirm. Second, the court masque was the earliest use in England of perspectival staging, a way of seeing that privileged the monarch in offering a proper view only to him. Furthermore, this privileged sight of royalty is also a fulcrum on which the masque as a whole pivots. Throughout his career, Jonson's masques attribute the transformations they dramatise to royal power as it is revealed, 'discovered' in the setting of the masque, or as it is made present in the watching figure of the monarch. In the early *Masque of Blackness*, it is James as a sun king or *roi soleil* 'Whose beams shine day and night, and are of force / To blanch an Ethiop, and revive a corse' (224–5). Light is his currency, and sudden illumination the means by which his force is registered. In *Blackness* and its sequel, *The Masque of Beauty*, it works to take off the stain of a dark skin from the 'daughters of Niger', but its properties are more generally beneficent:

His light sciential is, and, past mere nature,
Can salve the rude defects of every creature.
(*Blackness*, 226–7)

By the time of Jonson's final court masque in 1631, this act of reformation had been rehearsed many times and in many different circumstances.

But Jonson's career as a masque writer is not a simple repetition of the same formal procedures. In fact, this invocation of the royal presence is partly responsible for the masque's formal development, particularly in anchoring the Jonsonian elaboration of the *antimasque*. From *The Masque of Queens* (1609) onwards, Jonson's court masques incorporated a prelude to the masque proper which offered more of an outlet for writerly invention than the dancing that followed. As the ambiguity of its name indicates, it not only preceded but also opposed the action of the masque, providing a foil for the image of royal power presented in the spectacle of the masquers themselves – indeed, providing something for royal power to *act upon*. Customarily acted by players from the professional companies, it offered the spectacle of low comedy, vice, licence and its inevitable circumscription by the king's writ. It incorporated such themes in a binary logic which generated a series of differing if structurally equivalent transgressors: the witches of *Queens*, the alchemists and 'imperfect creatures' of *Mercury Vindicated from the Alchemists at Court* (1615), the sins of *The Golden Age Restored* (1616), the carnivalesque unconscious of 'Fant'sy' in *The Vision of Delight* (1617), the rude Celts of *The Irish Masque at Court* and *For the Honour of Wales* (1613, 1618), are all tamed or banished through their encounters with Stuart power.

This structure does not account for all of the masques. In *Christmas His Masque* (1616), for example, the popular urban festivity presented is not tempered by its contact with the courtly elite, but remains robustly in possession of itself and the performance space. By contrast, *The Gypsies Metamorphosed* (1621), commissioned by the royal favourite Buckingham **[31, 33]** and performed three times before James in 1621, featured Buckingham himself and members of his circle as the seemingly 'low' or transgressive gypsies. The form, that is to say, remained flexible, a point which can sometimes be lost in the critical emphasis on royal authority and the masques' repeated narratives of marginalisation and transformation. This flexibility is actually evidence of the masque's occasional nature, its root in particular times and places that Jonson's account of his masques strives to obscure or at least to relegate to a lesser significance. These occasions themselves, furthermore, could be complex negotiations of different forces and meanings. Though they share the king's presence as an organising centre, entertainments stemming from the patronage of the Queen, of Prince Henry, of Buckingham or other nobles, or those commissioned from London's civic authorities and institutions, might be read as configuring monarchical vision and visibility in differing ways. Indeed, much of the recent critical attention given to the masques has developed precisely the suggestions to this effect to be found in Jonson's own texts **[202]**. What are we to make, for example, of the multiple reference points provided by the *Entertainment at Britain's Burse*, an interlude in praise of trade commissioned by Salisbury **[27]** and performed before the king at the opening of the New Exchange in 1609 (Knowles 1999)? In whose interests might this be said to speak? Why did Jonson not seek to publish it, thus ensuring that it slipped from view for nearly four centuries? Such artefacts demonstrate that an attention to the Jonsonian masque as a genre needs to accord due significance to its nature as event, that this at least partially *constitutes* it as a genre. Perhaps it is not quite as easy to separate out the 'removed mysteries' from their 'present occasions' as Jonson himself claims.

Further reading

The Jonsonian masque has received a very significant share of critical attention in recent years, following the pioneering work of D. J. Gordon (1975), and that of Greg (1952), Orgel (1965), Orgel and Strong (1973) and Orgel (1975). Lindley (1984) and (1995) gathers essays on and examples of Jonson's work, considering it alongside the efforts of others. Goldberg (1983) considers Jonson's masques as exercises in an absolutist scheme of royal self-representation, a view challenged in Butler (1991), (1992b, 1993b, 1994, 1998), Butler and Lindley (1994) and Lindley (1986). The politics of the masque is also the explicit focus of Parry (1993), and of the collection of essays in Bevington and Holbrook (1998). Feminist critics have argued that the patronage of Queen Anne in particular needs to be factored into our reading of Jonson's work: see for example Aasand (1992), Wynne-Davies (1992), Lewalski (1993) and McManus (1998). The masque's binary opposition of centre to margins, masque to antimasque, and Jonson's deployment of 'marginal' figures, has attracted the attention of critics concerned with the discursive structures of political oppression. See Gossett (1988), Hall (1995), Siddiqi (1992) and Smith (1998) for some differing engagements with this topic.

PART III

CRITICISM

(a) INTRODUCTION

This section focuses on the critical responses that Jonson's work has provoked over the years, and indeed continues to provoke in ever-increasing volume. The sheer variety and range of Jonson's work means that these critical responses cover a disparate array of both formal and thematic issues, addressing not just the substance of Jonson's writing (assuming for the moment that that is easily separable) but also its generic affiliations. Analysis of his work, that is to say, plays an important part in the history of critical thinking about drama, the masque, and poetry. Furthermore, the four centuries over which Jonson has been read in a manner recognisable as 'literary-critical' ensures that there is already a huge body of work devoted to the analysis of Jonson's own, substantial *oeuvre*. What follows is therefore necessarily selective, dealing at length with significant landmarks in the critical writing of the later twentieth century while only giving an outline of influential elements in its prehistory. The subsections which follow have been arranged to reflect both attention paid repeatedly to certain topics and the particular lines along which the critical assessment of Jonson's drama, masques and poetry have – at times separately – developed. Within this framework, the reader will find that particular topics have been revealed or transformed by the attentions of critics writing from various theoretically informed positions. Thus, for example, the development of feminist criticism made possible an engagement not only with the ways in which Jonson writes women, but also with the broader functioning of the language of gender and sexuality in his work. Similarly, comprehension of Jonson's configurations of authorship and of carnival were developed distinctively by critics working from a Marxist inheritance, and then reworked again in the light of New Historicist concerns.

(b) ON NOT BEING SHAKESPEARE

For nigh on four centuries the reputations of Jonson and Shakespeare have been locked together in an often stifling embrace. As we have seen in Part II, Jonson's own writing acknowledged and worked through the example and contrast of his great contemporary [111]. Yet while Jonson's reputation stood higher than Shakespeare's at the former's death in 1637, and he was for some years held up as the exemplar of English letters, in the criticism of his fellow laureate John Dryden and others towards the end of the seventeenth century we can detect a change in the relative assessments of the two dramatists which was to have devastating effects on the formation of attitudes to Jonson. As early as 1662 the antiquarian Thomas Fuller compared them in the following terms:

> Many were the wit-combats betwixt [Shakespeare] and Ben Jonson, which two I behold like a Spanish great galleon, and an English man of war; Master Jonson (like the former) was built far higher in learning; solid, but slow in his performances. Shakespeare with the English man of war, lesser in bulk, but lighter in sailing, could turn with all tides, tack about and take advantage of all winds, by the quickness of his wit and invention.
>
> (Craig 1990: 237)

This might appear at first sight to be a fair assessment of differing but equal virtues, contrasting strengths; but, as Richard Dutton has pointed out, the vehicle for the comparison – especially less than a century after the Spanish Armada – insinuates its own victory of Shakespeare's native powers over the suspiciously foreign qualities of his adversary in wit (Dutton 1996: 141–2).

The stage was thus set for the eighteenth century elevation of Shakespeare to the unrivalled position of national poet, the figure who was to metamorphose at the turn of the nineteenth century into the exemplary genius of Romantic imagining. This was the task taken up by those who set out to edit Shakespeare's works for the readers of the age. What better way to establish his credentials than by corralling Jonson into the role of his Other, the negation against whose darkness the glory of Shakespeare would appear ever more strongly in its true luminescence? What is more, this was now not just an assessment of relative literary merits. The attacks fused a delineation of Jonson's writerly demerits with a harsh assassination of his character, sometimes drawing on forged documents to 'prove' the case for the prosecution. Jonas Barish, one of the twentieth-century critics whose work has done so much to re-establish Jonson's reputation, takes up the story:

> Eighteenth century critics ... competed with each other in ascribing ignoble motives to Jonson. They charged him not only with parody but with plagiarism, with scurvy attacks on his fellow players, with a want of decency and decorum. They imagined, and gloated over, scenes of discomfiture in which he was forced to acknowledge Shakespeare's superiority. Attempting to account for the gifts he

received from noble friends – money, books, hospitality – one critic reached a sage diagnosis: blackmail. The noble friends were paying him to keep his mouth shut...

To the extent to which they articulated their own motives, the critics aimed to deify Shakespeare, to show that in the precise degree to which Jonson was raucous, hostile, and vindictive, Shakespeare was gentle, mild and forbearing ... But this ostensible purpose, however perverse in itself, concealed, one suspects, a deeper one: the desire to find a suitable victim to maul and mangle ... The elaborate tenderness for Shakespeare that expresses itself by inventing calumnies against Jonson seems, at length, sadistic; it masks precisely the ferocity that is projected onto Jonson. It comes at last to have about it, in however attenuated form, the atmosphere of a witch-hunt, or a lynching-party.

(Barish 1963: 2–5)

Where the eighteenth century Shakespeareans had castigated Jonson for his supposed personal failings, the Romantics found his work and model of poetic function sorely lacking in the qualities that they themselves prized most highly. If Jonson was not quite so clearly the evil Spaniard, his work was still all too evidently a peculiar, unnatural kind of craft:

Jonson as poet was chided for his failure to chant, to soar, to cast spells; Jonson as playwright was reproached with a failure to create life-like and endearing characters. Romanticism, with its interest in individual personality, was beginning to cherish psychological portraiture. At the same time, while wishing to hear the unique accent of the individual soul, it wished also to hear the still sad music that bound soul to soul. Shakespeare satisfied on both counts, Jonson on neither. Shakespeare's characters possessed some of the mysteriousness of real people; they seemed part of nature rather than literature... Jonson offered no such satisfactions. His characters – so it was charged – were not individuals but blueprints of types, or else, on the contrary, they were so frantically individual, so rampantly eccentric, that they ceased to seem human altogether ... Moreover they belonged not to life but to literature, and to a laboured, unspontaneous sort of literature at that ... They were not, furthermore, the sort of people one wished to live among ... In Jonson, as Hazlitt witheringly observed, one always finds oneself in low company.

(Barish 1963: 7)

127

From such assumptions twentieth-century critics took their cue. For a brief period, around the turn of the century, scholars found what seemed like secure historical grounding for the bitter rivalries with which Jonson's name had been indissociably linked by eighteenth-century calumniators in the 'War of the Theatres', that brief flurry of libels and lampoons involving, primarily, Jonson, Marston and Dekker **[24, 54]**. This was now expanded to take in further playwrights and many more plays (see Small 1899 and Penniman 1897) – including Shakespeare. Yet in the Modernist reassessment of Romantic assumptions came a challenge to the basis on which Jonson's low personal and critical standing had been established. If not actually beginning the process, it was T. S. Eliot who most notably jettisoned the critical inheritance and set out to confront Jonson anew. His famous essay began with the acknowledgement – perhaps missing from Barish's later, more obviously polemical, history of Jonson's reception – that the habitual contrast between Shakespeare and Jonson did not always seek to show that the latter was not worthy of respect. The problem, rather, was that the qualities for which he could be respected were precisely those which made him unreadable:

> The reputation of Jonson has been of the most deadly kind that can be compelled upon the memory of a great poet. To be universally accepted; to be damned by the praise that quenches all desire to read the book; to be afflicted by the imputation of the virtues which excite the least pleasure; and to be read only by historians and antiquaries – this is the most perfect conspiracy of approval. For some generations the reputation of Jonson has been carried rather as a liability than as an asset in the balance-sheet of English literature.
>
> (Eliot 1928: 104)

While not entirely eschewing the unfavourable comparison with Shakespeare, Eliot finds in Jonson the model of a writer whose readability and lack of immediate appeal go hand in hand – in other words, a Jonson who redefines (as Modernism itself does) the protocols of readability:

> The immediate appeal of Jonson is to the mind; his emotional tone is not in the single verse, but in the design of the whole. But not many people are capable of discovering for themselves the beauty which is only found after labour; and Jonson's industrious readers have been those whose interest was historical and curious, and

those who have thought that in discovering the historical and curious interest they had discovered the artistic value as well. When we say that Jonson requires study, we do not mean study of his classical scholarship or of seventeenth century manners. We mean intelligent saturation in his work as a whole; we mean that in order to enjoy him at all, we must get to the centre of his work and his temperament, and that we must see him unbiased by time, as a contemporary.

(Eliot 1928: 106)

For Eliot, then, to whose Modernist tastes reading meant 'intelligent saturation', Jonson appeared as a vital precursor, one made newly visible by the literary shift announced in Eliot's own work. Here was the possibility of reconnecting study with artistic value, retrieving intellection from the clutches of other disciplines and restoring it to its rightful place in the making and reading of literature.

Highly influential though it was, Eliot's essay did not succeed in banishing the invidious comparison forever. Writing in 1938, and *en route* to the impeccably contemporary conclusion that the criticism of Jonson's works should operate 'in terms of pattern and colour', the American critic Harry Levin argues that 'Jonson adopts the attitude of society, Shakespeare the viewpoint of the individual, which is finally more real. Jonson's instrument is logic, Shakespeare's psychology; Jonson's method has been called mechanical, Shakespeare's organic' (Levin 1938: 53). His essay is just one of many occasions on which the old *pas de deux* has been dusted off and set in motion once again, yet is far from being the most strident invocation of the ancient curses against Jonson. That honour belongs to an essay which, itself provoked by Eliot's attempted uncoupling of Jonson's reputation from Shakespeare's, also came from an impeccably contemporary source – the American journalist and critic Edmund Wilson:

To an intelligent and sensitive man of any school of thought, Shakespeare appears sensitive and intelligent. But Ben Jonson, after Shakespeare, seems neither. Though he attempts a variety of characters, they all boil down to a few motivations, recognizable as the motivations of Jonson himself and rarely transformed into artistic creations ... Jonson also lacks natural invention, and his theatre has little organic life. His plots are incoherent and clumsy; his juxtapositions of elements are too often like the 'mechanical mixtures' of chemistry that produce no molecular reactions ... Nor has he any sense of movement or proportion: almost everything goes on too long, and while it continues it does not develop. Nor is his taste in other matters reliable. His puns, as Dryden complained, are sometimes of a stunning stupidity; and when he is dirty, he is, unlike Shakespeare, sometimes disgusting to such a degree that he makes one sympathetic with the Puritans in their efforts to clean up the theatre. His reading of Greek and Latin, for all the boasting he does about it, has served him very insufficiently for the refinement and ordering of his work, and usually appears in his plays as either an alien and obstructive element or, when more skilfully managed, as a padding to give the effect of a dignity and weight which he cannot supply himself.

(Wilson 1952: 205–6)

Wilson is not content simply to rehearse what are, after all, familiar complaints. Instead he roots them all in a psychoanalytically-inspired characterisation of Jonson as an 'anal erotic' personality, displaying the disorders of pedantry, avarice and obstinacy (which latter is somehow extended to defiance, irascibility and vindictiveness):

> Now, Jonson had all these qualities. He was a pedant, whose cult of the classics had little connection with his special kind of genius. There is something of the 'compulsive', in the neurotic sense, about his constant citing of precedents and his working into the speeches of his plays passages, sometimes not translated, from the Greek and Latin authors ... as if they were charms against failure ...
>
> (Wilson 1952: 207)

Wilson goes on to claim that Jonson also shows evidence of the parsimony or avarice characteristic of the 'anal erotic', a tendency traceable to 'an attitude towards the excretatory processes acquired in early childhood':

> Jonson certainly exemplified this tendency, and he exhibited it in a variety of ways. His learning is a form of hoarding; and allied to it is his habit of collecting words ... The point is that Ben Jonson depends on the exhibition of stored-away knowledge to compel admiration by itself. And the hoarding and withholding of money is the whole subject of that strange play *Volpone*.
>
> (Wilson 1952: 208)

There is much more evidence, Wilson thinks, that can be adduced in unifying all the defects with which Jonson had been charged under the one, all-embracing diagnosis. Yet although the condition is clearly chronic, and the prognosis not good, Wilson does detect at his essay's end one glimmer of hope for poor Ben. He is, we learn, redeemed by his active recognition of Shakespeare's merit, a recognition imagined in a manner reminiscent of the eighteenth-century Shakespeareans:

> In his elegy on Shakespeare especially, in estimating him above all their contemporaries and setting him beside the greatest of the ancients, he does justice to all that is noblest in his own aspiring nature, which had to drag so much dead weight, all that is soundest and most acute in his own cramped but virile intellect. The one thing he really loved was literature, and having served it as well as he could, no touchiness of personal pride could keep him from honouring one who had been fitted to serve it better.
>
> (Wilson 1952: 220)

Jonson can only be redeemed, in other words, in recognising that he has lost, acknowledging the comparison with Shakespeare as the single valid horizon within which his value can be assessed. For Wilson, Shakespeare remains the last word on Ben Jonson, whatever attempts might be made by Eliot and others to suggest other criteria for assessment. Yet it was precisely such other criteria that the burgeoning discipline of literary criticism was by the mid-twentieth century more able than ever to supply.

(c) CLASSICISM

It is a commonplace of Jonson criticism to highlight his engagement with his Greek and Roman precursors, the literary greats of a golden age, and to acknowledge the extent to which his work wears that engagement on its sleeve, foregrounding the processes of reading, of translation and quotation as central to his practice of writing. No one has ever thought to dispute the influence of Terence and Plautus on his early comedies [43], or the extent to which the differences between Ovidian, Horatian, and Virgilian exemplars provide a play such as *Poetaster* with much of its dynamic [54]. The importance of Tacitus's historical writing for Jonson's Roman tragedies [57], or of Martial's epigrams for his own adventures in that genre [103, 108] has never been in doubt, while the relevance of classical Stoicism and the explicit imitation of Horatian and Juvenilian satire [103] remain uncontested observations. What has never been finally resolved is the significance of this 'classicism' for the critical assessment of Jonson's work, what it makes possible and what it precludes, and how – finally – it relates to the theatricality of his work.

Jonson's classicism is a crucial reference point in both Eliot's and Wilson's essays. For Wilson, Jonson's classical learning is the paradigmatic example of the 'dead weight' that drags his work down. It is an almost faecal obstruction, a blockage which prevents his own writing from reaching the heights of Shakespeare's. In the end, his attachment to it merely shows his awareness of his own limitations, as if he were hoping that such elevated company might actually disguise his own flaws, or work as 'charms against failure'. Jonson's relationship to his own learning appears in this account to mimic the relationship of the miser to his gold in *The Case is Altered* **[43]**: it is a strangely unproductive stockpile of wealth, indicative only of its hoarder's failings and destined to bring him no real return. At first sight, Eliot's warning against reading Jonson in the manner of the antiquarians seems to share this dismissive attitude to Jonson's classicism. But even in questioning the value of such scholarly approaches to Jonson, Eliot restates the case for a 'beauty which is only found after labour', and therefore for the value of 'study'. Classicism re-emerges as a kind of industrious reading, an attitude to texts that stresses the importance of the work their reception requires. The association of artistic value and intellectual labour – a cornerstone of Jonson's own characterisation of his 'Works' – reappears in its separation from an aesthetically blind antiquarianism.

Classicism, then, describes both the active assumption of a Greek and Roman literary inheritance, the wearing of such influences on one's sleeve, and a series of assumptions about the ways that art should be approached, the sort of satisfactions it should give. Both of these readings of classicism are crucial to the ways in which criticism after Eliot has characterised the forces shaping Jonson's work. Important work by the American critic Wesley Trimpi, for example, identified in Jonson's poetry a distinctively 'plain style', a quality which marked Jonson's distinctive difference from other writers of his time (Trimpi 1962). For Trimpi, this plain style was the product of Jonson's classicism, the deliberate imitation and adaptation of certain classical genres and categories. The plain style was more concerned with argument than with rhetorical ornamentation, with matter rather than words (Trimpi 1962: 5–6). It could be traced particularly to the urbane, satirical *sermones* of Horace, a conversational kind of writing which eschewed heightened language or the grand gesture, and was also a crucial feature of the epistolary writing of humanist authors admired by Jonson such as Vives **[9]** (Trimpi 1962: 60–75). The humanist cultivation of the plain style prepared the ground for Jonson's own stylistic characteristics, and this classical inheritance provides the terms and concepts for describing those characteristics.

Where Trimpi locates classicism in Jonsonian style, other critics have considered it primarily a matter of content. Katharine Eisaman Maus, for example, traces Jonson's significant debt to 'Roman moralists', great classical writers including Seneca, Cicero and Horace who devote much effort to examining the bases on which the good life might be lived. These figures, she suggests, 'are, or claim to be, ethically serious writers. The virtues they most appreciate are often austere ones: temperance, self-reliance, fortitude, altruistic self-sacrifice' (Maus 1984: 5). Furthermore, their concerns provide the explanatory key to Jonson's own work:

> Once the nature and extent of the Roman moralist influence is understood, various Jonsonian idiosyncrasies – his techniques of characterisation, his critical stance, his bias toward certain dramatic and poetic genres, his preference for certain kinds of plot, his unusual relationship with his theatrical and literary audience – all begin to seem the inseparable consequences of an inherited frame of mind.
>
> (Maus 1984: 20–1)

Thus, for example, the nature of the 'free' friendship celebrated in the Cary-Morison ode **[109]** derives from Roman moralist strictures on friendship and its relationship to moral strength or weakness (Maus 1984: 115–17); thus, also, the importance to the dramatic structure of Jonson's earlier plays of the climactic trial scene: it is the place where the 'civilized community' of which Roman moralists write can be brought into being (Maus 1984: 126–7).

If Trimpi's account of Jonson's style, and Maus's claims regarding the Roman moralists, might on occasion make his work seem almost to disappear into its classical precedents, other critics have been more concerned to identify Jonson's ability to absorb and reconstitute those influences. This is of course a direct rejection of Wilson's charge that his learning was an obstruction which lay, unabsorbed, in the path of his creativity, and it is with direct reference to Wilson that George Parfitt's account of Jonson's classicist style was elaborated:

> Jonson's use of classical material in his poems, in fact, shows his mind moving easily from original statements to borrowed ones, adapting the latter where necessary to fit the new context. The unobtrusiveness of the loans also needs to be noticed: care is

consistently taken to make the loan fully part of the total fabric
and it is very seldom that either the material which is borrowed or
the original expression of it is allowed to stand out from its English
context. The very high level of assimilation should be enough to
free Jonson from charges of pedantry or of wishing to show off,
for pedantry is an attitude of mind, a failure of mental proportion,
rather than the inevitable result of erudition and love of accuracy
... The bulk of Jonson's poetry shows no concern to make the
poet's learning obvious and none to make loans literal translations.
His classicism is something finer than this and more subtle: an
attempt to show how classical attitudes and ideas could be relevant
to Renaissance England.

(Parfitt 1976: 108–9)

The process of assimilation described by Parfitt is qualified, also in
the context of Jonson's poetry, by Richard Peterson. His work depicts
Jonson the classicist not as a hoarder but as a labourer, working on his
classical inheritance in order to establish, in the process of quotation
or repetition, new contexts in which such an inheritance might extend
its capacity for meaning:

Read as wholes, the poems of praise show the poet enlarging his
relationship to the living subject by evoking precise ancient ideas
and situations and turning them in such a way that several distinct
allusions work together intriguingly and unexpectedly in the
context of Jonson's larger argument. Used in this way, the poet's
materials are not inert and suppressed 'sources', merely a part of
the genesis of the poem, but allusions meant to be recognized –
signs in the finished work that its originality, organization, and
continuing life depend on suggestive links to the great writers of
antiquity. Jonson's moral statements, then, are not so much
'commonplaces' or 'topoi' as careful echoes of particular ancient
literary contexts.

(Peterson 1981: 3)

Peterson outlines a process of 'turning' to which he claims Jonson
subjects his sources, the conversion which does not simply leave them
unaltered and alien in the Jonsonian text, but which refrains also from
rendering them entirely unrecognisable in their English incarnation.
His 'digestion' of the classics, in other words, improves on the simple
assimilation described by Parfitt. Paraphrasing Jonsonian ideals, Peterson
comments:

'Fullness' and good digestion are everything in imitation. What all bad imitators have in common is a failure to turn or transform borrowed materials, whether they openly 'confesse' this in a gush of mere learning or attempt to conceal it in a spirit of imposture which constitutes theft – and perverts the ideal of a bold incursion into the works and thoughts of another to claim a part for oneself.

(Peterson 1981: 16–17)

When Richard Dutton turned his attentions to the poet's critical writings he found a process not dissimilar to that outlined by Peterson in Jonson's relationship to his classical inheritance. But where Peterson's Jonson is more or less fully in control of his allusive resources and their deployment, Dutton finds a more anxious figure, and one more susceptible of explanation in political terms. In *Discoveries*, for example, what might look like the poised 'turning' of classical sources could also be described in a very different way:

Even at their most magisterial, the elements he assembles in this way are more circumspect and psychologically fraught than a modern reading may readily suggest; to recycle the authority of earlier writers is not always complacent conservatism, but can betray the fragility of your own authority, exposing foundations of sand.

(Dutton 1996: 13)

In fact, Dutton goes on to suggest that the clearest outline of Jonson's classicist creed, the 'Dedicatory Epistle' prefaced to *Volpone* **[69]**, might indicate that the elaboration of his classical principles and their explicit derivation from Greek and Roman sources aim to mark out a space for literature apart from the unwelcome attentions of government agencies:

[The Epistle] laid the groundwork for a *modus vivendi* for writers for the next century or more, as they defined their literature in terms of formalistic and moralistic neoclassical laws and the authority of the ancients, and so largely avoided confrontation with the laws and authority of the state which licensed their self-expression.

(Dutton 1996: 97)

Jonson's classicism, in other words, involves more than a negotiation between past and present, ancient and modern; also constitutive, though largely hidden, is a negotiation with the extra-literary forces of the present.

While Dutton imagines those forces in the guise of political authority, for Lorna Hutson they take on other, more broadly social forms. 'Classicism' can be illuminated as the way in which literate early modern people tackled and understood the world around them, stemming neither from an antiquarian fascination with the distant past, nor from a desire to mark out a terrain insulated against the attentions of the political present:

> Sociologists, bibliographers and historians of the book have increasingly made literary critics aware of the way in which the physical form of a text (as a printed quarto or folio, a broadsheet, a manuscript copied for circulation, etc.) situates that text in a network of practical interests, political projects and social and familial relations. Nowadays, for example, when we think of Latin and Greek classics, we tend to imagine a venerable body of texts of historical and linguistic interest but largely irrelevant to the advance of science, technology or the arts in modern society. In the period in which Jonson came to greatness as a dramatist, however, the new editions and translations of classical texts that were pouring from printing houses all over Europe were evidently being commissioned and marketed for their practical relevance to everyday life. The advent of the printing press had transformed the potential of classical and modern texts – even poetry and drama – as resources in the transmission of information. Regular pagination, standardized editions, modern commentaries and the invention of the subject index all contributed to the capacity of the book as an object for the storage and retrieval of reliable knowledge.
>
> (Hutson 1998: xv)

What this situation produced, says Hutson, was 'a culture of bookish self-improvement' in which a figure such as Jonson plays an exemplary role:

> Evidence of Jonson's immersion in and fascination by this culture is everywhere in his writings. We find him, for example, pursuing a fashionable interest in the contemporary relevance of ancient warfare in his meticulous annotation of a book of Greek military tactics ... while, in the chilling boudoir scene in his tragedy *Sejanus*, where a Roman matron plans the murder of her husband, Jonson

footnotes realistic details on the weather hazards of Roman cosmetics with reference to Martial, one of his favourite Latin poets.

(Hutson 1998: xvi)

Classicism, that is to say, was not a display of obscure – at best – or redundant – at worst – learning, but an encyclopaedic, instrumental knowledge, a way of putting the stored up erudition of the past to use in the pressing circumstances of the present.

(d) THEATRICALITY AND ANTI-THEATRICALITY

Whatever its source or character, classicism requires a necessary bookishness. It is swallowed by, swallows, or negotiates a relationship with the great works of the ancients, all processes which involve education, careful reading and detailed study. For a long time Jonson's critics have, with Wilson, understood this as an impediment to his dramatic art, as the quiet study vies with the noisy theatre and the silent privacy of reading is set against the public fellowship of performance. Jonson's classicism and his theatricality have been understood as mutually exclusive; his works, even his plays, have been read as in some way self-confounding, the theatrical incarnation of an over-riding 'anti-theatricality' that issues from his elevated conception of the ancients and the circumstances – books, schools – in which they might be encountered.

The fullest exposition of this standpoint has been provided by Jonas Barish, in his book *The Anti-theatrical Prejudice*. Barish brings together from Jonson's poems, plays, masques and other writings a litany of evidence which seems to align the dramatist with those of his contemporaries who despised the theatre and all its works. There is Jonson's educated disdain for the entertainments of the ignorant, for example, a disdain that often seems identical with a patrician dismissal of 'low' culture, and his separation of himself as 'poet' from those others, mere 'playwrights'. In Barish's hands, though, anti-theatricality amounts to a lot more than simple snobbery. He cites the distinction drawn in Jonson's prefaces to his early masques **[117]** between the soul of the masque – its words – and its earthly body, the visible spectacle or performance, as instancing a particularly forceful elevation of text over performance (Barish 1981: 140–43). Because text is the enduring part of the masque, that which doesn't decay into the lost realm of the

137

past, it can be accorded priority over performance, identified as its essence and original: 'what endures, for [Jonson], has substance' (Barish 1981: 143). This is further reinforced, suggests Barish, by the Jonsonian privileging of the plain, stable and solid, that which simply is what it appears to be, and is capable of remaining that way despite the buffeting of circumstance. This 'prejudice' also marks the dramatic works for which Jonson is most celebrated:

> When we turn to the plays we find that in them Jonson does not shed his anti-theatrical bias. Rather, he builds it in: he makes the plays critiques of the instability they incarnate. The plays show us change as something to be shunned, by presenting us with foolish characters determined to embrace it.
>
> (Barish 1981: 145)

Chief among these characters are the gulls, those who are not true to themselves, and the rascals such as Volpone, Mosca or Face, who constantly shift their shapes and appear in the guises of others. An attachment to the theatrical necessity of costume is another marker of a suspect fondness for the transitory and insubstantial:

> Wherever we look, then, within the plays or outside them, in structure or in moralizing comment, we find a distrust of theatricality, particularly as it manifests itself in acting, miming or changing, and a corresponding bias in favour of the 'real' – the undisguised, unacted, and unchanging. This is reinforced by a preference for simplicity as against ornament.
>
> (Barish 1981: 151–2)

Yet Barish would not want to suggest that this use of the theatre to condemn theatricality could be a simple, plain or stable process itself. Instead, it is the very source of the plays' persistent fascination:

> It seems likely, in short, that it is precisely the uneasy synthesis between a formal anti-theatricalism, which condemns the arts of show and illusion on the one hand, and a subversive harking after them on the other, that lends to Jonson's comic masterpieces much of their unique high tension and precious equilibrium.
>
> (Barish 1981: 154)

Others have followed Barish's lead, particularly – as we will see below [151] – by locating an anti-theatrical gesture in Jonson's self-fashioning as an 'author', and in his determination to make books out of his plays, to supplant performance with writing. Some critics have also recognised the 'uneasy synthesis' of which he speaks, finding both anti-theatricality and a tendency to prevent that anti-theatricality remaining unproblematically in charge. Robert Watson, for example, sees in Jonson's dramatic writing a series of parodic moves, satiric assaults on a folly which is explicitly theatrical. The dramatist's satiric energies, though, in seeking to encompass the theatrical norms of his day, end up reaching corrosively into the alternative standards established in his own works:

> Just as Jonson's on-stage surrogates such as Volpone and Face seem constitutionally unable to stop creating complications and simply enjoy their profits, so Jonson himself seems unable to switch off the parodic mechanism that generated his triumphs and relax on his satiric laurels. Instead, he turns that mechanism against his own dramatic pattern. These plays reveal Jonson's increasing doubts about the adequacy of satiric wit as an end in itself, reflected in an increasing willingness to parody the motifs of his own kind of city-comedy.
>
> (Watson 1987: 10)

For other critics, however, the assumption of an initial or governing 'anti-theatricality' has been more obviously problematic. Rather than see Jonson as an author engaged in a futile attempt to escape the conditions in which his writing took form, there is a more positive assessment of the theatrical not as an inevitable constraint but as a positive pole of attraction. Anne Barton's important study of 1984, for example, is pointedly devoted in its title to *Ben Jonson, Dramatist*, and her detailed treatment of all the extant plays is prefaced by the initial insight that 'Jonson's classicism was balanced, moreover, by a compensating attraction towards the irregular, the gothic, the contemporary and the strange. The rage for order which shapes his work is almost always met and, in a way, substantiated by an equally powerful impulse towards chaos and licence' (Barton 1984: x). This is perhaps not far from Barish's suggestion of a 'subversive' fascination with theatricality; but the interplay between 'bookishness' and 'spectacle' is configured sufficiently differently to suggest that theatre is not that which classicism cannot ultimately escape, but that which classicism cannot ultimately capture – a rather different way of imagining the inter-relation of this pair of concepts.

While Hutson's recent observations on classicism dispute any easy opposition of learning to spectacle, the monstrous, or the contemporary, others have sought to make good the radical promise of Barton's opening claim. Perhaps the most notable attempt has been that of Peter Womack, whose innovative work explicitly sets itself the task of paying attention to the plays as 'scripts for the theatre' (Womack 1986: ix). He traces, for example, the particularly theatrical contexts of Jonsonian character-writing, emphasising that his way of doing so is very much in debt to the circumstances for which the plays were written and might be difficult to comprehend without reference to them. In particular, he suggests that Jonsonian character is not the product of realist theatre, of the absolute separation of actors and audience by the proscenium arch, nor of the assumption that what we as an audience apprehend are the persons and personalities of 'realistic' individuals. Rather, he suggests, Jonson's writing of character is something that emerges not only from a different set of general assumptions about what a character is (here, the ready acceptance that character is a kind of writing rather than the hidden depths of a personal interior) but also from the very different conditions of performance that pertained in the early modern theatre. In such conditions, with the audience seated all round the galleries and privileged spectators on the stage itself, there is no categorical breach between actors and audience – the kind of illusion that can be offered, and the place that the apprehension of it as illusion might have in the transaction between players and spectators, is necessarily different. The key to understanding Jonson's drama, and what it can do, suggests Womack, is to take these circumstances seriously, and not to assume that Jonson's work emerges simply from his reading.

This does not produce an inert and singular Jonson, if only because theatre and theatricality are shown to be multivalent sites of conflict. Significantly, Womack suggests that it is classicism itself which plays a large part in the structure of these conflicts. He contrasts what he describes as the classicist ideal of a singular, referential, authoritative language – best exemplified in early modern England by Latin, and written as the language of authority in a figure such as Cicero in *Catiline* **[64]** – with the language that emerges on the Jonsonian stage, and is highlighted in games of 'vapours' and the canting of the plays' underworld inhabitants **[8, 85]**. Here we find not singular sense or meaning but the non-sense or at least unfixed sense of opaque sound, a babble of 'signifiers' which fail to communicate a transparent meaning: 'words are deception, junk, noise'.

> Thus the comic corollary of Jonson's linguistic classicism is a hypersensitive consciousness of the anarchic and unverifiable plurality of the vernacular. Living speech, speech as polymorphous

social interaction, appears by the dry light of the absolute Latin ideal to be a monster, endlessly doubling, compartmentalising, contradicting and parodying itself, travelling ever further outwards, in its illicit dynamism, from some pristine centre of truth and sense.

(Womack 1986: 103)

This opposition, Womack suggests, makes life difficult for the pretence that is theatre. It cannot be truth, or meaning, nor can it transparently communicate it – it always and necessarily shows itself to be playing a role, standing in for that which it pretends to be. This makes it suspect, fundamentally inauthentic, within the model of language and truth described above:

Once all propositions are so organized that they can be subjected to a single separation of those which are the case from those which are not, the act of deliberately adopting a role falls ineluctably into the category of illusion.

(Womack 1986: 109)

Womack finds this harsh judgement on theatre at work in Jonson, exemplarily so in Augustus's interruption of Ovid and Julia's masquing in *Poetaster* **[55]**. He suggests that the *unmasking* that takes place there, and which is such a crucial part in the denouements of so many of Jonson's other plays, shows 'a rough scepticism about the validity of the theatre':

In Jonson ... the mechanics of disguise are at once flaunted and demystified. Inductions and on-stage spectators play double-edged games with the factitiousness of the spectacle; the business of getting hold of costumes required by the intrigue is prosaically stressed; asides point up the gap between mask and face; false identities are assumed unconvincingly and – as in Sir Politic Would-Be's doomed attempt to pass himself off as a tortoise – exploded with brutal laughter. The *indignity* of theatre, the level at which it's a matter of creaking contrivances, false whiskers, funny voices, is harshly insisted on. The text homes in on something flatly derisive in the act of coming out of costume: the message of the brackish nonchalance with which a scar is peeled off, or a foreign gown dropped on a chair, is 'There's no such person – you've been had.' The theatre is not so much a magician, eliciting the secret potentialities of signs, as a buffoon, repeatedly sandbagged by the refusal of things to be anything other than what they ironically are.

(Womack 1986: 111–12)

141

The theatre is, in this register, disreputable: a trick, a jape, a wind-up, and we are its victims. It is, in fact, our faith in theatre that theatre seeks to undo.

Significantly, Womack also claims that another, related and definitively Jonsonian motif arises from the same circumstances, and is similarly exemplified in *Poetaster*:

> It might be called the figure of the absent magistrate. Caesar's sudden arrival is the sudden death of the illusion: the mask is neutralized by his presence, and this shows how his absence – the absence of legitimate authority – was the condition of its virtue all along. This typifies Jonson's theatrical structures: the performance space is cleared by suspending the function of the magistrate... Everywhere, the theatre opens when the true court closes down, and closes when it opens. It plays the role of the other, not only to the law of nature, but apparently to the law of the realm as well.
>
> (Womack 1986: 112–13)

Here, then, theatricality is characterised in explicitly political terms, as the 'other' of authority, its subversion. But it is not necessarily the content of theatre, what any play says, that makes it so – it is the very form of theatricality which, in the context described by Womack, ensures that it is positioned against authority. Jonson's work, he claims, embodies the struggle between a didactic theatre of classicist imagining, and the corrosive 'other' this ideal attempts to obscure. And this, too, is a political struggle: a work against the language and the performance of authority, a work performed by theatricality itself.

Womack's emphasis on the dependence of the Jonsonian canon on the practice of theatre, an emphasis which suggests that Jonson's work is not always in flight from its origins but perhaps draws its strength from them, is shared by Richard Cave. In Cave's study of the plays as performance texts Jonson is identified as a writer who is keen to exploit the theatrical circumstances of his art. Cave highlights the use of framing devices – inductions, prologues and the like – as a sign of Jonson's far from embarrassed exploration of the meaning and power of theatre itself, his willingness to 'expose to an audience what one might term the mechanics of performance' (Cave 1991: 3). Thus, for example, *Cynthia's Revels* begins with a dramatised squabble between three boy actors, in which the players who will embody the characters in the narrative appear to the audience first as players. The audience of Jonson's drama is required to engage with the play on two levels at least, as a fictional narrative and as the explicit staging of that narrative, and to be aware that what it witnesses is always a performance. Such an effect is achieved through the conscious manipulation of the conventions of performance: in his reading of *Epicene*, for example, Cave focuses on the climactic removal of the wig as the moment which crystallises the play's interrogation of the social functioning of signs of gender **[77, 126]**. He draws attention to the differences in meaning between such a moment on the all-male stage of the early modern era and its reproduction under modern conditions of performance that would not permit such a shockingly swift and easy transformation of a character's gender (Cave 1991: 62–75). For Cave, this transformation undermines the policing of the boundaries between normal and deviant forms of masculine and feminine behaviour, since 'if it is an acceptable social practice in particular circumstances [i.e. on the stage] for boys to become women how can we in all integrity make prescriptions about what constitutes a proper normality in gender-relations and sexual behaviour?' (Cave 1991: 71). In the raising of such questions, too, the firm distinction between acting as doing and acting as playing begins to tremble. 'The result,' claims Cave, 'is an experience of theatre that is exciting because combative, teasing, subversive, witty, dangerous' (Cave 1991: 170) – not perhaps the adjectives one might associate with Barish's anti-theatrical dramatist, repressing his pleasure in the possibilities of performance with a prolonged shudder of mandarin disgust.

(e) LOOSE AND GATHERED SELVES

While the critical exploration of Jonson's relation to the theatre has provided, as Womack demonstrates, an opportunity to read for the politics of his dramatic works, these debates have also drawn sustenance from other questions – raised in discussion as much of the poetry as of the plays – regarding the Jonsonian self, its inhabitation of the figure of the author, and its relation to authority in all its forms. Indeed, it was a reading of the poetry which compelled Wesley Trimpi to declare that Jonson's 'plain style' brings the reader close to an encounter with the poet himself, *as* a self:

> A poem in the plain style offers the reader the intimacy of a specific situation and its context of feeling. The generalizations, either stated or implied, arise out of particular detailed experience and are persuasive because the reader is encouraged to participate in the experience rather than simply acquiesce in a moral precept ...

The intimacy between the poet and the reader is strengthened by the urbanity of tone that has traditionally given the plain style its vitality. It is the urbanity which claims the experience as the writer's own but which, at the same time, recognizes that it is relatable to the experiences of others and that the relationship might be valuable.

(Trimpi 1962: 236–7)

While Trimpi found in the urbane style of the poetry the opportunity to apprehend Jonson's poetic self, Thomas Greene described a thematics of selfhood running throughout the body of Jonson's work. Greene's influential essay of 1970, 'Ben Jonson and the Centered Self', begins by noting the significance of the symbolic circle for his writing. Jonson's own emblem, the image of a broken compass which cannot therefore trace a circle, is identified as a statement of the problem from which his work departs, and to which it always returns:

It contains a kind of transparent enigma, to be solved in this case by the reading of its author's canon. For the orbis – circle, sphere, symbol of harmony and perfection – becomes familiar to the student of Jonson as one of his great unifying images. In a sense, almost everything Jonson wrote attempts in one way or another to complete the broken circle, or expose the ugliness of its incompletion ... In Jonson, the associations of the circle – as metaphysical, political, and moral ideal, as proportion and equilibrium, as cosmos, realm, society, estate, marriage, harmonious soul – are doubled by the associations of a centre – governor, participant, house, inner self, identity, or, when the outer circle is broken, as lonely critic and self-reliant solitary. Centre and circle become symbols, not only of harmony and completeness but of stability, repose, fixation, duration, and the incompleted circle, uncentred and misshapen, comes to symbolize a flux or a mobility, grotesquely or dazzlingly fluid.

(Greene 1970: 325–6)

In the masques Greene discerns the too-easy evocation of a centred harmony, an assertion of a stable order gathered round the central figure of the monarch which yet reaches out to encompass the whole world. In the non-dramatic verse, by contrast, he finds praise of a 'centred strength' or 'fixed stability' that lacks such grandiose scope. 'On the whole,' he suggests, 'the circles of the lyric verse shrink toward their centre, toward the Stoic individual soul, self-contained, balanced, at peace with itself even in isolation' (Greene 1970: 330). This is a 'gathered self', centred and coherent, and thus securely 'at home' even if beset by dangers from outside. Its 'equilibrated energy', its fixed stability, ensures that even in its journeying it is freed from the threat of flux or struggle:

> He travels well who in a sense never travels (or travails) at all, who circumscribes hell with his courage and whose mind knows no exile, keeping one foot still upon his centre, compass-like, and lives through tempests, here in his bosom and at home.
>
> (Greene 1970: 333)

Such a still, stoic self is contrasted in Jonson's poetry with 'the ugliness of the uncentred, ungathered selves, whose disorientation always seems related to some principle of discontinuity. The self which is not at home paints, feigns, invents, gossips, alters its manner and passion as whim or necessity dictates' (Greene 1970: 331).

In the poetry, Greene claims, Jonson stages the confrontation between these two principles of selfhood. Perhaps not surprisingly, their confrontation is also literally staged in the plays. Here, we witness 'a recurrent pattern of domestic invasion', from Jacques de Prie's fears of intruders in *The Case is Altered* **[43]** to Morose's sense of the threat offered by the noise of the outside world in *Epicene* **[75]** (Greene 1970: 335–7). The vulnerability of the house is a symbol of its owner's failure to be a properly gathered self; the repeated violation of its borders in Jonson's drama presents 'scattered evidence to suggest a strain of half-repressed envy for the homeless and centrifugal spirit'. In *Volpone*, says Greene, we find 'the greatest, though not the only work, to deal with that strain and make it into art'. The title character is an exemplary shape-shifter, a 'Protean man … without core and principle and substance':

> For *Volpone* asks us to consider the infinite, exhilarating, and vicious freedom to alter the self at will once the ideal of moral constancy has been abandoned … Volpone demonstrates the ultimate hectic development of Machiavelli's shifty pragmatism, and raises it from a political maxim to a moral, even a metaphysical state of being.
>
> (Greene 1970: 337).

Yet, of course, it all turns out badly for Volpone and for the other inhabitants of the play who would live by the same commitment to mutability. 'To multiply the self is to reduce the self', suggests Greene, adding that 'Jonson's drama ... reflects as we have seen the horror of a self too often shifted, a self which risks the loss of an inner poise' (Greene 1970: 343, 344). While he also goes on to show how *The Alchemist* and *Bartholomew Fair* might reveal 'a Jonson less jealous of the centred self's prerogatives, more warmly and less ambiguously tolerant of the histrionic personality' (Greene 1970: 347), his analysis continues to insist upon the defining contrast between these two possibilities of the self. It is an opposition reiterated by Ian Donaldson as recently as 1997, when he suggests that:

> Central to Jonson's thinking about the nature of personal identity is a contrast that is developed extensively throughout his drama and his non-dramatic verse between *the gathered self* – collected, consistent, contained, morally stalwart but tending towards stodginess and solipsism – and what might be called *the loose self*, a personality more labile and mercurial, ready to shift opportunistically from one role, one voice, one stance to another, and another; a self that in its very instability is at once deeply attractive and deeply untrustworthy.
>
> (Donaldson 1997: 42)

(f) AUTHORIAL SELVES

In the terms of this opposition – fixity versus flux, substance versus show, endurance versus transitoriness – we might be justified in finding more than a slight echo of the conflict between the classicist word and theatrical performance set out in Barish's analysis **[137]**. Yet that opposition has also been taken up by critics keener than Greene, Donaldson or Barish to *historicize* the Jonsonian self, to account for its dynamism through reference both to early modern discourses and practices of identity, and to the historical conditions in which such constructions of selfhood were generated. Much of this work has been undertaken in the wake of Stephen Greenblatt, the pioneering New Historicist critic whose *Renaissance Self-Fashioning* (1980) opened up both the terrain of such investigation and established the method-ological justification for analysing selfhood as a cultural construction, and therefore as an entity whose exact shape and dynamic at any historical moment is necessarily specific to the particular structures of power and forms of discourse characteristic of the culture in which it is generated. Richard Helgerson, in an important work tracing the literary self-presentation of Spenser, Jonson and Milton, suggests that the qualities of Greene's gathered self can be understood historically as pertaining to a Renaissance ideal of the 'laureate self', 'a virtuous, centred, serious self, characterized by its knowledge of and fidelity to itself and the governing ethos of the age' (Helgerson 1983: 102). This laureate self differs from Greene's, for a start, in being necessarily authorial – it is a *writerly* identity that is here held up as the normative ideal against which contemporary varieties of authorship (some not even worthy of the name) can be judged. Second, in its 'fidelity to the governing ethos of the age' this is a simultaneously *authoritative* self, one which bases its claim to significance on an asserted proximity to centres of cultural and political authority – it is just this proximity which makes it a 'laureate' as well as an authorial self. In Jonson's early works Helgerson locates an attempt to establish himself as just this elevated kind of author, comparing the self-presentation of the writer's critical function in *Every Man Out of His Humour* **[50]** to Spenser's equivalent declaration of laureate intent in *The Shepherd's Calendar*:

> In these two poems of literary self-presentation, each published when its author was in his mid-twenties and each proclaiming by its dedication, Spenser's to Sidney and Jonson's to the Inns of Court, its author's alliance with the amateur elite of his generation, Spenser and Jonson adopt the fashionable mode of their time only to criticize and partially detach themselves from it. They thus establish themselves as poets but let it be known that they are poets of an unusual sort. And for each, the aspiration that sets him apart from his contemporaries also directs him toward the monarch, who is central to the higher and truer poetic identity that he seeks.
>
> (Helgerson 1983: 139)

Such declarations of laureate intent, though, do not necessarily add up to the achievement of laureate selfhood, and Helgerson goes on to trace the ways in which such intent issues in paradox and difficulty. *Volpone*, he suggests, with its address to the Universities and its didactic aspirations **[69]**, also constitutes an attempt on Jonson's part to claim for himself the standing of a laureate. Yet since such a status was defined against the supposed baseness of the theatre, such a claim could proceed only by the disavowal of its own form:

> So long as the pressure to define himself remained strong, so long, that is, as the accurate construal of his status remained in doubt,

147

he could be a laureate poet in the theatre only by opposing the theatre, by unmasking the moral emptiness of its mimicry, its metamorphoses, and its plotting. Unless he held fast to the good man's station as unmoved spectator, the poet risked being implicated in the madness of the 'turning world'.

(Helgerson 1983: 161)

To Jonson's eventual achievement of a place in the Jacobean sun Helgerson attributes a subsequent softening of tone and attitude in subsequent plays – the established laureate no longer needed to press his claims quite so insistently. Yet he also suggests that what survives of Jonson's attempt to live up to the status of laureateship is as much the bustle of the attempt as the serenity of achievement. We read in him not the static self-identity of simply *being* a laureate but 'the labour of self-presentation', all the commotion of *becoming* which ultimately cannot be obscured:

His work is an agon, an unresolved struggle of the self against the very conditions of its expression. But that struggle gives Jonson's plays, poems and masques much of their troubling power – and it has made Jonson himself one of the most enduring presences in our literature.

(Helgerson 1983: 184)

If he has *presence*, then, it is as the laureate's failure to coincide with himself. Or, as Ian Donaldson has also put it, describing Jonson's determination to achieve through imitation the authorial, laureate status of his classical forebears:

Literary personality, for Jonson, did not consist in the achievement of a unique and unprecedented voice, in the finding of some essentialist *self*; it consisted rather of the gradual assumption of another self, in a process of deliberate play or travail through which one laboured to become the sort of person one most hoped to be. It was in this spirit and with these ends that Jonson sought diligently to become 'the English Horace'.

(Donaldson 1997: 39)

It is the gap between imitator and imitated marked by the necessary and incomplete process of 'assumption' which prevents 'literary personality' from settling into the bounded unity of a self at all. The author, in other words, is both the closed, centred circle and the breach in such self-identity made by the necessary attempt to achieve it. This anatomy of the authorial psyche is perhaps not too dissimilar from that of the 'humorous' personality depicted and condemned in Jonson's early plays **[44]**; but in these circumstances, 'loose' and 'gathered' are not mutually exclusive alternatives to be exalted at the expense of their opposite, but necessarily implicated in the thought of each other. Jonson's personal emblem, a broken compass that cannot trace a complete circle, encapsulates both these possibilities.

Bruce Thomas Boehrer, too, has attended to the laureate dynamics of Jonsonian selfhood. For Boehrer, though, this is a matter which appears most strikingly in bodily terms, and specifically those that cluster around the processes of eating and digestion. 'Jonson's much celebrated self-transformation', he writes, 'occurs very largely in alimentary terms':

> Scholars have often focused on the long, concerted spiral of upward social mobility that characterizes Jonson's career; as far as I know, however, no one has concentrated on the digestive troping of this mobility. In fact, Jonson's career can be described as a kind of inverted figurative peristalsis [the process by which food is passed down the oesophagus towards the stomach]. The life which began so inauspiciously atop a Westminster sewage conduit in time attaches itself to the pre-eminent aesthetic and culinary monument of early Stuart culture: the royal banqueting house at Whitehall. In the process, Jonson crafts himself into a regular fixture of Jacobean and Caroline entertainment.
>
> (Boehrer 1997: 6)

Furthermore, claims Boehrer, Jonson configures his own authorship in such terms. The writer and the cook are regularly if troublingly aligned in his work, while the process of digestion figures not only as a means of comprehending the ways in which the good author ingests and absorbs the works of his predecessors but also as an analogue for the position of authorship itself:

> The digestive tract offers Jonson a good metaphorical equivalent for the situation of authorship exactly because both are subject to flux and contingency: the multiple media and markets within which Jonson worked find their parallel within the interrelated processes of consumption, ingestion, excretion, and indigestion, as well as in the shifting social and material ground upon which those processes play themselves out.
>
> (Boehrer 1997: 40)

Finally, the correlation between Jonson's 'literary self-expansion', his assertion of significant laureate selfhood, and the corpulence which is explicitly mentioned in his work is itself not simply coincidental. In both aspects, the poet 'reaches out to the world in order not so much to embrace it as to engulf it' (Boehrer 1997: 206). Selfhood, Boehrer argues, is a corporeal matter, and alimentary processes are crucial to the possible configurations of Jonson's theory and practice of authorship.

For a number of critics, it is the figure not of the gut but of the book which best represents authorial identity. Richard Newton describes the ways in which Jonson claims the printed book as the manifestation of his writerly status, such that the 1616 folio, for example, gives us not only the works but also a clear concept or practice of authorship:

> In Jonson's work we first find a poet appearing in texts which are decisively made for print – in texts proclaiming their own complete-ness, aware of their own permanence, and creation of their own context ... Jonson establishes the printed text as the primary object of literature. Then, to aid in this project, he appropriates for his text new sources of authority, in particular classical authority. Finally, he imbues his texts with a pervasive thematic reference to the authority and textuality that he is seeking to establish. The result of these efforts is the birth of the printed book in English literature.
>
> (Newton 1982: 34)

Completeness, permanence, an imperviousness to the pressure of context – these are the qualities of print which are also, by the same means, the qualities attributable to the book's author. The classical text, itself a phenomenon of print culture, thus appears as a means of ratifying this Jonsonian model of authorship not by its content, its themes or imagery but in the completion and permanence indicated by its form. If these are some of the qualities attributable to laureate status, they are here reconfigured as a claim to authorial *autonomy*, an autonomy that signals an independence from monarchy as much as from any other would-be determinant of selfhood. Timothy Murray identifies the process of publishing a dramatist's works in the expensive, elite folio format as the mark of just this claim, and this was of course a process which Jonson himself did much to initiate. In this way, the playwright:

> finds himself in the elite company of Chaucer and Spenser – in addition to classical authors, theologians, historians, and scientists

whose texts were often entombed in folios. The magnificent shape of these books embodies particularly well the increasing system of 'self-crowned laureates' which Richard Helgerson depicts as the dominant literary tradition of Jonson's age, a tradition directing the poet 'towards the monarch, who is central to the higher and truer poetic identity that he seeks' [Helgerson 1983: 139–40]. Yet ... the folio collections might also signify the distinction between a bookish dramatic tradition and the laureate status that poets acquired through identification with the monarch ... Suggesting a relation different from Helgerson's equation of laureate and princely subject, the folios assume, in many respects, their own sovereign right of authorial succession.

(Murray 1987: 51–2)

While the process of 'self-crowning' of which Helgerson writes might imply a slightly more complex relation to monarchical authority than Murray allows, his claims for the function of print in establishing the meaning of authorship are strongly made. In essence, he suggests that print is the means by which the stuff of theatre is made legitimate, where legitimation involves the recoding of plays as the works of an autonomous, originating author. Such recoding is achieved through the conversion of playtexts into printed books, and is thus also an evocation of authorship as a bulwark against the moral and philo-sophical dangers represented by theatricality itself. The drive to secure an ideal of authorship, in this reading, is motivated by the kind of anti-theatrical prejudice described by Barish **[137]**.

The role that the book plays in the configuration of authorship is depicted rather differently by Sara van den Berg. Working from a pers-pective informed by Freudian psychoanalysis and the development of Freud's thinking by the French psychoanalyst Jacques Lacan, a 'science' which takes the dynamic organisation of selfhood as its major concern, she sets out to explore both the contradictory processes that constitute the authorial self and the means by which these contradictions might be ameliorated. She notes, for a start, that 'in the humanist model of identity, an individual can take as an ideal the status of an autonomous, unified subject':

That Jonson subscribed to that model is inscribed everywhere in *Epigrams*. Yet subjectivity is always contingent, associative, relational, and incompletely knowable in any one act or even in the aggregate acts of a person. Jonson himself admits failures of language and autonomy. In poems to friends and patrons, he often protests that he cannot say what he feels or fully express what he

151

knows ... The poet, despite his confident stance and humanist hope, is not really sure how to define himself.

(van den Berg 1991: 118)

The self, in other words, cannot quite close on itself: authorship, in this model, seems as much the dogged pursuit of an ideal by its failure as in other accounts.

This dynamic selfhood, though, is the sign of a loss or failure of a slightly different kind, a loss which is in fact constitutive of selfhood *as such*. Following psychoanalytic models, she suggests that in order to come into being as an individuated self the infant must experience a traumatic separation from a supposed union with the mother, and the division of its world into the self and the 'not-self'. Yet just this process, which gives the self its identity, marks it with the trauma of the imaginary unity it has lost in coming into being. This uncomfortable situation is alleviated by the taking up of 'transitional objects', items that are invested with the status both of self and of not-self or 'other', becoming 'the me/not me in which self and other are reunited in an act of substitution or symbolic play'. For Jonson, she claims, the book is just such a 'transitional object', and literature a 'transitional phenomenon [that] could serve the twin needs of separation and individuation, of loss and gain' (van den Berg 1991: 125). Even as they serve to replay the constitutive processes of individuation, the book, and authorship, play a symbolic role in the painful paradoxes of selfhood.

For Joseph Loewenstein, the determinants of the dynamic practice of authorial autonomy lie elsewhere, though they remain associated with the printed book. Influenced by the Marxist suggestion that artistic activity is a material process, happening within the shaping contexts of specific modes and relations of material production – the particular arrangements within which the production and consumption of all the resources involved in the reproduction of human life are organised – Loewenstein's essay 'The Script in the Marketplace' reminds us that dramatists working for the early modern commercial theatre did not 'own' their plays [13] in the modern sense of holding their copyright. They were the property of the company, or of the stationer to whom they might be sold. He points out that Jonson or his printer, William Stansby, somehow managed to secure the rights to the author's back catalogue in preparing his folio of 1616, and thus managed to bring together a group of plays under the name of their writer, despite the fact that they had been written for or performed by different companies, and had previously appeared in book form, if at all, under various imprints. The developing laws identifying books as property, as commodities for exchange in the growing market economy of early modern England, made this possible – Jonsonian authorship emerges on the back of changes taking place in the economic practices of the country as a whole. The gathered, authorial, autonomous self, that is to say, arose as an idealised figure of *self-possession* from economic practices which enabled the products of artistic labour to be owned privately and disseminated through trade. Needless to say, suggests Loewenstein, this condition of his authorial status is thoroughly occluded in the Jonsonian text, in which appeal is made precisely to other models of non-autonomous authorship, such as patronage, or to a classicist conception of authorial significance which makes no mention of economics at all. *Epigrams* 3, 'To My Bookseller', for example, tellingly forbids any attempt to advertise Jonson's book to interested consumers:

> Giving the bookseller leave to esteem the volume according to its sales, but refusing to condone any active appeal to a consuming public, Jonson presents himself as a man ambiguously engaged with the literary marketplace. He dedicates all of his newly recovered plays in the Folio either to people or to institutions, adapting the modern technology of dissemination to an archaic patronage economy. His are among the first dedicated texts of *printed* drama in the history of the English theatre, and the sense of novelty ought to outweigh the sense of regression here. It is a *neo*-conservative move, a groping forward toward later authorial property rights within a bourgeois cultural marketplace, but modelled on the ethos of the classical *auctor* and the economics of patronage: the investment of proprietary rhetoric in the author of a printed play is a major step toward the modernization of authorship.
>
> (Loewenstein 1985: 109)

Reasons for this refusal or inability to acknowledge the enabling conditions of his authorial standing have been offered by other critics. They have pointed out how Jonson's eagerness to distinguish his own activity as author from the less reputable status of hacks or jobbing playwrights identifies such lesser forms of writerly life as contaminated by their dependence on the burgeoning market for plays and printed books. In a densely argued investigation of *Bartholomew Fair*, to which we will return in more detail below **[171]**, Peter Stallybrass and Allon White have described how 'Jonson was attempting to dissociate the professional writer from the clamour of the marketplace and to install his works in the studies of the gentry and the libraries of the universities'

153

(Stallybrass and White 1986: 76). The fair and the theatre, they suggest, are paradigmatic sites of that 'clamour', where the market itself might be defined as low, popular and transgressive. Yet the term 'professional' carries with it not only connotations of authority and independence but also the sense of selling one's services or labour as a commodity in the market – and Jonsonian authorship hovers uncertainly between these alternatives, trying to obscure the latter with the former through ritual gestures of exclusion. Such gestures might be understood as congruent with the kinds of recoding which Timothy Murray describes, in that they serve to mark the division between legitimate and illegitimate forms of writing:

> As 'master-poet', then, Jonson constituted his identity in opposition to the theatre and the fair. Through the imaginary separation of the scholar's study and library from the theatrical marketplace, Jonson simultaneously mapped out the divisions ... between the 'author' and the hack ... In the image of the fair, the author could rewrite the social and economic relations which determined his own existence; in the fair he could stigmatise the voices which competed against his own and reveal just how 'dirty' were the hands which sullied his 'pure' wares.
>
> (Stallybrass and White 1986: 77)

In thus marking the estrangement of the author from a market understood as this space of the low or the popular, Jonson set the parameters for subsequent elaborations of authorship as individualism, as the self-possession of the centred, gathered subject, elaborations which are thereby relocated in the determining circumstances of their emergence in a thoroughly historicist manner:

> In separating self from the popular festive scene, authorship after Jonson gradually developed in accordance with the ideal of the individual which was emerging within bourgeois culture – the individual, that is, as 'the proprietor of his own person and capacities, for which he owes nothing to society' (quoted in Fish 1984: 26). Authorship became a visionary embodiment of this ideal to the degree that it represented itself as transcendent to the 'common' place of the market.
>
> (Stallybrass and White 1986: 77)

(g) AUTHORITY AND AUTHORSHIP

If these configurations of autonomous authorship appear both as product of and defence against the intruding hand of the market, other attempts to historicize Jonson's authorial selves have specified different determinants and constraints. One of the most potent possibilities, given Jonson's 'laureate' status, is suggested by his relationship to the monarchy, and to King James in particular. While Helgerson's ideal of the laureate author implies – if it does not over-emphasise – a necessary relationship between government and poetry, and Jonson himself wrote of the parallels between poets and kings **[104]**, the most thorough and complex description of this relationship has been provided by Jonathan Goldberg. Drawing on the investigations into the symbolic vocabulary and apparatus of political power undertaken by the American anthropologist Clifford Geertz, Goldberg situates the author in relation to the king by way of an aphoristic declaration that allows the identification of discourse, symbols, and stories as the substance of power, rather than their designation as the properties of a separate, subordinate realm: ' "The real is as imagined as the imaginary," and the actuality of politics requires the fictions of poets' (Goldberg 1983: 55). This is not a strange declaration that everything is imaginary, fantastic, unreal – simply the assertion that the power to shape and organise the world always takes place through a repertoire of signs and symbols, systems of meaning-production shared with the activities that are sometimes held apart as 'literature'. Consequently, authorship and kingship might both be understood as dealing in this repertoire, this production and reception of meanings which are simultaneously means through which relations of power are established. Goldberg's book sets out to trace the ways in which Jonson's texts and James's authority share in these processes, and in doing so produces an extremely close identification of Jonson's writing with James's strategies of government. For example, Goldberg finds in James a contradictory figure, who governs through a public visibility which is paradoxically simultaneous with an asserted remoteness from the eyes of his subjects. His claim to govern *personally* and *absolutely* makes of his private person a profoundly political entity; it also turns his person into a public sign of his authority. He is both author of meanings and the text to be read, and in James's claims regarding the ways in which government took place *through* representation we find the identity of poetry and kingship of which Jonson wrote, and of which James – whose 'Works' were also published in 1616 – was a living, yet symbolic, embodiment.

Goldberg, though, goes much further in aligning Jonson's writing with this royal poetics. For example, in describing the identification of private needs with matters of state in *Volpone* he suggests an echo or an instance of James's absolutist bringing together of the personal and the political, a conjunction which is the opposite of the Venetian, republican separation of public and private life, itself the target for the play's corrosive attentions (Goldberg 1983: 74). Mostly, though, it is the masques which stage this unity of power and representation. They are not monolithic entities, if only because the contradictory processes of royal power they serve to enact are not static or one-dimensional, and Goldberg goes out of his way to trace the dramatisation of those circuitous processes (Goldberg 1983: 120–46). Nonetheless, all is contained within the triangular structure of representation, poetry and kingship, a structure which both allows the poet to figure kingship as a kind of writing, and enables kingship to underwrite the power of poetry in return. Jonson and his royal master are locked into a mutually sustaining, if grimly exclusive, embrace.

It is the exclusivity which has led to the strongest dissent from Goldberg's subtle, complex and intricate analysis. Critics have argued that Jacobean government could not and did not operate *absolutely*, solely through the person of the king, in the manner which Goldberg's identity of power and representation implies. Which is not to say that power was not exercised through, and written as, a repertoire of symbols or a practice, to some extent, of representation. It is just that its operations may not have been quite so *singularly* Jacobean as Goldberg suggests. For Robert Evans, the crucial system is the network of patronage relations within which Jonson necessarily operated and in which James's role was hugely significant but not singular. This network existed both as an ideal, distinguished by 'reciprocity and *noblesse oblige*' and a rather messier set of 'imperfect, inadequate, frustrating, or uncertain arrangements' which were the perennial object of authorial complaint. These supposed defects of the system were far from contingent impediments to its functioning, however, as 'the very irregularity and unreliability they complained about was one of the actual system's most typical features, and helped to underscore the subservient relationship of writer to patron that the system actually fostered' (Evans 1989: 29). What this insecurity generated was a framework in which the author's activities belie any claims to a centred stability, or gathered stasis: the authorial self was constituted in a set of competitive relationships with other potential clients for the patron's favour. Such circumstances, he claims, ought not to be excluded from attempts to account historically for the Jonsonian configuration of the author:

> The proliferation of print, the growth of capitalism, the rise of ever-purer forms of Protestantism, the increasing centralization of political power – all of these forces inevitably affected the tone and conduct of patronage relations. But since these forces themselves evolved in contexts variously shaped by patronage, they were themselves influenced by it.
>
> (Evans 1989: 26)

Similarly, Martin Butler has argued that the 1616 Folio itself reveals the determining influence of the 'micropolitics of interest and obligation, competition and local advantage' that shaped the environment in which Jonson operated (Butler 1993a: 379). Where Evans imagines the competition between authors as a crucial factor, Butler locates patronage itself as a means by which the competition and factionalism of the court proceeded. In contrast to Loewenstein, then, he suggests that the patronage economy was itself at odds with a model of non-market based authorial autonomy, setting local political considerations against the ahistorical authority of the neo-classical *auctor*, and sets out to trace the marks such a conflict leaves on the *Works*:

> Examination of the arrangement of Jonson's Folio does suggest how much the public role of poet continued to be a game of negotiation, coded stance and strategy even in a volume which exploits the technologies of print so successfully. The Folio may be articulated as a volume of Works, timelessly detached from events and enshrining the power of the author, but the play of contingencies is still emphatically present in its interstices and silences. Jonson's authorization of himself cannot proceed irrespective of the pressures of the political environment within which he was working, and the posture of independence which he sought to promote was subject to professional tensions which his volume could partly efface but from which it could not escape altogether.
>
> (Butler 1993a: 388)

While Butler joins Stallybrass and White in invoking Jonson's professionalism, he adds to that term, with Evans, the sense of an ability or need to thrive within the unpredictable and perpetual shifts in political influence, obligation and allegiance which characterised the practice of patronage within the Jacobean court. Thus, too, his work distinguishes itself from Goldberg's account of Jonson's relationship to James. Where Goldberg identifies contradiction and conflict as moments in a strategy of royal self-representation, a self-representation given (back) to the king in Jonson's texts, Butler's emphasis suggests that this symbolics of power is more clearly a space of negotiation between contrasting, differently directed sets of interests. The critical consequences of this for the reading of the masques are outlined below **[200]**. If it continues to allow Jonson's authorship to be allied to the representation of power, it does so by placing him in to some extent in the intersection *between* authorities rather than eliding him with a singular royal authority.

If Goldberg sought to identify Jonsonian authorship and Jacobean rule, for others it has appeared more helpful to oppose the one to the other. Annabel Patterson, for example, has sought to trace the operations of authority on the author through the notion of censorship. In her analysis Jonson's work appears as revelatory of the operations of a repressive authority: *Sejanus*, for example, 'actually dramatizes the hermeneutics of censorship' in the trial of Cordus **[60]**, staging the conflict between different conceptions of what a text can or should say (Patterson 1984: 52). As she goes on to say, 'when political censorship is *acknowledged* by a writer as his context, the tensions between self and society are likely to have been brought within reflective reach' (Patterson 1984: 58). In such a situation, the autonomous, authorial self emerges as a consequence of censorious intervention in the business of writing, as, 'marked and shocked, the self gathers itself together, and declares itself an autonomous state' (Patterson 1984: 122). In Patterson's picture, though, there is little room for the writer whose selfhood is not a defence against censorship but the capacity to exercise censorious judgement, or even – as Jonson himself sought – to be the censor himself **[31]**. And, as Richard Dutton has shown, the operations of censorship through such offices as the Mastership of the Revels were much more than the business of prohibiting and controlling, the exercise of a singularly negative authority (Dutton 1991). Regulation did not simply oppose authorship to authority – it allowed their interplay in ways which were far more subtle and complex than this repressive model could allow.

Tracing that interplay is the work of Richard Burt's investigation into Jonson's place in the early modern practice of censorship. He reminds us of 'Jonson's own theatre of punishment,' in which he 'symbolically branded, beat, or purged the bodies of poetasters and censurers, invoked a muse of fire to torch the writing of libellous informers and seditious slanderers, from whom he could distinguish himself as a loyal servant of the court' (Burt 1993: 4). Yet this does not mean that we should assume that Jonson simply spoke for authority, or that his poetry can be easily subsumed into the operations of a monolithic power. Rather, Burt proposes that 'we think of censorship broadly as a mechanism for legitimating and delegitimating access to discourse':

> Censorship in its usual sense – the repression of sedition, libel or blasphemy – was only one mechanism for regulating the circulation of discourses, exchanges of power between institutions, transfers of status markers from one institution to another, and so on which marked the emergence of a licensed and relatively autonomous aesthetic domain. To define literary censorship as an activity that legitimates and delegitimates discourses and their modes of circulation means broadening the term, so that its negative, repressive function is seen as only one of many regulatory mechanisms.
>
> (Burt 1993: 12–13)

Censorship, in other words, does not just say 'no'. In saying 'no' to some practices it says 'yes' to others, it *licenses* them as legitimate and protects them from interference. What that suggests to Burt is a need to understand the legitimating role played by such 'positive' practices as Jonson's literary criticism, by the protection of a patron, or by a paying public's exercise of its faculty of judgement. All these, in separating out the legitimate from the illegitimate, played their part in this broadened discourse of censorship; yet they also contributed to a *crisis* of legitimation, in that the boundaries between allowed and forbidden, proper and improper, were not clearly and finally in place, because they were being defined and redefined by different regulatory sites:

> The equivocal meaning of *licence* (both liberty and licentiousness) indicates the difficulty in maintaining a distinction between legitimate poetic liberty and libel or blasphemy. The multiple licensing authorities of court and market alternately affirmed and dissolved the distinctions by which a text was receivable as legitimate and poetic or transgressive and nonpoetic.
>
> (Burt 1993: 13–14)

And as a writer whose work crossed the boundaries between these 'multiple licensing authorities', the authorial Jonson was necessarily at odds with himself, especially in his attempts to establish a clear standard for a unified practice of literary criticism – and thus manifested what Burt describes as a 'neurotic' or 'decentred' subjectivity:

> In order to 'fit in' with one audience, Jonson willingly censored himself; yet the censored criticism emerged in another context. He couldn't say everything he wanted to say in any one place or in any one medium. Jonson was both limited and licensed in a given sphere – the theatre, the tavern, the court, the country house, the study. The same may be said for the media he used – speech, manuscript, print, or marginalia – in the vernacular or in Latin. In displacing the problems he saw in one practice, such as theatrical performance, onto another, such as print, Jonson needed to construct a new set of distinctions (the reader ordinary versus the reader extraordinary, as in the prefaces to *Catiline*) to solve the new problems this displacement opened up. In moving from one site to another, Jonson produced finer and finer distinctions between censure and vulgar censure, or between 'good' and 'bad' libel, as when he delegitimated in 'Ode to Himself' the 'vulgar censure' of *The New Inn* ... These paradoxical displacements, I suggest, constitute a neurotic subjectivity not reducible to an opposition between freedom and repression.
>
> (Burt 1993: 47)

Thus it is that Jonson can paradoxically commit crimes in trying to arraign them, and the censurer can make of himself an object for censure:

> He ends his epigram 'To Prowl the Plagiary,' *Epigrams* 81, by threatening the plagiarist, 'if thou leave not soon, I must a libel make' (8). Jonson contentiously censured his censurers, libelled his libellers, in order to exclude them from his critical community ... He transgressed the boundaries between legitimate and illegitimate censorship, between licensed critique and transgressive libel, which grounded his authority.
>
> (Burt 1993: 64)

So the poetic, authorial self is neither at one with political authority nor constituted in opposition to it, but internally divided by an ever-shifting boundary between the allowed and the forbidden. This condition, Burt suggests, is best exemplified in the Jonsonian corpus by *Bartholomew Fair*, which not only explicitly appeals in its framing apparatus both to theatrical and court milieus, but also includes explicit play on the ambiguity of 'licence' and 'liberty' in its portrayal of the puppet show **[88]**; while the use and abuse of Overdo's warrant and Cokes's marriage licence also draw attention to the potential instability of just the practices of legitimation that Burt has identified with the broad function of censorship. Importantly, this and preceding models of authorial selfhood shape, as we might expect, the possible *political* functions and consequences that can be inferred for Jonson's writing – the exploration of authority's place in their structure presumes as much. In subsequent sections we will examine the ways in which these and other contexts, in all their variety, have defined those functions and those consequences.

(h) DRAMATIC WORKS: ETHICS, POLITICS AND HISTORY

For a long time, the claims made in such prefatory material as the framing device of *Every Man Out of his Humour*, *Volpone*'s Dedicatory Epistle or the brief Prologue to *The Alchemist* shaped the idiom of the criticism such plays provoked. The satirist's claims to be in pursuit of moral reformation have helped to ensure that Jonson's works for the stage were read as single-mindedly *ethical*, and could be comprehended entirely within the horizons of this reformatory impulse. Edward Partridge, for example, averred that Jonson's drama is marked by the evocation of a 'transchanged world' of inverted values in which ethical decorum was hideously reordered, but that such an evocation took place within the overall purpose of setting the world once more to rights:

> Jonson inverted the values which are commonly accepted and made those inverted values the real values of the world which he dramatically created. For instance, most people say that they worship God, but live as though they worship money or worldly power. To ridicule such folly and to arouse the scorn that such impiety ought to call forth, Jonson created an imaginative world in which money or food or sensual experience is regarded as divine; thus, Volpone, Mammon, and Peniboy Senior worship gold, sacrifice to it, and live for it. All things within the Volpone or Mammon world are measured by such inverted values ...

In such a 'transchanged' world sin becomes piety, devils appear as angels, and blasphemy is the true religion. This sense of inversion or perversion appears in some form or another in most of Jonson's plays, but most clearly in *Volpone* and *The Alchemist*. In part, Jonson hoped that, if his plays could show men how preposterous their manners and natures had come to be, they would go and sin no more ... Like all masters of irony, Jonson celebrated the good obliquely: he made the foul ridiculous.

(Partridge 1958: 63, 69)

Partridge cites as an example of this process Volpone's celebrated opening speech, in which his gold is addressed in religious language **[71]**. Devotional terms become the metaphorical expression of Volpone's attraction to money, and also provide a means whereby that fascination may take on the apparent respectability of a moral system, assuming the ethical mantle of Christianity with its vocabulary (Partridge 1958: 72–7). The same process is repeated in the language of *The Alchemist* and in the later plays. So it is primarily in his deployment of imagery that Jonson indicates the means whereby the moral perversion takes place: such metaphorical expressions breach the proper decorum of language which ought to prevent values from becoming twisted round in this way. In a play such as *Epicene*, this process of perversion is explicitly related to the imagery of gender **[76]**. The play's women are represented as unnatural, breaching decorum in allowing the female body to take on masculine attributes, and thus proving themselves – as Madam Centaur's name indicates – monstrous. The play's men, by the same token, are equally 'perverse'. Those who are not, like Daw and La Foole, 'warped by the Amazonian natures of these epicene women' (Partridge 1958: 170) are still sexually ambiguous: Partridge alights on Truewit's comment regarding Clerimont's fondness for his 'ingle' in the play's opening scene **[77]**. So the play itself is a dramatisation of distortion, and though Partridge explicitly claims that it does not manage to assert a clear morality of the natural, the normal and the decorous, the comedy of inversion implies such a framework:

Though the play offers no final answers, it suggests throughout that the various answers dramatized in the physical and verbal action of the play are comic in so far as they violate certain standards of what is masculine and what is feminine, as well as what is natural and artificial in dress, behaviour, and beauty.

(Partridge 1958: 176)

The difficulty for Partridge, and for critics of a similar cast of mind, is that the sense of ethical purpose which he claims underlies Jonson's dramatic works seems to be betrayed by the apparently tolerant endings given to such plays as *The Alchemist* or *Bartholomew Fair*, in which a proper moral order is not obviously asserted, and no ethical justice is superimposed, as in *Volpone*, on dramatic narrative. His sense of the interdependence of linguistic decorum and moral order offers a route out of these difficulties with endings in serving to tie the Jonsonian text to an ethical purpose *despite* the thrust of the narrative. Yet by the time he wrote *The Broken Compass*, other critics had already queried the assumption that these formal features of the works could so easily bear and preserve a timeless moral burden. In an important work published in 1937, L. C. Knights had related Jonson's work to the economic 'background' of his time, in particular the development of new capitalist ways of organising the production and exchange of commodities, a new identification of wealth and power with money – now not just a means of exchange but a 'store' of wealth, 'capital' – as well as land, and therefore changing social circumstances as a new class, the 'bourgeoisie', began to emerge to challenge the pre-eminence of the aristocracy and landed gentry. The society of Jonson's time was, therefore, marked by an awareness of a new order emerging from the midst of a 'traditional', agrarian, medieval view of the world. Jonson's work could be aligned with the articulation of opposition to such a new order, as the dramatisation of an 'anti-acquisitive attitude' that registered its emergence with some discomfort. His satire was thus not timelessly moral, concerned with unchanging conceptions of virtue and vice, but contemporary and even topical. The portrayal of 'projectors' in *The Devil is an Ass*, for example, not only stemmed from such epochal changes, but actually put them on stage (Knights 1937: 212).

Even so, Knights did not for a minute dispute that Jonson's plays were definable by their satiric, corrective purposes, nor that the economic circumstances to which he had opened up the drama were themselves in the end reducible to the moral terms presupposed by those definitions of satire. 'Attacks on the new order,' he argued, 'took the form of attacks on individuals ... The diagnosis was moral rather than economic. Or, to put it another way, the dramatic treatment of economic problems showed them as moral and individual problems – which in the last analysis they are' (Knights 1937: 176). It is this that more recent attempts to attend to the ethics and politics of Jonson's drama have been keenest to dispute. Knights, like Partridge, presupposes the obviousness, integrity and fundamental reality of the site of moral

BEN JONSON

problems: the autonomous individual who thinks, acts, judges according
to ethical principles and can be located within an ethical scheme. Yet,
as we have seen **[146]**, critical accounts of selfhood and authorship in
Jonson might query just such an assumption, particularly when they
suggest that this model of the autonomous, self-authoring self is itself
the product of historical, social and economic circumstances. Rather
than social questions being reducible in the end to morals, it is morality
which is in the end reducible to society.

 This at least is the substance of Don Wayne's 'attempt to redefine
the relationship between Jonsonian drama and its sociohistorical
context' (Wayne 1982: 103). Arguing that Jonson's drama of humours
amounts to 'a rudimentary social psychology', a recognition that 'the
dislocation and division of the human subject ... are functionally related
to historical disjunctions in the social organization of reality', he insists
that this should prevent us from positioning Jonson's works as merely
exemplifying an 'anti-acquisitive attitude', for 'while they may be
satirizing the acquisitiveness associated with an incipient mercantile
capitalism, the dramatists are themselves caught in something of a
double bind concerning the place of their own work in this new
economic, political and social context.' Jonson's 'own identity as poet
and playwright – and therefore his personal transcendence of the still
rigid social hierarchy in which he lived and wrote – depended on the
same emerging structure of social relationships that he satirized in his
plays' (Wayne 1982: 105, 106, 107). This is the same double bind that
other critics, as we have seen, have located in the Jonsonian structure
of authorship and its unstable authority **[154]**; here, Wayne takes it
up as a means of describing the inadequacy of the basis on which
'ethical' accounts of the plays are based. What Knights describes as an
essentially ethical concern, 'acquisitiveness', Wayne locates within the
complex transformations of human identity and relationships which
he suggests are brought about by the development of new socio-
economic processes. Jonson's plays, which voice ethical concerns and
serve moral ends, but which simultaneously reveal the ways such
concerns and ends change over time and under social pressure, cannot
therefore be reduced to merely serving such ends. Ethics, in other words,
has a history – and Jonson's drama is revelatory of precisely that fact.

 Wayne's revision of Knights is an attempt to politicise the reading
of Jonson's drama in a particular direction. It is not simply that he
does not think that the plays can be adequately understood as
repudiating passions or follies which are the permanent stuff of human
nature – greed, lust and so on; more importantly, he considers that an
account of their functioning should not be constrained within the

model of a satirist consciously and purposively working through the definition and treatment of a problem. What Jonson thought he was doing, in other words, however that can be defined, is not the appropriate horizon of interpretation. Rather, the plays should be read within a framework which locates them in broader social practices and discourses – a terrain that Wayne describes as 'ideology' – which both determine the forms and limits of what can be said and are themselves shaped and altered by changes in the basic economic structure of society. This is a *political* reading in that it draws on a model of culture derived from the Marxist view of history as a 'material' process, and also periodises that history in accordance with the Marxist view of successive epochs defined by their characteristic *mode of production* – of which capitalism is the most recent. Consequently, it insists that the model of human nature presumed by moralistic criticism to be the basis for its activity is at worst illusory, and at best a local, historically contingent formulation of what it means to be human. To forget its contingency is to mistake it as natural, unchanging and unchangeable – to recover that contingency is to suggest that it might one day be changed. Thus, a critical reading of Jonson's drama which historicizes the ethical opens it up to politics, and links the practice of literary criticism to the broader pursuit of social change.

This orientation of historical criticism to contemporary politics has had a profound impact on Jonson studies in the last twenty years. As is demonstrated below, it has not just been Marxism which has provided the means – feminist criticism, for example, has allied the study of the organisation of gender relations in history to contemporary political demands. While some among such political critics have sought mainly to integrate Jonson's texts into the broader social structures and changes – such as the emergence of capitalism – whose analysis is the basis of their approach to history, others have set out to trace the ways in which Jonson's writings might be implicated in the *reproduction* of the power relationships characteristic of the society in which they were written. But these power relationships need not only be of the primarily economic kind emphasised by Marxism: they might instead be organised around the axes of gender, race or sexuality, for example. Encouraged by the New Historicist account of the interdependence of power and representation, such critics have joined Jonathan Goldberg in describing Jonson's work – the masques serving as the clearest example here – as a full participant in the symbolic reproduction of power **[155, 203]**. Alternatively, others have pointed to the plays as instances of the disruption or subversion of those very structures. In either of these cases the politics of the *criticism* is largely internal to literary or cultural studies itself – what is sought is a revision of the understanding of the part that literary texts can play in the political arena. A yet further way of considering the political meanings which might be located in Jonson's works has involved the identification of the political alignments, conflicts and institutions of his age – the court, Parliament, the church and so on – and the placement of Jonson's texts as political acts within such matrices. Here, the sense of what Jonson thought he was doing – which need not perhaps play much of a part in the styles of political criticism described above – makes something of a return. In other words, this is a form of criticism which understands Jonson's works as playing a role in the explicit political disputes of his age: he is understood to be a self-conscious political agent, and his works testify to his choices and commitments as much if not more than to the deep, discursive structures of power characteristic of his age.

In truth, much critical work has not found it necessary or possible to separate out these different ways of understanding Jonson's politics. It is not simply that Marxists, feminists and New Historicists have drawn on and incorporated each other's strengths, important though such interchange has been. As significant has been the engagement of all these tendencies with the thought of the conscious political agent or actor. They all manifest a profound concern with the place of subjectivity or selfhood within the symbolic operations of power, and Jonson – whose engagement with such questions, as we have seen, has been the focus of repeated critical attention – has not been absent from such accounts. In any description of the differing debates around the politics of his drama, all the tendencies outlined above can be seen in a variety of configurations.

(i) DRAMATIC WORKS: CARNIVAL

One of the most persistent concerns for those who would give an account of the political functioning of Jonson's drama has been its representation of popular festivity. Here, concerns about authorship, authority, classicism and theatricality come together to provide the coordinates for a myriad of interpretations. In his *The World Upside Down* Ian Donaldson averred that Jonson's plays take 'the festive idea as a starting point to explore questions of social freedom and social discipline, social equality and social distinction' (Donaldson 1970: 20). He is keen to associate Jonson's work with the celebratory mode of popular carnival, and in readings of *Epicene* and *Bartholomew Fair* he sets out the terms on which such an association might be made. Both plays present 'a picture of a farcical and Saturnalian society in which normal social roles are inverted':

> By this means he compels us to attend to questions which are far from farcical, and which are concerned principally with problems about social order; with the problems of what Jonson called 'licence' and 'liberty'.
>
> (Donaldson 1970: 20)

Here, in other words, we find the same representations of inversion that Partridge noted, but which are now to be recognised as of their time. In *Epicene*, the travesty wedding ceremony to which Morose is subjected is related to the early modern festive practice of *charivari*, a kind of 'public defamation' by means of noise to which appropriately un-festive victims are treated. *Bartholomew Fair* borrows its mood from the festivity of the fair itself, the liberty of holiday to offer an alternative to the workaday world. The sense of a time apart is heightened by the identification of the play's festivity and the festivity of theatre itself, which offers the possibility of exceeding its limits in offering the continuation of revelry at the house of Adam Overdo, the comic figure of authority (Donaldson 1970: 59–71). But this festivity, says Donaldson, is ultimately contained: 'the play does not come to rest at a point of tolerant, festive anarchy' (Donaldson 1970: 71). For it is ultimately surrendered to the purposes of King James, its satirical portrayal of Overdo's exertions matching James's own criticism of rulers who overreach themselves, or – as Donaldson points out – overdo it:

> 'The power to judge', the epilogue declares, is finally that of King James himself; and it is significant that the king is asked to judge not simply ... whether the play is a good one or a bad one, but whether or not Jonson has abused his privilege as a writer, whether he has turned royal 'leave' into 'licence'. The play's leading question is now turned against the writer of the play himself. The final appeal to the king re-affirms, with the lightest of touches, but nevertheless with something of the effect of the entry of the main masque after the anarchy of an anti-masque, the existence of a real and workable social order with James at its head.
>
> (Donaldson 1970: 71–2)

Jonsonian festivity, then, ultimately reaffirms the social order from which it momentarily excuses itself – it is to that extent a *conservative* phenomenon. Furthermore, as Donaldson points out, the *charivari* to which Morose is subjected in *Epicene* is not a celebration of freedom from social constraints but the punishment of those who breach such constraints: not only misers and misanthropes but also mannish women and womanish men, domineering wives and henpecked husbands.

For subsequent critics, the festivity of Jonson's middle comedies has been readable in other ways and through other frameworks. For Leah Marcus *Bartholomew Fair* presents a similar picture, of drama surrendering itself to royal judgement. But she sets this in the context of royal policies of the early years of the seventeenth century, in particular a determination to contain the growth of London and its influence, and to revivify country sports and holiday pastimes which were thought amenable to the royal view of the country's government and of activities appropriate to its different social strata. *Bartholomew Fair* thus becomes a rebuke to the city and an assertion of royal authority over it:

> Bartholomew Fair has suffered from a vacuum of authority: its judges lack judgement and its reformers fail to reform. Since Londoners cannot manage to curb the vices of their own fair, they are disqualified as censurers of its equivalent, the theatre. By demonstrating that the major contemporary arguments against the drama apply equally to the fair, Jonson dilutes their force against either. The ultimate power to criticize, licence, and order the drama, and by extension the fair as well, is left to the King of England.
> (Marcus 1986: 59)

Jonson's work is thus here explicitly consonant with royal policy, not just with general conceptions of the role of the monarch or a broader, seemingly conservative, practice of popular festivity.

This account of the middle comedies is strongly challenged by a number of works. For some, Mikhail Bakhtin's reading of Rabelais **[84]** offered an invaluable resource. He identified and linked particular carnival motifs which critics have subsequently located in all manner of texts. Inversion, for example, was joined by the image of the marketplace as the site of an inclusive, collective festivity which acknowledged no boundaries between participants and spectators, and was also the place for a kind of popular language which contradicted the singular, unambiguous, authoritative official word. This festivity was characterised by a non-hierarchical banquet which acknowledged no social boundaries. Furthermore, the self-contained, clearly bounded body of the 'individual' was contrasted with the 'grotesque body', a corporeality which was permeable, open to the world, never fixed but constantly in the process of generation, regeneration and degeneration, ingesting and excreting – a body of movement, process, or 'becoming' to contrast with the hard, impermeable surface of the individualised, static body of 'being'. But in his account of carnival festivity Bakhtin did more than simply describe a centuries-old cultural practice. He also insisted that it had a particular value as a model of cultural subversion, a defiantly political challenge to 'official orders' everywhere. It not only demonstrated the impermanence of the established structures of authority, debunking their claims to be natural and unalterable, it also offered the prefiguration of the forms of collective identity, of popular community, which could not only work to transform the world but also establish the basis for a new social dispensation (Bakhtin 1968: passim).

It has been the apparently *critical* function of Bakhtin's theory of carnival which has most appealed to readers of Jonson's comedies. For Peter Womack, the theatre is readily identifiable as the space of carnival, a place where the singularity of the official order, the absolutism of monarchy, is challenged by the multiplicity of other voices and other faces that the pretence of drama located simultaneously in the figure of the actor-in-performance. Here, the single Truth of the 'official order' was replaced by the dialogue between different voices, the opening up of the possibility of other truths, and the prison-house of individuality was broken open by the unstable identity characteristic of the *player*. Womack gives as one example the double reading to which the performance of sickness put on by Volpone is susceptible:

> Read as representation, it depicts a lie; a criminal stratagem whose success signifies only the folly and greed of those who are taken in by it ... Read as performance, on the other hand, Volpone's sickness is a kind of carnival: a celebration, against the rigid categories of official culture and legality which the first reading takes for granted, of the ceaselessly dying and renewing body, its devouring and discharging laughter, and the invincible resourcefulness with which it provokes fresh transformations. In this context, the parodic vaunting of the tricksters doesn't so much enforce as undermine the authoritarian barrier between what is and what could be: they're artists, transmuters of nature, concluding there's naught impossible. And if the authorially controlled plot endorses the ethical condemnation of lying and cheating, the *show* is riding shamelessly on the flight in the face of truth: that is, the moralism of the text is dialogised by its complicity with its own staging.
>
> (Womack 1986: 143)

In being staged, that is, the play works against its own ostensible purpose – it speaks in two voices, the certainty and fixity of monologue replaced by the doubleness of dialogue, and in so doing undermines the singular meaning and authority to which it might be thought to be subject or to give voice. Despite such possibilities in performance, though, *Volpone*'s inversions of the official order ultimately produce merely its mirror image, a kind of 'travesty court' presided over by Volpone himself which produces not a carnivalesque celebration of generation and regeneration but 'a parodic apotheosis of money':

> Its cold and abstract utopianism takes the form, not of a saturnalian 'banquet for all the world', but of an infinitely large pile of precious metals.
>
> (Womack 1986: 74)

The political promise of the carnivalesque is more clearly made good, however, in *The Alchemist* and *Bartholomew Fair*. The house in which all the action of the former takes place is a 'self-referring image of the theatre' (Womack 1986: 118) in which acting is marked clearly as politically challenging: linked to desire, and thence through the motif of alchemy to the possibility of political change **[82]**. As Womack puts it, 'what Subtle is really forging is not just a licence to print money, but a charter to remake the world in accordance with human desire' (129). Yet the fact that such carnivalesque significance exists in the work of a spokesman for the 'official order' like Jonson means that it is to some degree marked as illicit and occult – utopia becomes an underworld, and its activities are associated with the horrifying freedoms of a plague-driven collapse of, or abdication by, proper authority. In *Bartholomew Fair*, though, this subordination does not take place – carnival is fully realised in its festive environs, its peculiar confusions of time, its refusal to posit one authoritative place from which a singular truth can be seen and the 'falsity' of theatre identified and condemned:

> The Fair is evidently an equivalent of the alchemist's shop or Volpone's sick-room: a space where stable identities dissolve in ambivalently proliferating forms of desire and which, in its asymmetrical combination of utopianism and deception, is the theatre's own self-reflected image. But ... the popular-festive note, which I've described as repressed and distorted in the other plays, here seems to be struck directly.
>
> (Womack 1986: 145–6)

In the multiple points of view of the play, in which all the characters appear as 'spectacles' for each other, the carnivalesque aspiration to bring together in its multiplicity 'the whole body of the people' is finally met, while in the Induction the line between audience and spectacle is also crossed: they are invited, in the tradition of carnival, to participate in the show:

> The scene is a spoof, a piece of parody-legal clowning ... which acknowledges that the relationship between the show and the audience can't really be bound by formal agreements, and at the same time invites the audience to play at being parties to such a contract ... The act of coming to see the play is retextualized as participation in a game.
>
> (Womack 1986: 158)

What this produces, Womack argues, is a challenge to the kinds of dramatic procedures familiar from the court masque, that apotheosis of the 'official order' which identifies the king himself as the single authorising viewpoint from which the truth can be seen and known. The play is a kind of uncontained *antimasque*, given not to the monarch but to his uncontainable, festive other:

> By removing this upside-down comic form from its proper place in the iconography of absolutism and staging it in the public theatre, Jonson arrives at an uncrowned celebration, a masque for the people.
>
> (Womack 1986: 159)

While Womack identifies the liberating thrust of carnival with the fair, and both with theatricality, other critics have been more circumspect. Peter Stallybrass and Allon White have argued that Bakhtin's representation of the carnival marketplace is itself a simplification, that rather than being a 'pure outside' to the official order, a utopian 'no-place' utterly set against such constraints, the festive marketplace of the fair ought instead to be viewed as a hybrid space, a 'crossroads' where the opposites of commerce and pleasure, work and play, usefulness and wastefulness can be commingled. It is, they say, 'a gravely over-simplifying abstraction therefore to conceptualise the fair purely as the site of communal celebration' (Stallybrass and White 1986: 29, 30). Much cultural labour, they suggest, was expended in the dominant, bourgeois culture which developed with capitalism, on trying to separate out these two sides to the fair, to unpick its hybridity. Yet that effort was also haunted by the fact that the separations achieved kept threatening to melt away: the legitimate was always haunted by the fact that it only made sense, that it owed its identity to, its *difference* from the illegitimate. The strength they find in Bakhtin's analysis is that although it sometimes insists on the absolute separation and opposition of official and unofficial cultures, of order and festivity – a separation which would allow the oppositions between work and play, serious and silly, high and low to remain happily in place, consigning carnival to the role merely of the low – it also, perhaps contradictorily, imagines the grotesque as *precisely* the process of hybridisation which caused so much trouble to attempts to keep those oppositions properly in place. As Stallybrass and White explain, the pig is the perfect symbol of this hybridity, this confusion of opposites: in many cultures, it blunders across boundaries between the human and the animal, the clean and the dirty, food and excrement.

All this has a clear relevance for a reading of *Bartholomew Fair* in particular. In Ursula, the pig-woman, that hybridity finds its vibrant expression:

> In Ursula, the overcoming of the confines between bodies, and between the body and the world, is dramatized. She is, indeed, the go-between, not only in her role as bawd and as the mediator between the fairgoers and food, but also in the symbolic function-ing of her bodily processes which move continuously between the inner and the outer. At the same time, the boundaries of the body, gender and status are destabilized.
>
> (Stallybrass and White 1986: 65)

Yet though Stallybrass and White here locate festivity in Jonson's fair, they do not share Womack's willingness simply to identify the theatre with a carnivalesque opposition to the official order. Rather, as we noted above, they find in Jonson an example of the attempt to police the boundaries, not to transgress them: his play does not become one with the carnivalesque fair, but in its Induction separates itself from what it represents, and separates itself too from the 'low' audience crowded into the Hope theatre to watch it. This cleansing strategy, they suggest, can never be finally accomplished however vigorously it is pursued:

> Disgust bears the imprint of desire, and Jonson found in the huckster, the cony-catcher [that is, con-man] and the pick-pocket

an image of his own precarious and importuning craft. Proclaiming so loudly how all the other plays were mere cozenings, did not Jonson pursue the perennial strategy of the mountebank who decried the deceptions and the false wares of others the more easily to practise his own deceptions and pass off his own productions as the 'real thing'?

(Stallybrass and White 1986: 77)

It is not, therefore, a matter of celebrating *Bartholomew Fair* as a properly popular drama: it is a question of diagnosing the place it occupies in the production, transgression and reproduction of political limits and boundaries, the cultural demarcations which generate and are always threatened by the possibility of hybridity, of contamination.

This 'diagnostic' stance is taken in a different direction by Jonathan Haynes in his attempt to delineate *The Social Relations of Jonson's Theatre* (1992). He sets out to trace the relationship between Jonson's drama and the social conflicts of its age, focusing on what he describes as the realism of the Jonsonian text, a description deserved by an art 'thick with social references and so clearly social in its intentions' (Haynes 1992: 10). This approach is justified by such features of the text and the theatre's role as an element in 'a historical process of social representation' (5); Haynes's book outlines the routes by which the theatre became established as an arena both for this process and for the kinds of competition or social conflict that might be represented on the stage. He suggests, too, that Jonson actually develops a sociological account of his world, rather than being simply or mainly symptomatic of it. The focus of his account is on the social changes and conflicts brought about by the growth and spread of the capitalist mode of production, its organisation of the material processes of life. In *The Alchemist*, for example, Jonson manages to 'formulate a new conception of criminality', which places it in 'a new structure of economic and social opportunities':

Subtle and Face and Doll represent new social possibilities, are figures of and for new spaces, fissures and energies in London society; their operation may go up in fumes at the end of the play, but the vast, restless, generative metropolis does not dissolve.

(Haynes 1992: 99)

He compares the play's configuration of criminality to that developed in the non-dramatic writing on crime of the period, and finds in Jonson a mapping of underworld activities on the model of capitalist enterprise rather than other models of confederacy. The play implies, he claims, that 'the fundamental problem is not the appearance of a new criminal profession ... but a new economy, working through both society and the underworld' (Haynes 1992: 109). Rather than allow the separation and stigmatisation of the criminal as 'Other', a different kind of person and society altogether, the play suggests a more 'subversive' conclusion:

> The Alchemist is specific about the terrain of criminal activity without containing and demonising it within a subculture: the points of contact, and the negotiations of the border with straight society, are of the greatest interest. The underworld is not the antithesis of society, but its continuation, its shadow.
>
> (Haynes 1992: 118)

Continuing in this sociological vein, he relates Bartholomew Fair to the changes confronting the fair in Jonson's time, when its character as a time and place apart from daily business was being eroded. In fact, he locates those changes precisely in the play's refusal to embody the principle of collective festivity, 'drawing us away from participation in the festive marketplace and toward a criticism of it' (121). He suggests that rather than bringing together the people as a whole, the play keeps in place precisely the distinction between underworld and 'straight' society that Womack finds notable only by its absence. In the persons of Quarlous, Winwife and Grace Wellborn we find those who keep themselves apart, and in so doing fail to succumb to the festive reordering which befalls the other characters coming into the fair from the outside. Furthermore, he finds in the Induction further evidence of Jonson's separation of theatre from carnival:

> The Fair, still very much alive in Smithfield, is being represented in a commercial theatre, before a paying audience, at a different time of the year. It is thus torn out of its social context and made into an object of art, and Jonson wants to be sure his audience sees the difference, that they reconstitute themselves as the proper sort of audience, not as a crowd in the festive mode.
>
> (Haynes 1992: 130)

In the 'Articles of Agreement' presented to the audience Haynes locates stipulations which very carefully prevent them construing themselves as a festive crowd, and insist on their responsibility to act autonomously, exercising a judgement which is strictly individual. This Haynes relates to the fair's subsumption into the general structure of capitalist exchange, as the marketplace of Bakhtinian political possibility is reshaped in taking its place in the general, workaday practices of the market.

(j) DRAMATIC WORKS: GENDER AND SEXUALITY

If the political force of Jonsonian festivity has been one of the most productive debates to gather round Jonson's middle comedies in the last two decades, another has been generated by the development of feminist criticism over the same period. This criticism has been concerned not just to explore the representation of women in literature but more profoundly to address the cultural functioning of gender, the operations of the language of gender, the relationships between the social habitation of gendered identities and a supposedly pre-social, bodily 'sex', and the relationships of the structures which support the binary opposition of masculine and feminine to those which police the division of sexuality into hetero- and homo-, straight and queer. The political force of such criticism is similar in many ways to that attributed to Marxism: if it can somehow show that our understanding of the ways in which we are gendered is not the apprehension of unchanging features of human identity, but historically specific and culturally forged, then it becomes possible to envisage that things might be otherwise. Furthermore, if the social dominance of men can be recast as a human act and not a state of nature, what was beyond the realm of political endeavour becomes a clear space for political intervention. Reading literary works so as to question what earlier readers had thought beyond question becomes one form that such intervention might take.

Where *Bartholomew Fair* has been the *locus classicus* for critical thinking around the politics of festivity, *Epicene* has joined it as one of the major sites for feminist work. At first this play might seem merely to confirm the challenge or opportunity for feminist criticism offered by Jonson's writings: the play, Kathleen McLuskie is not alone in claiming, is staunchly and obviously misogynist in its workings. As she says, 'if there is a central position *vis à vis* women in the play, it is one of avoidance' (McLuskie 1989: 170). Nonetheless, it is precisely the structure of that misogyny, how it works to define what woman means, how it might fail to cohere as an account of gender difference, and what it might reveal about the links between women's oppression and other social structures that is of interest. Moving from *Epicene* to

175

Catiline, McLuskie argues that femininity is written 'as part of a symbolism of consumption and luxurious excess which dominates Jonson's satiric view of the world' (McLuskie 1989: 179). Here, though, the misogynist condemnation of women actually helps to expose the ways in which women circulated as objects or commodities in transactions between men in early modern culture. In *Bartholomew Fair* such a logic is fully in view, since 'the fate of Grace Wellborn holds the action together, and she is quite explicit about her status as a "commodity", bought by Justice Overdo and handed, against her will, to Bartholomew Cokes' (180). Yet there is perhaps a problem here. If, as McLuskie says, 'no one escapes from the relations of the market, not the audience in the theatre, who may only judge according to the value of the seats, and not the author himself' (181) – if, in other words, *everyone* is subject to the processes of commodification that she describes – then it is hard to see how Jonsonian misogyny can reveal women's *gender-specific* relation to commodification and market exchange.

This is a challenge taken up in the works of other feminist critics. Karen Newman notes that women have been identified 'as goods themselves, and inversely, goods are often feminized' (Newman 1991: 133). They are exchanged by men, given in marriage, in order that their reproductive capacity should be properly allied to the purpose of extending male bloodlines – providing, that is, sons and heirs for their husbands, and joining together families that are identified with and by the name of the father. And yet women are also paradigmatic *consumers* of goods. Their relationship to commodification is therefore not fixed or stable – they are objectified as goods, but escape such objectification in being consumers. This escape is itself figured as an escape from the control of fathers or husbands, as the woman's 'supposed desire for goods is linked to her sexual availability' (134); one move along the figurative chain, her sexual looseness is also troped as the garrulousness of the talkative woman. The talking woman is not only immodest but transgressive – her speech challenges the order of things which makes public speaking a male prerogative. Her presence in the marketplace, as either a buyer or a seller, is equally a direct affront to masculine control of public life and public spaces. Newman traces the place of this complex of misogyny and anxiety through the text of *Epicene*, showing how the ways in which women are *characterised*, and the ways in which consumerism and authority are *gendered*, reinforce each other, while such languages always describe in order, finally, to *judge*. Yet even as they do so they reveal their own logical flaws and inconsistencies:

In *Epicene*, the talking woman represents the city *and* what in large part motivated the growth of the city: mercantilism and colonial expansion. Consumption, like female talk, is presented as at once stereotypical (women all do it) and as unnatural (women who do it are masculine, hermaphroditical, monstrous). Critics of *Epicene* typically discuss its female characters in terms of the opposition between the hermaphroditical, monstrous, epicene women and the cultural norm – women who were chaste, silent, and obedient. The play's satire depends on shared, if unrepresented, assumptions about behaviour appropriate to women that position the audience to perceive the collegiates' activities as reprehensible. Such readings join Jonson in his censure by assuming the implicit norm as positive and 'natural' rather than culturally produced. In Jonson, woman is the focus of cultural ambivalence.

(Newman 1991: 137–8)

In an innovative reading of *Bartholomew Fair*, Shannon Miller has connected such accounts of the symbolic functioning of woman with the motif of carnival which, as we have seen, has proved an enduring concern for political criticism. In so doing, she has provided an exemplary instance of how the concerns of feminist criticism have redrawn even apparently comprehensively radical accounts of the plays' political possibilities. Noting that Bakhtin's notion of the grotesque body is not gender specific, she suggests that its defining openness to the world, its involvement in generation, nonetheless implicitly mark it as female (Miller 1996: 75). She also points out that this is an already transgressive femininity, given to all the connotations of looseness, incontinence and uncontrollability associated with the 'naturally grotesque' woman. She goes on to map this contrast between the openness of the grotesque, female body and the closed, defined space of the classical or official body on to a redefinition of the relationship between carnival and the marketplace. As capitalism developed, and the forms of economic exchange associated with it became more pervasive, the old conception of the distinct, enclosed marketplace gave way to a new practice of the market as an amorphous, decentred entity, existing throughout society and therefore identifiable at no single place within it. This, she claims, resulted in an anxiety which attached itself to the figure of the uncontrollable woman, an available cultural analogue for such disturbances:

The movement to control the female body can be seen as an analogous move to contain the threatening carnival object as

177

women become the vessels for anxiety about a changing economic system ... The woman, then, becomes an index not only of men's anxieties about the uncontrolled and potentially uncontainable woman, but also of economic concerns to which she is frequently compared.

(Miller 1996: 80)

In *Bartholomew Fair*, this is the reason why the carnivalesque overflowing of boundaries is explicitly gendered in the bodies not only of Ursula but also those of Mistresses Overdo and Littlewit. It is also, therefore, the site of a concern about the loss of control over such carnivalesque entities and indeed over the feminised fair itself, eluding all attempts to confine them within manageable borders:

The historical division between the market and the carnival is erased through the female body as a carnivalesque economy is projected onto the overflowing uncontainability of the grotesque woman ... Chaotic, consuming, and destructive, women become figures for the marketplace itself.

(Miller 1996: 94)

Here, then, the political thrust of carnival is rewritten to take account of the place within it of the figure of gender. What makes Miller's essay doubly interesting is its identification of the carnivalesque, the undoing of the official order, with the processes of capitalist commodification and exchange that Haynes, for example, positions as the historic enemy of carnival. In this she deploys the double vision, inherited from Marx, which sees the transition to capitalism both as the death of old forms of popular, collective life and also a revolutionary challenge to a rigid established order. If Jonson is located on this cultural faultline, then his writings are a crossroads of many differing political trajectories.

It is this doubleness which has also enabled recent feminist challenges to the commonplace assumption of Jonsonian misogyny. Helen Ostovich, for example, has examined *The Magnetic Lady* as an exploration of what happens when women escape their roles as 'female bodies whose reproductive power men appropriate as vehicles for transmitting and securing property' in order to 'reappropriate maternity and motherhood in the course of their own pursuit of independent pleasure or profit' (Ostovich 1994: 425). In this play, such a realm is not allowed to thrive for long, being marked as transgressive and in need of masculine correction **[97]**. Yet against this, in another article,

Ostovich sets Jonson's portrayal of the dilemma faced by Frances Fitzdottrel in *The Devil is An Ass*, a dilemma she connects to the problematic construction of aristocratic femininity in early modern culture:

> Frances Fitzdottrel … must choose between her tyrannical fool of a husband and her sensitive admirer – essentially a choice between being perceived as honest (by sticking to her marriage vows), or dishonest (by reaching out for love and rational companionship). In this dilemma, Jonson stresses that she has every justification for preferring adultery: hence, the difficulty of her decision. Her desire for independent self-government in sexual matters is closely bound up with her desire for independent control of her real property, both impossible in common law where the marital authority over both sexuality and property is the husband. Despite Jonson's modern reputation for misogyny, his sympathetic treatment of Frances suggests that his relationships with women in London … alerted him to complex models of female behaviour… How does a woman resist the gender ideologies of her day, define her identity as separate from her husband's, or locate a private space where she may discover and act on her own values?
>
> (Ostovich 1998: 155)

Her new thinking of Jonsonian misogyny has also been presented in relation to *The New Inn* (Ostovich 1997), opening up further interpretative possibilities. From the feminist concern with gender and identity has risen, too, an innovative interest in questions of sexuality, which in the last decade has achieved a new prominence in literary studies. Such questions are not properly separable from consideration of gender, since so much of the language of sexual difference and identity invokes distinctions between desires. Real men, it is assumed, desire women; a man who loves a man cannot really be a man. Desire was notably at issue in the culture of Jonson's England, if in ways that do not necessarily map onto contemporary models of sexual identity. Yet Jonson's work might seem an unpromising source for this kind of investigation. In fact, as Mary Beth Rose has argued of *Epicene*, it is notable for its neglect of romantic love, for its lack of concern with the representation of heterosexual desire:

> No matter how vicious the satire, sketchy the portrait, or deflected the treatment, city comedy frequently relies on the romantic comic convention of desired marriage to conclude the action within festive

traditions and retain a comic tone. Jonson, however, does not merely deflect or de-emphasise marriage in *Epicene*; he calls attention to this romantic convention by inverting it. *Epicene* ostentatiously depicts not the construction but the undoing of a marriage, ending not in a promise of consummation, but in a declaration of impotence.

(Rose 1988: 58)

Julie Sanders, Kate Chedgzoy and Susan Wiseman have also noted this absence, and suggested that Jonson's dramatic world is one that, if still possessing its fair share of marriages, lacks a sense of a *normative* heterosexuality, a default configuration for desire as properly directed *across* gender boundaries it also sustains (Sanders, Chedgzoy and Wiseman 1998: 19). While Rose goes on to suggest that *Epicene* holds Dauphine up for admiration as the character who most clearly escapes the pull of desire of any kind, she also acknowledges that the play's blankness regarding heterosexual love accompanies a tolerance – if no more than that – of the possibility of homoerotic desire. Mario di Gangi has made this possibility the focus of important work, in which he sets out to explore 'how homoeroticism operates within orderly and disorderly master-servant relationships' in early modern drama (di Gangi 1995: 181). In doing so he emphasises the lack of a single category of the transgressive homosexual, under which all homoerotic acts or events are marked as socially, ethically unacceptable; he is keen to ascertain why it is that some are identifiable as 'sodomitical' or transgressive, and some are not. Contrasting the servant-master relationships between Mosca and Volpone in *Volpone* and Epicene and Dauphine in *Epicene*, he argues:

Volpone suggests that when transgressive of marriage, inheritance, and hierarchical authority, a partnership between master and servant can be powerful and profitable, even attractive, but is liable to be unstable and self-destructive. Authorized by his wanton master to violate social propriety, Mosca eventually overturns the master-servant hierarchy itself. On the other hand, Dauphine's maintenance of a well-born boy, because it is a temporary, socially and erotically orderly relationship, gives him intellectual mastery without the risks of personal intimacy and affection that undo Volpone. In *Volpone*, an erotically disorderly master-servant relation is integral to the social disorder threatened by class mobility and the non-reproductive (or monstrously reproductive) household. The erotically orderly relation between master and servant in

Epicene, on the other hand, bolsters the social order by re-establishing an heir's proper inheritance and by allowing him to humiliate disorderly men and women.

(di Gangi 1995: 192)

Same-sex desire, in other words, takes its place within other frameworks of legitimation and its opposite. Tracing its place in Jonsonian drama allows us, once again, to see what we have previously overlooked, or to look in new ways at elements which seemed to appear in only one possible guise. We could usefully contrast, for instance, the identification of 'inversion' in Partridge's account of *Epicene*, above, and the ways in which the terrain denoted by such a motif has been remodelled and reorganised in the recent criticism discussed here.

(k) DRAMATIC WORKS: GOVERNMENT AND COMMUNITY

While this may be one way of attending to the politics of Jonson's drama, another important strand has started not from such broad accounts of social structure and its challenges, but from the consideration of the explicit politics, the politics of court and parliament, of religion and of monarchy and commonwealth, which was another labile feature of early modern England. We have considered, above, Goldberg's account of Jonson's assimilation to James's government policies, an assimilation he traces in *Volpone* as much as in the more clearly topical masques; Marcus's account of festivity, too, explores Jonson's festive drama in its relationship to such policies.

It might perhaps be expected that Jonson's Roman plays could provide further evidence for locating the early modern political resonances of his drama as a whole. Certainly, these have always seemed an obvious locus of political interest, if sometimes in very particular ways. B. N. de Luna, for example, has produced a detailed if somewhat strained attempt to find in *Catiline* 'a classical parallelograph on the Gunpowder Plot of 1605' (de Luna 1969: 360), in which the events of that year find allegorical expression in the events of Cicero's Rome. Jonson's play, so de Luna suggests, is essentially a *pièce à clef*, in which there is a one-to-one correspondence between Roman characters and English political figures. Few have endorsed de Luna's ingenious scheme, though that isn't to say that parallels between the Elizabethan and Jacobean courts and the Rome of *Poetaster*, *Sejanus* or *Catiline* have not been suggested. Thomas Cain has recently argued that *Poetaster* contains specific commentary on the fall of Essex, and is evidence to support the contention that Jonson himself was aligned with the Essexians at the time **[23, 55]**. The play's motifs of slander and false accusation can be shown to be a reflection of the concerns expressed by those close to Essex in the wake of his downfall:

> Far from being an apologist for the anti-Essex faction, *Poetaster* shows him satirizing the machinations which friends and sympathisers believed had trapped Essex, and mocking as at best an over-reaction the accusation of treason.
>
> (Cain 1998: 53)

While such an approach looks for the specific reference to local issues or events, other avenues are opened up by exploring the relationship between Jonson's work and the political ideals developed in his classical sources. In a pair of related essays, the historian Blair Worden has sought to show how Jonson's Roman tragedies reveal an engagement with early modern political concerns precisely through their deployment of the work of Roman historians. As we have noted above **[57]**, the translation of the writings of Tacitus and others was understood by contemporaries to be a political activity, and *Sejanus* itself dramatises the dangers into which the historian might drift. Worden argues that Jonson's location of subject matter in Tacitus suggests a clear orientation towards the political issues of his time:

> In selecting the reign of Tiberius, and particularly the career of Sejanus, for his play, Jonson seized on the section of Tacitus's writings that made the deepest impression on readers of the late Renaissance. Jonson's generation became ever more troubled by the growing ostentation and duplicity of courts, and by the mounting influence and vaulting ambition of upstart favourites at the expense of ancient noblemen and ancient virtue: themes which are at the centre of *Sejanus his Fall*.
>
> (Worden 1994: 77)

Worden suggests, too, that the play contains specific allusions to the Essex affair, but that it is the Germanicans, not Sejanus, who can be identified with Elizabeth's fallen favourite. In his departures from his Tacitean source, Jonson makes his Rome more like the early modern English court in its workings not in order to allegorise recent events but to present a more general critique of the court through the rhetorical resources provided by classical history:

In *Sejanus his Fall*, tyranny prevails because the ruling class has allowed itself to be corrupted. The English ruling class, thinks Jonson, has likewise betrayed its responsibilities. He is dismayed by the decay of antique and austere noble values.

(Worden 1994: 86–7)

In a more recent essay on Jonson's use of Roman sources in *Catiline*, Worden again aligns Jonson with a critical reflection on questions of state which, if pertinent in Jacobean England, are not *only* applicable to its situation:

Whereas the earlier play ends with the overthrow of Sejanus, the later one concludes with the triumph of Cicero, who has gradually replaced Catiline as the principal figure of a narrative which centres on the conflict between the two men. The conflict belongs to a larger movement of events that extends our attention beyond the fate of individuals to that of the society for whose destiny the central characters contend. Jonson guides us towards that perspective by intimating that the conspirators, though they seek to destroy Rome, are representative of its failings ... Catiline's conspiracy is a symptom of a process of decay which his defeat cannot halt. Though Catiline is overthrown, Caesar, the eventual destroyer of the republic, survives.

(Worden 1999: 157)

The real political complexity is to be found in Jonson's portrayal of Cicero. Here, he pits the less than flattering account provided by his principal source, Sallust, against the versions of events to be found in the historical Cicero's own speeches. What Jonson produces, according to Worden, is a carefully nuanced account of how virtue might triumph in the fallen world of corrupt courts or states, an example which serves to illustrate a general debate taking place in the political cultures of early modern Europe, but also one with specific reference to the Stuart circumstances in which Jonson was writing. In other words, it is precisely Jonson's engagement with the issues arising from his contemporaries' appropriation of classical history that ensured that his Roman plays would be relevant to the politics of Jacobean England, while simultaneously preventing them from slipping into the status of a 'parallelograph'. In the end, their political reach was both widely *and* precisely focused: they served to connect the troubling events of Tudor and Stuart rule to the explanatory vocabulary and political possibilities of a classical historiography which praised not monarchy, but republicanism.

The Jonson who emerges from Worden's essays is a figure working, through his assumption of the position of historian, to establish critical distance between himself and the court in which he operates; that distance, in this account, is measured in his willingness to deploy a language that emphasises republican virtue and the tyrannies of monarchical government. This is clearly not the Jonsonian corpus of Goldberg's account, but it nonetheless forms part of a surprisingly irresoluble debate around the political affiliations of the first Stuart laureate. More than the Roman plays, though, it has been the later works which have been the focus of most recent dispute. While critics have often been willing to accept the model of a loyal poet, broadly in agreement with the king's domestic and foreign policy ambitions, as an accurate account of Jonson's relationship to James, the late flowering of his dramatic talent at the turn of the 1630s has in recent years been thought to indicate an alienation from the Stuart government of King Charles I. Anne Barton has suggested that his work from this time exhibits a 'nostalgia' for the era – and by implication, the government – of Queen Elizabeth. Identifying *A Tale of a Tub* as clearly a late work, she sees the deployment of a deliberately archaic style of comedy and dramatic language as a contribution to this 'harking back' to a golden age against which the present can only be compared to its disadvantage:

> Jonson in 1633 seems to have been looking back to the mid-sixteenth century, near the time of his own birth, when Elizabeth really was a maiden queen, the Armada had still to be fought, and the works of Sidney, Spenser, Shakespeare and Donne were all waiting in the wings. Nostalgia, by definition, is always concerned with times and places that are lost. The 'Wise men of Finsbury' in the play tend to be fascinated by their parents' or godfathers' time, or by their youth in the reign of King Edward or Henry VIII. For Jonson, however, it is the present of the comedy, the re-created Elizabethan world in which he has placed these characters, that exerts the emotional pull. The nostalgia of the dramatis personae in *A Tale of A Tub* is enfolded by that of the poet who invented them, a man slowly coming to believe that he had once lived in a Golden Age without recognizing it at the time.
>
> (Barton 1984: 336–7)

In this reading *The Sad Shepherd*, too, takes its place in the framework of nostalgia, as 'Robin Hood's memory of a bygone time' of freedom, play and plenty 'presents an idealized picture of the pleasures of Elizabeth's reign' (Barton 1984: 349). Yet Barton's idea of Jonsonian nostalgia, to some extent bolstered by David Norbrook's similar suggestions regarding the same plays in his *Poetry and Politics in the English Renaissance* (Norbrook 1984: 246–7), and by Leah Marcus's arguments that these texts offer critical reflections on court attitudes to rural festivity (Marcus 1986: 133–9), has been challenged by Martin Butler. Butler argues that Jonson's last three completed plays in fact demonstrate a continuing congruence between his monarchical ideal of government and those of the Caroline court:

> For all that these three plays are a kind of Jonsonian experiment, in which Jonson explores new forms, conventions and motifs, the ideological assumptions which the plays serve and underwrite have not undergone substantial revision, ... Jonson was still concerned to construct fables which reaffirmed rather than called into question the social and political hegemony of the court.
>
> (Butler 1992a: 185)

The New Inn, for example, with its dramatisation of an aristocratic revival and Prudence's wise and benevolent monarchical rule, seems to be envisaging a rapprochement between the King and those among his aristocratic subjects who had been affronted by the supremacy of Buckingham, only recently ended by the favourite's assassination. In the critical frame of *The Magnetic Lady*, 'Jonson carefully establishes that the literary misinterpretation against which he struggles is the same voice of licentiously free censure that dogs his royal master' (Butler 1992a: 176–7), so reinforcing the identification of poet and king of which he had already often spoken. Moreover, the nostalgia for a mid-Tudor golden age that marks *A Tale of A Tub* is itself consonant with the royal policy of opposing a social polarisation disruptive of established rural life and preserving traditional festivity. In this period, Butler argues, such polarisation created 'village notables' who were often of puritan inclinations, and it was these who not only sought to suppress country sports, but also presented some of the most fervent opposition to the ecclesiastical policies of Charles's government. This, then, is a nostalgia of a distinctively Caroline kind. As Butler concludes:

> The plays educate as well as legitimate: they promote images of how responsible authority should act and of what the good society should be. But in the context of the loss of consensus which was the political legacy of the 1620s, [Jonson's criticism of royal policy] was circumscribed by the political needs of an increasingly embattled court, and had to be contained within actions which

were serviceable to the ideological outlook of Whitehall. Ultimately the plays had to work towards the dispelling of reservations about Caroline government, and to operate within an attitude that remained at root deferential and respectful towards royal power.

(Butler 1992a: 185)

But Butler's own conclusions have recently been subject to challenge. Julie Sanders, like Worden, has explored Jonson's debt to the republican language and ideas of his classical sources, and has also argued that this debt extends beyond the Roman plays. Whereas her reading of *Catiline* suggests that Jonson's deployment of republicanism is not a simple assumption of its language and principles, her analysis of both the major comedies and the late plays maintains that it is an unacknowledged component of these apparently non-Roman works. *Volpone*, for example, witnesses an engagement with the republicanism of Venice which goes beyond the attack on such political structures found in the play by Goldberg **[156]** (Sanders 1998a: 38–9). Similarly, *The Alchemist* dramatises the fall of a 'pseudo-republic' in the criminals' joint-stock venture **[79]**, but equally insists on re-establishing the republican community in its appeal to the approbation of the audience in the playhouse (88). In the later plays, where the strict outlines of a republican polity are less clearly visible, Jonson nonetheless pursues the evocation of 'alternative communities', forms of sociality which are at odds with the court culture of Stuart England. The Light Heart Inn, for example, is a space apart, in which a critical distance from the priorities of the Caroline court can be established – its evocation of the community of a Parliament, in particular, might not allow its easy identification with the 'personal rule' favoured by Charles **[95]**. Sanders concludes, boldly, that 'Ben Jonson was a republican', though this is not an assertion that goes unqualified:

in the sense that he registered the potential and difference of all theatrical and literary communities and used his skill as an author to dramatize and mobilize them.

(Sanders 1998a: 187)

Jonson's republicanism, then, encompasses a focus on the lineaments of existing communities, the possibilities for change, and the ways in which drama might mediate between them. It is a way of reasserting that his drama is irreducibly political, because – in many different ways – it is irreducibly social. If he is the King's poet, such readings suggest, he is necessarily the poet of community too.

(1) POETRY: DISCRIMINATION IN HISTORY

Critical accounts of Jonson's non-dramatic poetry have often taken the structure of the *Epigrams* as a convenient point of entry into the broader body of this work. The nominative strategy there pursued has been the occasion for commentary seeking to explicate the peculiar features of a poetry that abstains, for the most part, from the praise of God or a beloved, refusing elaborate allegory or pithy conceits. Jonson's distinctiveness seems to lie not simply in his style but also in the particular function his poetry sets for itself – for that reason, attention to matters such as the 'plain style' (Trimpi 1962) **[132]** has required the accompaniment of a criticism attendant to questions of purpose.

We can look again to Edward Partridge's work for an exemplary instance of such a criticism. In an article devoted to the *Epigrams* he articulates what he sees as Jonson's dedication to setting forth the characteristics of 'a new aristocracy, one of worth, not merely blood', making the collection 'a book of moral heraldry' (Partridge 1973: 155). Crucial to this strategy is the Jonsonian habit of naming his heroes, gathering under their proper names the qualities which can be attributed to them, and putting at the centre of his poetic project the chronicler's concern with the facts and deeds of an age:

> He was moved more by what actually happened than by what one could imagine happening. Fancy is finally less moving to him than fact. More important than the talismanic significance of Pembroke's name is its designative function: it points to a man who actually lives, who does certain verifiable things, who has a particular character and historically accountable relationships. Jonson, one must see, has an historian's sense of the holiness of fact. He put his faith, as his great heroes, Camden and Savile and Selden, did, in 'things' – in what men actually do or have done, how men really live or have lived. It is not what the mind fancies that fascinates him but what the mind faces – that external world where the mind discovers itself in discovering the things it must work with.
>
> (Partridge 1973: 194)

For Partridge, then, Jonson is crucially implicated in producing an evaluative account of history – helping to secure places in the pantheon for the great figures of his age, those whose personal qualities are sufficient to qualify them for a place. Simultaneously, those who remain nameless in the satirical epigrams attacking their vice or folly are denied admittance to the roll of honour, and thereby punished for their manifold failings.

Assessing this account of the *Epigrams*, Don Wayne – whose Marxist revision of another monument of Jonson criticism, L. C. Knights's *Drama and Society in the Age of Jonson* (1937), has been described above **[164]** – was struck by Partridge's willingness or desire 'to accept the "facts" at face value' (Wayne 1979: 82). Rather than dispute the account, for example, of Pembroke's nobility that Partridge seems to take on trust from Jonson's encomiastic strategy, Wayne seeks to examine and contextualise the very activity of noting and describing historical 'fact' that Partridge's article attributes to the poet. What he finds significant is the Jonsonian assumption – apparently unquestioned by Partridge – that the praise of virtue consists of an enumeration of the differing quantities of particular, discrete qualities that can be gathered together under particular proper names (Wayne 1979: 95). And this particular configuration of the praise of virtue as observation and enumeration – as, that is to say, largely a matter of noting quantifiable 'facts' – he relates not primarily to the development of the knowledge-producing methods of the natural sciences in the work of Jonson's contemporary Francis Bacon, but centrally – in Marxist style – to the development during Jonson's age of capitalist social relations. Such relations configured human capacities and lifetimes as objects or commodities, quantifiable according to the universal numerical standard of monetary value. Jonson's enumerative poetry is therefore not *wrong*, simply, to praise in this way – if not true for all time it is at least true to the historical features of its society, and the critic's role is to point up this complicity:

His literary output shows a deeper perception of the developing structure of relations in seventeenth century England, a perception (if not an understanding) of the general phenomenon ... of the objectification of human relations in the exchange of commodities, and of the tendency of the commodity relation to become a universal structuring principle of society not only in the strictly material forms of exchange but in the symbolic forms as well.

(Wayne 1979: 97)

Wayne goes on to argue that such relations intrude into Jonson's sense of his own position as praiser, too. Jonson's epigrams display not the objectivity and detachment of a quasi-scientific stance, but instead reveal his participation in the competitive market for social prestige. They offer, in Wayne's account, a doubled perspective: on the one hand, Jonson stands as the unmoved enumerator of praiseworthy qualities, endowed with the ability to associate proper names with particular virtues; on the other, he secures the authority of his praise by associating himself with these *already* great names:

> The irony of his relationship to the great (if not the good) who are celebrated in the *Epigrammes* is that the authority of the name 'Ben Jonson' as a properly credentialed witness of his time depended on those names which appear to designate the 'facts' of virtue and nobility in these poems.
>
> (Wayne 1979: 100)

The kind of analysis pursued here in relation to *Epigrams* is taken up again by Wayne in his book-length study of Jonson's most celebrated poem, 'To Penshurst'. He repeats, for example, the argument he advances against Partridge's attitude to Jonsonian claims in suggesting that 'most of the criticism devoted to "To Penshurst" [is] little more than a rephrasing of the poem's central themes, and an acceptance at face value of the direct statement and orderly composition that characterize the poem on the surface'. Furthermore, he finds in the poem the same path he noted in his earlier study, along which the work travels in order to 'expose the assumptions on which its method is based' (Wayne 1984: 33, 37). Thus, he explores the ways in which the poem's language of nature, home and family serves to legitimate the Sidneys in a number of different registers at once:

> We are made witness to a magical Nature which bestows itself freely upon an Edenic 'lord' and 'lady', and a real Nature that the poem legitimates as the property of an actual ruling family.
>
> (Wayne 1984: 127)

Bringing such registers together is a way of reconciling the contradictions experienced, Wayne suggests, by the aristocracy in an age when their power and the means by which it was justified are under threat from the growth of a new, capitalist way of organising economic activity and its attendant cultural consequences. The fly in the ointment, once again, is what the poem reveals about the authority of its own claims and judgements: Jonson's intrusion into the poem focuses attention on the social basis of his praise of the Sidneys. His assertion of his own freedom to judge takes place in terms which threaten to contradict those in which the title of the Sidney family has been legitimised.

A complex series of readings, Wayne's was not the first attempt at a Marxist criticism of Jonson's poetry. His study of 'To Penshurst' had been memorably preceded by the distinctive Marxist analysis of Raymond Williams, whose own lifelong critical project aimed not only to delineate the intricate ways in which the involvement of culture in the social processes of capitalism could be understood, but also to recast the meaning of the term 'culture' in such a way as to revalue the popular culture of the past and prefigure the culture of a democratic, socialist future. In his book *The Country and the City*, Williams argued that 'To Penshurst' was as notable for what it concealed as what it revealed. Taking issue with a critical propensity to take Jonson's evocation of a 'natural order' at face value, Williams argues that this little Eden in which the fish, flesh and fowl of the estate leap unbidden onto the Sidneys' table is only made possible by the poem's systematic exclusion of the fact of labour, the 'curse' to which humanity – in the biblical narrative – was subjected following its expulsion from paradise:

> What is really happening, in Jonson's ... celebrations of a rural order, is an extraction of just this curse, by the power of art: a magical recreation of what can be seen as a natural bounty and then a willing charity: both serving to ratify and bless the country landowner, or, by a characteristic reification, his house. Yet this magical extraction of the curse of labour is in fact achieved by a simple extraction of the existence of labourers. The actual men and women who rear the animals and drive them to the house and kill them and prepare them for meat; who trap the pheasants and partridges and catch the fish; who plant and manure and prune and harvest the fruit trees: these are not present; their work is all done for them by a natural order. When they do at last appear, it is merely as the 'rout of rural folk', ... and what we are then shown is the charity and lack of condescension with which they are given what, now and somehow, not they but the natural order has given for food, into the lord's hands. It is this condition, this set of relationships, that is finally ratified by the consummation of the feast.
>
> (Williams 1973: 32)

What Williams perceives is a mystification that is constitutive of Jonson's vision of Penshurst, one which serves to exclude the labour of the estate's workers not only from the poem but, in a longer view, from the narratives of English history and the English countryside, as if the whole of both were not only the property but also the doing of a small echelon of virtuous noblemen. The epochal emphasis of Marxist criticism has been complemented by an attention to the part played by Jonson's non-dramatic verse in the more explicit and localised political dramas of his age. David Norbrook's analysis in his *Poetry and Politics in the English Renaissance* positioned Jonson's writing carefully, and in detailed fashion, in the high politics of the age, the factions and struggles which marked the first forty years of Stuart rule. Despite their associations with the Sidney family, famed for their own association with a radical Protestantism, the poems of *The Forest* are not marked as oppositional to the pacific Stuart court in Norbrook's account:

Throughout 'The Forest' the emphasis is on peaceful activities; Sidney and Wroth devote their energies to cultivating the land, whose fertility Jonson constantly emphasises. Imagery of natural growth runs through the volume. The one reference to Sir Philip Sidney alludes not to his restless Protestant internationalism but to a tree planted at his birth and now flourishing under the Stuart peace … The poems give the sense of a nation which, whatever its faults, is essentially harmonious and well-ordered and reflects credit on its governors …

The very title of 'The Forest' has courtly associations. Strictly speaking an area could be a forest whether or not it had any trees: the term defined an area which was outside, 'foris', the normal common law and subject directly to a special forest law. The initial purpose of a forest was to allow the monarch to hunt freely and without interruption: in the words of an Elizabethan treatise, the protection of wild beasts in forests 'is for the delight and pleasure of the King onely, and his nobles, and for no other end nor purpose'.

(Norbrook 1984: 184–5, 190)

Though Norbrook suggests a close alignment of Jonson's and King James's aims and principles, his account of Jonson's later years suggests some alienation from the court of his son, Charles, though this is not argued from an analysis of the non-dramatic verse. For Annabel Patterson, another critic keen to locate Jonson's work in the political conflicts of his time, the later work gathered finally as *The Underwood* suggests a similar sense of estrangement from the centres of power. Read 'in the sequence Jonson provided,' she suggests, 'we can discover in it a lyric narrative, a socio-political autobiography' (Patterson 1984:

49). A volume which presupposed its emergence under conditions of literary censorship, it speaks obliquely and in a doubled voice, and in so doing produces 'a retrospective of Jonson's career, a retelling of his relations with the state, the stage, friends, patrons, politicians; and inserted between the occasional poems are intermittent assertions of autonomy' (Patterson 1984: 126). This retrospective is only available, though, to the reader who examines the arrangement of the collection – for it is as much in the poems' recontextualisation and juxtaposition in this form, as in what they openly declare, that the meaning of the sequence appears:

> What the *Underwood* poems require of their readers is a simult-aneous recognition of when and for whom they were first written; of how those original occasions serve as one of the conditions of their placement in the new historical structure of the volume, a structure inevitably affected by the poet's own processes of after-thought; of what new relationships and interactions are formed between them by this process of collection, which is also recollection; and of how these new relationships are both the effect of textual juxtapositions – key terms which tie them together in ways that could not have been foreseen when they were first written – and extratextual reverberations – conditions of meaning that have accrued to them since they were first written because of what history has subsequently wrought upon their subjects.
>
> (Patterson 1984: 127)

The sense of a Jonson alienated or marginalised from the centres of power which Patterson gleans from the spaces between the poems in *The Underwood*, a reading predicated on her assumptions about the place of censorship in the literary production of the early Stuart period **[158]**, is not one upheld by Martin Butler's synoptic account of the poet's relations with the courts of James and his son. Starting from Jonson's own characterisation of himself in the Folio dedication to *Cynthia's Revels* as the Jacobean court's 'servant, but not slave', Butler argues that his poetry 'sought to manage and shape the heterogeneous forms of Jacobean power' (Butler 1996: 69). Thus the social relations of virtue implied in *Epigrams* offer 'a code of obligation which cuts against the unregulated pursuit of courtly reward, and implies an ideal economy in which aristocrats ought to act as responsible servants to the Crown's political needs' (Butler 1996: 79). 'To Penshurst', in Butler's account, is a site for the elaboration of this 'ideal economy'. Whereas the estate of

Jonson's sometime patron Cecil, for example, had been an example of the kind of extravagant and ostentatious building denigrated in the poem, Penshurst offers a contrast:

> The project of 'To Penshurst' is to find values in the Sidney life-style which offer a more productive model than this for the relation-ship between aristocrats, the monarch and the realm. The Sidneys are presented as stewards of their domain, landlords whose ownership is justified by the life of exemplary discipline which they lead. They are neither self-aggrandising courtiers nor an oppositional 'country' party, but channels of influence between centre and periphery, who instil into their locality attitudes of obligation which render it tractable to Stuart power ... Penshurst is neither a status-free Utopia nor an oppositional counter-community set against the court, but a perfect court in the country, a reproduction in little of what the good state ought to be ... The Sidneys seem less owners than deputies, servants to the royal master who arrives at the poem's culmination, their good stewardship channelling his authority outwards to the realm at large.
>
> (Butler 1996: 82–3)

Though the poetry of Jonson's middle years might be easily assimilated to this mildly reformatory ideal, the later years of his career are acknowledged by Butler as presenting particular stresses for the loyal but not sycophantic poetic posture he assumed. His poems in praise of James's heir, for example, 'are remarkable for the difficulty they have in finding ways of making Charles's power sound persuasive. They insist on the King's piety and glory, and his status as an example to his people, but they are equally preoccupied with the inner political divisions which persist, in spite of the outward peace' (Butler 1996: 89). These stresses are not the signs of Jonson's own alienation and distance from Stuart ideals, however, but a mark instead of the troubles afflicting the Stuart reality. If Butler is required to concede that Jonson's last years were marked by nostalgia of any kind, as Barton and others have argued [184], he posits a slightly wistful hankering for the stability of James's reign, and not the more clearly 'oppositional' invocations of the cult of Elizabeth.

For other critics, it has been neither epochal nor local political antagonisms that have marked the engagement of Jonson's non-dramatic verse with its own age. Sara van den Berg has explored the forms of 'occasionality' taken by Jonson's poetry, the ways in which it articulates the events of which it writes and its own status as an utterance or event 'occasioned by a courtier's rudeness, a friend's achievement, a lady's rejection, a publication, a fire, an initiation' (van den Berg 1987: 35). Martin Elsky's exploration of the 'off-centred voice' that he argues is typical of the poems, one preoccupied with trying to advance the cause of virtue in hostile conditions, maps this dislocation onto Jonson's anxiety over the absence of linguistic and ethical consensus (Elsky 1989: 81–109). In *Jonsonian Discriminations* Michael McCanles has also sought to anchor the poetry in a characteristic concern with custom and conduct, seeing it as centrally occupied with the functioning in Jacobean culture of the signs of 'true nobility'. Jonson's poetry performs the job of discriminating the virtuous from their opposites, naming and identifying them, while at the same time recognising that the signs of virtuous nobility – wealth, status, titles, the praise of contemporaries – were not always bestowed where they should be, that they did not always indicate the possession of the qualities they ought to denote. Consequently, Jonson's poetry also takes upon itself the important function of distinguishing between the proper and the improper use of such signs. Furthermore, since such a recognition implicitly rejects the notion that those born with titles and status automatically or naturally possess 'true nobility', and accepts the possibility of its being taught and achieved, Jonson's poetry pursues the delicate didactic task of inculcating virtue in those whose status suggests that they ought already to possess it. Like Wayne, if from very different perspectives, McCanles and Elsky describe a poetry which is not only engaged in distinguishing virtue from vice but also explores or reveals the justifications on which such a claim to be capable of discrimination might base itself.

Such accounts find an intriguing counterpoint in Stanley Fish's much read essay on the poems. Fish is a critic particularly concerned with the paradoxes to be traced through the formal properties of literary artefacts, an emphasis which in this case leads him to see Jonson's verse as both promising to represent its objects – to name, describe or outline them – and failing to deliver on that promise. In so doing, he sets himself against the kinds of critical description of Jonson's verse which see it thoroughly enmeshed in the business of describing or representing virtue, deploying a 'plain style' which unproblematically and transparently points out and depicts the virtuous components of the social world. Fish is not suggesting, though, that Jonson's work fails to make discrimination among its objects a primary goal: in fact, his essay explicitly resorts to presenting the poems of praise in the role of a doorman, admitting only a few and excluding – among others – us, the readers.

Underlying this imagery is a striking claim about Jonson's apparent 'plainness'. Noting the hesitancy which marks the opening of many of the poems, Fish argues that this 'habit of beginning awkwardly is not simply a mannerism but is intimately related to the project of his poetry, and indeed represents a questioning of that project, since the issue always seems to be whether or not the poem can do what it sets out to do' (Fish 1984: 28). Representation features in the poetry as a suspect endeavour; it interposes a gap between the object represented and the subject who can only gain access to that object through the medium of its representation. This gap is a space just waiting to be occupied by error, dangerously capable of introducing *mis*representation into the communication between inhabitants of the world. Representations might not be adequate to their objects, or they might not be properly understood; praise, in such a situation, might always be misdirected or misread. Instead, suggests Fish, the poetry posits and celebrates a form of immediate communication among the virtuous which is effectively a kind of recognition: virtue is recognised by the virtuous, the self finding itself in the other. The process is tautologous, producing the circulating reflection of a 'community of the same'. Yet while this may seem a cunning way of circumventing the possible perils of representation, it is also in danger of rendering the verse pointless. For a start, the poems of praise 'continually proclaim their inability to describe or "catch" their objects' (Fish 1984. 33); furthermore, they are actually superfluous to the process of recognition they claim to foster:

> They present the objects of praise to themselves; they say in effect, "Sir or Madam So and So, meet Sir or Madam So and So, whom, of course, you already know". Once this is said, the poem is to all intents and purposes over, although the result paradoxically is that it often has a great deal of difficulty getting started since it is, in effect, all dressed up with nowhere to go. Epigram 102 says as much in its first two lines: "I do but name thee Pembroke, and I find / It is an epigram on all mankind".
>
> (Fish 1984: 34)

Consequently, Fish suggests, Jonson's virtuous community is one which is not at all susceptible to description. The ethical qualities which mobilise it remain tantalisingly out of bounds to representation, traceable only in the quasi-mystical reciprocal interactions between its members with which the poems instead engage:

This reciprocity, at once endlessly self-replenishing and defiantly excluding, is the essence not only of the transaction between Jonson's poetry and the community of its readers, but of the friendship that binds that community together and provides its true – that is, nonspecifiable – ties. Not surprisingly, although friendship is the constant subject of this poetry, it is a subject that is more invoked than described. Like Jonson's other master values, it is present largely as what cannot be presented or re-presented; it is at once known in advance and what cannot (in the usual discursive sense) be known. Although the question of record in a Jonson poem will often be 'What is friendship?', the answer can only be 'If you have to ask, you couldn't possibly know'.

(Fish 1984: 48)

Thus this community of the same remains too resolutely exclusive. Examining the closing couplet of *Underwood* 14, 'An Epistle to Master John Selden', Fish comes to rest on its final word, 'farewell':

Jonson reaches out (as he does in so many poems) to those with whom he is already sealed, and as he says to them a superfluous 'farewell' – superfluous because they fare well simply by being what they are – he says to the rest of us a farewell that has the unmistakable sound of a closing door.

(Fish 1984: 55)

At the essay's end, the question of motive is raised: 'Why would anyone write a poetry that does not persuade or teach or assert or present or represent or define or describe or incite?' And Fish looks for an answer to the patronage relationships within which Jonson wrote, the subordinate, dependent position in which his social standing placed him throughout his career, suggesting that this kind of writing represents 'a classic instance of a familiar psychological strategy':

The outsider who must rely on others for favour and recognition imagines himself as the proprietor and arbiter of an internal kingdom whose laws he promulgates and whose entrance he zealously guards, admitting only those he would 'call mine', to an elect fellowship.

(Fish 1984: 57)

Even a poetry that avoids representation, then, speaks ultimately of the cultural position from which it was written. For all his differences of emphasis or in particular readings, the poet we are left with by Fish is not too dissimilar to the figure imagined by other recent critics of the non-dramatic writings. Jonson's poetry of ethical discrimination is finally revelatory of the social structures of its historical moment.

(m) MYSTERIES AND OCCASIONS: MASQUES

Jonson's masques, too, have been much studied in recent years for their historical resonance. Dismissed for a long time as absurd and frivolous entertainments, their inclusion in the monumental twentieth century edition of Jonson's works produced by Herford and the Simpsons made them properly available for widespread academic study for the first time. At around the same time, the efforts of a number of pioneering scholars made it abundantly clear that there was more here to engage the critic's attention than had often been thought. W. Greg produced an edition of *The Gypsies Metamorphosed* which laid bare the complexities of tone, form and content of this long, later masque (Greg 1952), while Allan Gilbert's work on *The Symbolic Persons in the Masques of Ben Jonson* (1948) showed the richness and intricacy of Jonson's allegorical and emblematic language. Meanwhile, the essays of D. J. Gordon helped to situate Jonson's endeavours in a broader practice of ritual and image-making that encompassed art and architecture as well as poetry, and revealed too the wider European roots of these endeavours (Gordon 1975). These foundations enabled later critics to make broader interpretative claims regarding the masques, and thus to initiate the critical conversation around their significance which continues today.

Crucial to this conversation has been the work of Stephen Orgel. Both in his *The Jonsonian Masque* (1965) and *The Illusion of Power* (1975), as well as in his co-edited work on Inigo Jones's contributions to the genre (Orgel and Strong 1973), Orgel exemplified particularly influential positions regarding the nature of the genre and its relationship to the royal authority that occasioned it. For a start, his first book suggested that Jonson's conception of the masque's 'poetic' essence [117] should guide critical assessment of his efforts here, seeing in the masques a (sometimes) successful transformation of the external demands on the poet made by king and court into the internal structural dynamic of his work: 'What he achieved at his best was a synthesis of the world he wrote for and the world he created' (Orgel 1965: 109). Jonson's work strives to bring together contingent circumstances and unchanging truths, in such a way as 'to offer a moment in which a vision of an ideal becomes a poetic and dramatic experience – becomes, in other words, a reality' (Orgel 1965: 185). There is, then, a fundamentally *unifying* imperative at the root of Jonson's practice of the masque, a unification which takes place on literary or poetic terrain.

While John Meagher's book on *Method and Meaning in Jonson's Masques* (1966) paid more attention to the other components of the form – music, dance, light – it did so in order similarly to bring them together on the ground of symbolic meaning, and to see such symbolism as tending towards the figuration on earth of a transcendent ideal of beauty and virtue. For Jonson the masque-writer 'the task of perfection is arduous and urgent; for him the stones and the stars, even the loves and sports and frivolities of the court, join in pointing the way to the holy road of virtue and sing of the splendour of the palaces to which it leads' (Meagher 1966: 186). Yet Orgel's subsequent book on Jonson's contribution to the masque signals an important change of emphasis, away from tracing the symbolic articulation of an abstract ideal and towards a concern with the utility of such an ideal for the self-presentation of Renaissance monarchy. He describes the bifocal nature of a performance at court by professional players during the reigns of Elizabeth and her successors:

Now there were, properly speaking, two audiences and two spectacles. The primary audience was the monarch ... At these performances what the rest of the spectators watched was not a play but the queen at a play.

(Orgel 1975)

His own critical position is now closer to that of those spectators, examining ways in which the masque centred on the monarch and in so doing served not to make the ideal real, but to idealize and legitimate a political actuality. He focuses on the use of perspective staging at court masques after 1605, suggesting the political significance of such a way of presenting dramatic entertainments:

In a theatre employing perspective, there is only one focal point, one perfect place in the hall from which the illusion achieves its fullest effect. At court performances this is where the King sat, and the audience around him at once became a living emblem of the structure of the court.

(Orgel 1975: 10–11)

Furthermore, the actual content of the masques works in the same direction. The presentation of the House of Fame in the *Masque of Queens*, for example, valorises not an ideal virtue but the Jacobean court and its policies:

> The whole vision presents the Jacobean court with its own best image. Heroism is the royal consort; but the highest virtue is that of the pacific king, not a warrior, but a classical scholar and a poet.
>
> (Orgel 1975: 65)

In this way Orgel can argue that 'dramas at court ... were expressions of the age's most profound assumptions about the monarchy' (8) and that such assumptions worked largely to affirm royal power, its virtue and legitimacy. This power was performed in the content, form and staging of the masque, actualised as much as represented.

Jonathan Goldberg, whose description of Jonson's relation to the Stuart monarchy is examined above [155], draws for his own account of James's literary absolutism in the masques on Orgel's work. While his argument allows that the Jonsonian masque is not quite so univocally celebratory of Stuart rule, that indeed it even stages quite scurrilously subversive moments of resistance to the whole pattern of Stuart government, he nonetheless ties any contradictions or uncertainties to the multiple trajectories of the king's own practice and ideal of monarchy, making the masque still a mirror held up to him (Goldberg 1983: 57). For other critics, though, an examination of the circumstances which occasioned a masque and in which it was staged has suggested a rather different sense of the genre's function. David Lindley, for example, has drawn attention to the problematic circumstances surrounding three of Jonson's court masques (Lindley 1986). The first was *Hymenaei*, performed in celebration of the marriage of Frances Howard to the Earl of Essex in 1606; the others were commissioned for the same woman's marriage to Robert Carr some seven years later, after the acrimonious, embarrassing and ultimately murderous divorce between Howard and Essex had been finalised [30]. Lindley notes that on the publication of *Hymenaei* in the 1616 *Works*, when Howard had herself been disgraced for her part in Overbury's murder, 'all mention of its specific occasion was deleted', and that the edition also suppresses mention of the occasion of the two masques of 1613, *A Challenge at Tilt* and *The Irish Masque at Court*. Lindley traces their difficult interrelation, embarrassing for the Jonson of 1616 both severally and as moments linked by their joint membership of his poetic canon. His analysis of the awkwardness evident in the attempt to sever the masques from their occasions and otherwise to suppress the possibility of the later two embarrassingly recalling the first leads him to significant conclusions regarding the political functioning of panegyric, a poetry of praise:

> It is too simple to concur with the idealizing ambition of the masques, and mistaken to lift them out of their particular social and political context, since to do so is to falsify their contemporary aim and effect ... But, on the other hand, it would be equally misguided to dismiss Jonson's intellectual effort and didactic aspiration as superficial flattery and time-serving. For it is precisely in registering the complexity of the struggle within the poet's work to sustain the transmutation of the circumstances of the Jacobean court and its politics into self-sufficient myth that the true fascination of the genre lies.
>
> (Lindley 1986: 358–9)

Lindley's sense of the masque's uneasy relation to its own occasion has been complemented by Martin Butler's detailed readings of a number of masques. Butler acknowledges the force of both Orgel's and Goldberg's account of the masques' political functioning, while simultaneously recognising, with Lindley, the possibility of events, accidents or forces which might prevent them operating smoothly as the discursive instantiation of royal power. Drawing on a critique developed by the Marxist critic Lawrence Venuti (1989), he suggests that, in Orgel's account,

> each masque tends to testify identically to the authority of the royal gaze, representing the court as serenely reaffirming its unchanging sense of identity and purpose. In such a paradigm, the theatres of power which the masques presented are compellingly evoked, but their encompassing aesthetic structures seem strangely homogenized.
>
> (Butler 1998: 23–4)

Goldberg's image of royal doubleness, his model of the masque as consonant with James's own contradictory strategies of royal self-presentation, is seen in a similar way:

> Goldberg's stunning analysis of the masques as at one and the same time outrageously subversive and outrageously self-abasing interprets them as acts of rebelliousness which are countenanced

in order that they may be seen to be contained... In this perspective, the masques are invariably going to function as testimonies to the prison-house of Jacobean culture, glittering occasions on which the courtly elites danced in festive celebration of their own disempowerment.

(Butler 1998: 25)

Butler instead proposes another paradigm for the analysis of the political work of the masque, its relation to the monarch and the court whose occasions it marked:

I wish to suggest that other kinds of negotiations may also have been hosted by the masques, scenarios which did not simply reproduce an ineluctable oscillation between resistance and authority, but which were more in the nature of symbolic transactions between those who were competing for position in and around the courtly arena. These negotiations can be understood as acts of accommodation or realignment, give and take between differently empowered participants in the political process, transactions that served to shift, manoeuvre and reshape the forms in which power circulated.

(Butler 1998: 26)

The negotiations of which Butler speaks are those between different factions at court, between differing powerful courtiers, and also between the different households of James, his Queen, and his heirs, Prince Henry and Prince Charles. The very structure of royal government, its lack of a standing bureaucracy or machinery of enforcement and consequent dependence on powerful elites, as well as the mechanisms of patronage through which positions were distributed, all served in Butler's account to make the masques spaces in which 'James's authority was having to be negotiated rather than simply affirmed':

His masques must have been more like lobbying, in which groups of aspiring courtiers conducted a symbolic conversation with the monarch, designed to persuade him of their worth or to convince the court as a whole of their own importance in larger schemes. From the performers' side, the masques would have appeared to be acts of persuasion, in which the occasion was enlisted to give prestige to factions struggling for influence, or to advertise agendas of their own. The King presided over the fictions, but a great deal depended on who was paying, and within the fictions he might find that his situation was redefined, or that images were imposed upon him which offered different views of his obligations.

(Butler 1998: 29, 28)

Jonson's role in this was to enable such 'festive transactions' to take place, to accommodate differing interests within the single space of court festivity and the formal and thematic limits of praise of the king, and much of Butler's work on the masques has aimed to trace Jonson's performance of this delicate task. Yet his essays are also interested in the changing nature of royal rule over the earlier decades of the seventeenth century, the challenges to royal power and its ways of working that might be seen to disrupt the workings of the masque as well. In his readings of *Oberon* and *Neptune's Triumph*, for example, he finds evidence that 'the customary rituals of containment and legitimation did not, in fact, get performed as anticipated', and that 'faultlines in the structures of power were unusually apparent' (Butler 1998: 29).

Butler's well-researched and meticulous readings of Jonson's masques, of what they reveal both about the political functions of royal festivity and its limits, have been particularly influential. Other critics, though, have sought to complicate the 'absolutist' models of Orgel and Goldberg in different terms. For Barbara Lewalski it is an understanding of the role played by the court of Queen Anne which is crucial to this move. She identifies James's consort, the force behind Jonson's earliest court commissions, as pursuing a political agenda which was opposed to that of her husband not simply on the substantive issues of the day but also in more general ideological terms. The Queen's requirement that she and her ladies dance in black make-up, the requirement underpinning the concept and execution of Jonson's *Masque of Blackness* **[119]**, is read by Lewalski as a gesture of supreme 'subversiveness':

> Representing herself and her ladies as black African beauties, the Queen associates them with alien cultural practices and primitive energies, with the feared and desired 'others' imagined by contemporary explorers, and perhaps with the Amazons – always portrayed as dark-skinned and often assumed to be located in Africa or America.
>
> (Lewalski 1993: 31–2)

Furthermore, this evocation of an exotic 'otherness' does not in the end reproduce the negative evaluation of blackness as defect that the masque's language seems to promise: the dark-skinned women are not actually affected by the king's whitening powers, and remain as black at the end of the masque as they were at its outset.

For Lewalski, then, Jonson's masques are caught up in the Queen's occupation of the role of 'royal opposition' to the governing ideologies of her husband, a role exemplified in the challenge to white, male power presented by the valorisation of its black, female 'other' in *The Masque of Blackness*. And while her claims have seemed a little over-ambitious to some, her interest in the way in which the masques participate in writing or rewriting the broader political discourses of race and gender has been widely shared in recent years. In particular, critics have been interested in tracing how the binary structure of the masque – its division between dominant masque and subordinated antimasque **[119]** – parallels the polarised conceptual, discursive and political oppositions along these two axes. Suzanne Gossett has looked in detail at the representation of women in Jonson's masques, noting the confusions which emerge from the performance space being shared both by boy actors playing female parts and female masquers themselves, as in *The Masque of Queens* (Gossett 1998). Marion Wynne-Davies has focused on the same masque, finding in the witches of its antimasque figures who 'belong to a weirdly mutated "other world" which is efflorescent with bodily force and energy, and cannot be entirely circumscribed by the formal structures set against it' (Wynne-Davies 1992: 85). In other words, they enact a form of disorder that threatens the ordered opposition of masque and antimasque. This is apparent, too, in the language in which the legendary queens represented by the female masquers are described. They are apportioned qualities traditionally ascribed to masculinity and strongly at odds with their silence on the floor of the masque itself; in this way, a singular concept of the feminine is actually undermined. Recent work by Clare McManus has also focused on the figures of the female masquers in *The Masque of Blackness*, tracing the ways in which their physical presence and their distinctively theatrical appearance both works with and against the dominant ideologies of gender that the masque might be expected to perpetuate. Women were customarily associated with the body, a physicality necessarily inferior to the masculinity against which they were defined. Yet this very physicality also becomes the space in which 'an assertion of female sexual and political autonomy' can be made, as the aristocratic women of the masque embrace 'the indecorum of bare and blackened limbs' (McManus 1998: 110).

If the Queen's resort to black make-up in *The Masque of Blackness* has been read primarily along the axis of gender by some feminist critics, others have looked particularly closely at the masques' deployment of the racial 'other'. Yumna Siddiqi has explored the intersection between *Blackness* and the broader discourse of blackness in early modern England. While the African body is imagined as 'uncontrollable and potentially overwhelming' and 'potentially disruptive', it is also something to be desired as meriting 'refinement' (Siddiqi 1992: 145–6). Thus, the masque shows a complicity with a developing colonial discourse: in containing and holding the dark-skinned bodies of the female masquers within the embrace of Britain, an exemplary kingdom, the masque also figures 'a territorial claim to their African bodies' (Siddiqi 1992: 150). Kim Hall has effected a subtle demonstration of the interlocking of racial and gendered differentiation, noting the extent to which the discourse of 'blackness' was an established mode of assessing women's worth: while 'fairness' was prized, a relative darkness of complexion was a signifier of – but also synonym for – lower value in an economy of female beauty (Hall 1995: 128–33). Yet she also associates the discourse of blackness as exemplified in Jonson's masques with another of their recurrent themes – the transformation of England into the embryonic imperial power of Great Britain, a transformation particularly associated with the Stuart unification of English and Scottish monarchies. Blackness is both the 'other' against which the new imperium defines itself, enabling it to figure the superiority of its own European 'whiteness', and also the threat that confronts this new 'Great Britain' in its formative years, as established discourses of 'Englishness' themselves cede place and other cultures are confronted by colonial pioneers. *The Masque of Blackness* can be analysed as the site where these different layers coincide (Hall 1995: 133–41).

The attention of critics such as Hall and Siddiqi to the masques' implication in the discourse of colonialism is complemented by James Smith, who has argued recently that Jonson's deployment of an antimasque of Irish visitors in his *Irish Masque at Court* 'suggests the extent to which Ireland served as an alternative arena into which Jacobean society could conveniently displace compromising realities' (Smith 1998: 297). The disorderly behaviour of Jonson's Irish visitors echoes English judgements on resistance to Jacobean colonial legislation in Ireland (302–4). Thus, Ireland joins Africa as a site of threatening 'otherness', a space in need of exactly the kind of royal mastery celebrated in the masques. If, for these recent critics, the masques still speak eloquently of royal power, they do so in such a way as to reveal the workings and limits of a politics of identity, a politics that develops along the interlocking axes of gender, race and nation.

Further reading

The readings outlined here have taken their bearings from a myriad of methodological sources, and readers who wished to familiarise themselves with the broad, basic outlines of those sources could do worse than consult the conspectus provided by Barry (1995). The full range of Marxist criticism is illustrated and introduced by Eagleton and Milne (1995), while Moi (1985) remains a brief, helpful exposition of the terrain of feminist literary theory. Veeser (1988) contains a multitude of formulations of and responses to the challenge of New Historicism, while Bristow (1997) elucidates the theoretical challenges presented by the consideration of sexuality. The body of Bakhtin's thought, including his theory of carnival, is expounded in Vice (1997), while Raymond Williams's distinctive thinking on 'culture' has been outlined by Higgins (1999). The critical work of Stanley Fish is excerpted and introduced in Fish (1999). In addition to the Casebooks on individual plays noted in Further Reading in Part II, collections and anthologies of essays on Jonson's work include Dutton (2000), Harp and Stewart (2000), Butler (1999), Cave, Shafer and Woolland (1999), Sanders, Chedgzoy and Wiseman (1998), Summers and Pebworth (1982), Blisset, Patrick and Van Fossen (1973) and Barish (1963). Evans (2000) provides a compendium of modern scholarship on the major plays, while Magaw (1998) offers an index to the thematic concerns of recent work.

CHRONOLOGY

1572   Ben Jonson (BJ) born in Westminster, posthumous son of a
        clergyman; early in his life his mother remarries Robert Brett,
        a bricklayer.
1580s   Educated at Westminster school, under the tutelage of William
        Camden.
1590s   Apprenticed to his stepfather; enlists as a soldier and serves
        with English army in the Low Countries.
1594   Marries Anne Lewis.
1597   Acting with 'Pembroke's men'; first extant play, *The Case Is
        Altered*, written for the company; jailed for his part in the
        writing of a now lost 'seditious' play, *The Isle of Dogs*.
1598   *Every Man In His Humour*; kills Gabriel Spencer, an actor, in a
        fight; found guilty of murder but escapes the death penalty;
        converted to Catholicism during this spell in jail.
1599   *Every Man Out of His Humour*; imprisoned for the third time,
        for debt.
1600   *Cynthia's Revels*.
1601   *Poetaster*.
1603   Death of Queen Elizabeth, accession of James VI & I; death of
        Jonson's eldest son, Benjamin; *Sejanus His Fall*.
1604   Contributes to King's coronation entertainments.
1605   *Eastward Ho!* (with Marston and Chapman) leads to fourth
        imprisonment, BJ released after intercession by his patrons;
        involved in the aftermath of the Gunpowder Plot; writes *The
        Masque of Blackness* with Inigo Jones for performance at court
        by the Queen and her ladies.
1606   *Hymenaei* written for court celebrations of marriage between
        Earl of Essex and Lady Frances Howard; *Volpone*.
1608   *The Masque of Beauty*.
1609   *The Masque of Queens*; *Epicene*.
1610   *The Alchemist*.
1611   *Oberon*; *Catiline*.
1612-   In France as tutor to son of Sir Walter Ralegh.
1613   *A Challenge at Tilt* and *The Irish Masque*, in celebration of
        marriage of Frances Howard to Robert Carr, Earl of Somerset.
1614   *Bartholomew Fair*.

1616   Receives royal pension, effectively making him laureate;
        publishes *Works* in folio; *The Golden Age Restored*; *The Devil Is
        an Ass*.
1618   Walks to Scotland, stays with Drummond of Hawthornden;
        Pleasure Reconciled to Virtue.
1619   Honorary degree from University of Oxford.
1621   Writes *The Gypsies Metamorphosed* for Buckingham, royal
        favourite, performed before the King three times.
1623   Catastrophic fire destroys BJ's library.
1624-   *Neptune's Triumph For the Return of Albion* written to mark return
        of Prince Charles from Spain, never performed due to
        diplomatic difficulties.
1625   Death of James; accession of Charles I.
1626   *The Staple of News*.
1628   Assassination of Buckingham, Jonson questioned over verses
        in praise of his assassin attributed to him; suffers a stroke;
        awarded the post of City Chronologer.
1629   *The New Inn*.
1631   Final court masques: *Love's Triumph Through Callipolis*;
        Chloridia.
1632   *The Magnetic Lady*.
1634   *A Tale of A Tub*.
1637   Dies at Westminster, buried in Westminster Abbey.
1640   Posthumous second volume of works published under
        editorship of Sir Kenelm Digby.

BIBLIOGRAPHY

Aasand, H. (1992) '"To Blanch an Ethiop, and Revive a Corse": Queen Anne and The Masque of Blackness', Studies in English Literature 32: 271–85.

Abraham, L. (1998) A Dictionary of Alchemical Imagery, Cambridge: Cambridge University Press.

Ayres, P. (ed.) (1990) The Revels Plays: Sejanus, Manchester: Manchester University Press.

Bakhtin, M. (1968) Rabelais and His World, trans. Helene Iswolsky, Cambridge MA: Harvard University Press.

Barish, J. (1960) Ben Jonson and the Language of Prose Comedy, Cambridge MA: Harvard University Press.

—— (ed) (1963) Ben Jonson: A Collection of Critical Essays, Englewood Cliffs: Prentice Hall.

—— (1981) The Anti-theatrical Prejudice, Berkeley: University of California Press.

—— (ed.) (1993) Jonson: Volpone, Casebooks, Basingstoke: Macmillan.

Barry, P. (1995) Beginning Theory, Manchester: Manchester University Press.

Barton, A. (1984) Ben Jonson: Dramatist, Cambridge: Cambridge University Press.

Bevington, D. and Holbrook, P. (eds) (1998) The Politics of the Stuart Court Masque, Cambridge: Cambridge University Press.

Bland, M. (1998) 'Jonson, Biathanatos and the Interpretation of Manuscript Evidence', Studies in Bibliography 51: 154–82.

Blissett, W., Patrick, J. and Van Fossen, R. (eds) (1973) A Celebration of Ben Jonson, Toronto: University of Toronto Press.

Boehrer, B. (1997) The Fury of Men's Gullets: Ben Jonson and the Digestive Canal, Philadelphia: University of Pennsylvania Press.

Brady, J. and Herendeen, W. (eds) (1991) Ben Jonson's 1616 Folio, Newark: University of Delaware Press.

Bristol, M. (1985) Carnival and Theatre: Plebeian Culture and the Structure of Authority in Renaissance England, New York and London: Methuen.

Bristow, J. (1997) Sexuality, London: Routledge.

Burke, P. (1978) Popular Culture in Early Modern Europe, London: Maurice Temple.

Burt, R. (1993) Licensed by Authority: Ben Jonson and the Discourses of Censorship, Ithaca and London: Cornell University Press.

Butler, M. (1984) Theatre and Crisis 1632–1642, Cambridge: Cambridge University Press.

—— (1990) 'Stuart Politics in A Tale of a Tub', Modern Language Review 85: 12–28.

—— (1991) ' "We Are One Man's All": Jonson's Gypsies Metamorphosed', Yearbook of English Studies 21: 253–73.

—— (1991/2) 'Ecclesiastical Censorship of Early Stuart Drama: The Case of Jonson's *The Magnetic Lady*', *Modern Philology* 89: 469–80.

—— (1992a) 'Late Jonson', in Hope, J. and McMullan, G. (eds) *The Politics of Tragicomedy*, London: Routledge, 166–88.

—— (1992b) 'Ben Jonson's *Pan's Anniversary* and the Politics of Early Stuart Pastoral', *English Literary Renaissance* 22: 369–404.

—— (1993a) 'Jonson's Folio and the Politics of Patronage', *Criticism* 35: 377–90.

—— (1993b) 'Reform or Reverence? The Politics of the Caroline Masque', in Mulryne, J. and Shewring, M. (eds) *Theatre and Government Under the Early Stuarts*, Cambridge: Cambridge University Press, 118–56.

—— (1994) 'Ben Jonson and the Limits of Courtly Panegyric', in Sharpe, K. and Lake, P. (eds) *Culture and Politics in Early Stuart England*, Basingstoke: Macmillan, 91–116.

—— (1996) ' "Servant But Not Slave": Ben Jonson at the Jacobean Court', *Proceedings of the British Academy* 90: 65–93.

—— (1998) 'Courtly Negotiations', in Bevington and Holbrook (1998), 20–40.

—— (ed.) (1999) *Re-Presenting Ben Jonson: Text, History and Performance*, Basingstoke: Macmillan.

Butler, M. and Lindley, D. (1994) 'Restoring Astraea: Jonson's Masque for the Fall of Somerset', *English Literary History* 61: 807–27.

Cain, T. (1995) *The Revels Plays: Poetaster*, Manchester: Manchester University Press.

—— (1998) ' "Satyres, That Girde and Fart at the Time": *Poetaster* and the Essex Rebellion', in Sanders, Chedgzoy and Wiseman (1998), 48–70. (ed.)

Campbell, O. (1931) 'The Relation of *Epicoene* to Aretino's *Il Marescalco*', *Publications of the Modern Language Association* 46: 752–62.

Cave, R. (1991) *Ben Jonson*, Basingstoke: Macmillan.

Cave, R., Shafer, E. and Woolland, B. (eds) (1999) *Ben Jonson and Theatre: Performance, Practice and Theory*, London: Routledge.

Clare, J. (1998) 'Jonson's "Comical Satires" and the Art of Courtly Compliment', in Sanders, Chedgzoy and Wiseman (1998), 28–47.

Corballis, R. (1979) 'The "Second Pen" in the Stage Version of *Sejanus*', in *Modern Philology* 76: 273–7.

Craig, D. (1990) *Ben Jonson: The Critical Heritage*, London: Routledge.

—— (1999) 'Jonsonian Chronology and the Styles of *A Tale of a Tub*', in Butler (1999), 210–32.

Creaser, J. (ed.) (1978) *Volpone, or The Fox*, London: Hodder and Stoughton.

De Luna, B. (1969) *Jonson's Romish Plot: A Study of Catiline and Its Historical Contexts*, Oxford: Oxford University Press.

Di Gangi, M. (1995) 'Asses and Wits: The Homoerotics of Mastery in Satiric Comedy', *English Literary Renaissance* 25: 179–208.

Donaldson, I. (1970) *The World Upside Down: Comedy from Jonson to Fielding*, Oxford: Oxford University Press.

—— (ed.) (1985) *Ben Jonson. The Oxford Authors*, Oxford: Oxford University Press.

—— (1997) *Jonson's Magic Houses: Essays in Interpretation*, Oxford: Oxford University Press.

—— (2000) 'Jonson's Poetry', in Harp and Stewart (2000), 119–39.

Dutton, R. (1983) *Ben Jonson: To the First Folio*, Cambridge: Cambridge University Press.

—— (1991) *Mastering the Revels: The Regulation and Censorship of English Renaissance Drama*, Basingstoke: Macmillan.

—— (1996) *Ben Jonson: Authority: Criticism*, Basingstoke: Macmillan.

—— (ed.) (2000) *Ben Jonson*, Longman Critical Reader, London: Longman

Eagleton, T. and Milne, D. (eds) (1995) *Marxist Literary Theory: A Reader*, Oxford: Blackwell.

Eliot, T. S. (1928) *The Sacred Wood: Essays on Poetry and Criticism*, London: Methuen.

Elsky, M (1989) *Authorizing Words: Speech, Writing and Print in the English Renaissance*, Ithaca and London: Cornell University Press.

Evans, R. (1989) *Ben Jonson and the Poetics of Patronage*, Lewisburg. Bucknell University Press.

—— (2000) *Ben Jonson's Major Plays: Summaries of Modern Monographs*, West Cornwall: Locust Hill Press.

Fish, S. (1984) 'Authors-Readers: Jonson's Community of the Same', *Representations* 7: 26–58.

—— (1999) *The Stanley Fish Reader*, ed. Veeser, H., Oxford: Blackwell.

Foakes, R. and Rickert, R. (eds) *Henslowe's Diary*, Cambridge: Cambridge University Press.

Frank, J. (1961) *The Beginnings of the English Newspaper 1620–1660*, Cambridge MA: Harvard University Press.

Gilbert, A. (1948) *The Symbolic Persons in the Masques of Ben Jonson*, Durham: Duke University Press.

Goldberg, J. (1983) *James I and the Politics of Literature*, Baltimore: Johns Hopkins University Press.

Gordon, D. (1975) *The Renaissance Imagination*, Berkeley: University of California Press.

Gossett, S. (1988) ' "Man-maid, begone!"': Women in Masques', *English Literary Renaissance* 18: 96–113.

Greenblatt, S. (1976) 'The False Ending in *Volpone*', *Journal of English and Germanic Philology* 75: 90–104.

—— (1980) *Renaissance Self-Fashioning: From More to Shakespeare*, Chicago: University of Chicago Press.

Greene, T. (1970) 'Jonson and the Centred Self', *Studies in English Literature* 10: 325–48.

Greg, W. (1952) *Jonson's Masque of Gypsies*, London: British Academy.

Hall, K. (1995) *Things of Darkness: Economies of Race and Gender in Early Modern England*, Ithaca and London: Cornell University Press.

Hannaford, S. (1980) 'Gold is But Muck: Jonson's *The Case Is Altered*', *Studies in the Humanities* 8: 11–16.

Happé, P. (ed.) (1994) *The Revels Plays: The Devil is an Ass*, Manchester: Manchester University Press.

—— (ed.) (2000) *The Revels Plays: The Magnetic Lady*, Manchester: Manchester University Press.

Harp, R. (2000) 'Jonson's Late Plays', in Harp and Stewart (2000), 90–102.

Harp, R. and Stewart, S. (eds) (2000) *The Cambridge Companion to Ben Jonson*, Cambridge: Cambridge University Press.

Hattaway, M. (ed.) (1984) *The Revels Plays: The New Inn*, Manchester: Manchester University Press.

Hayes, T. (1992) *The Birth of Popular Culture: Ben Jonson, Maid Marian and Robin Hood*, Pittsburgh: Duquesne University Press.

Haynes, J. (1992) *The Social Relations of Jonson's Theatre*, Cambridge: Cambridge University Press.

Helgerson, R. (1983) *Self-Crowned Laureates: Spenser, Jonson, Milton and the Literary System*, Berkeley: University of California Press.

—— (1993) 'Ben Jonson', in Corns, T. (ed.) *The Cambridge Companion to English Poetry, Donne to Marvell*, Cambridge: Cambridge University Press, 148–70.

Higgins, J. (1999) *Raymond Williams: Literature, Marxism and Cultural Materialism*, London: Routledge.

Holdsworth, R. (ed.) (1979) *Every Man In His Humour and The Alchemist*, Casebooks, Basingstoke: Macmillan.

Hughes, P. and Larkin, J. (eds) (1973) *Stuart Royal Proclamations*, volume 1, Oxford: Oxford University Press.

Hutson, L. (ed.) (1998) *Volpone and Other Plays*, Harmondsworth: Penguin.

Kaplan, M. (1997) *The Culture of Slander in Early Modern England*, Cambridge: Cambridge University Press.

Kay, W. D. (1995) *Ben Jonson: A Literary Life*, Basingstoke: Macmillan.

Knights, L. (1937) *Drama and Society in the Age of Jonson*, London: Chatto and Windus.

Knowles, J. (1999) 'Jonson's Entertainment at Britain's Burse', in Butler (1999), 114–51.

—— (ed.) (2001) *The Roaring Girl and Other City Comedies*, Oxford: Oxford University Press.

Lanier, D. (1983) 'The Prison House of the Canon: Allegorical Form and Posterity in Ben Jonson's The Staple of News', *Medieval and Renaissance Drama in England* 2: 253–67.

Larkin, J. (ed.) (1983) *Stuart Royal Proclamations*, volume 2, Oxford: Oxford University Press.

Lee, J. (1989) *Ben Jonson's Poesis: A Literary Dialectic of Ideal and History*, Charlottesville: University of Virginia Press.

Levin, H. (1938) 'An Introduction to Ben Jonson', in Barish (1963), 40–59.

Levine, L. (1994) *Men in Women's Clothing: Anti-theatricality and Effeminization 1579–1642*, Cambridge: Cambridge University Press.

Lewalski, B. (1993) *Writing Women in Jacobean England*, Cambridge MA: Harvard University Press.

Lindley, D. (1986) 'Embarrassing Ben: The Masques for Frances Howard', *English Literary Renaissance* 16: 343–59.

—— (ed.) (1984) *The Court Masque*, Manchester: Manchester University Press.

—— (1993) *The Trials of Frances Howard: Fact and Fiction at the Court of King James*, London: Routledge.

—— (ed.) (1995) *Court Masques: Jacobean and Caroline Entertainments 1605–1640*, Oxford: Oxford University Press.

Loewenstein, J. (1985) 'The Script in the Marketplace', *Representations* 12: 101–14.

Mack, R. (1997) 'Ben Jonson's Own "Comedy of Errors": "That Witty Play," The Case Is Altered', *The Ben Jonson Journal* 4: 47–63.

Magaw, K. (1998) 'Modern Books on Ben Jonson: A General Topical Index', *The Ben Jonson Journal* 5: 201–47.

Marcus, L. (1986) *The Politics of Mirth: Jonson, Herrick, Milton, Marvell and the Defence of Old Holiday Pastimes*, Chicago: University of Chicago Press.

Marotti, A. (1972) 'All About Jonson's Poetry', *English Literary History* 39: 208–37.

Maus, K. (1984) *Ben Jonson and the Roman Frame of Mind*, Princeton: Princeton University Press.

McCanles, M. (1977) 'Festival in Jonson's Comedy', *Renaissance Drama* n.s. 8: 203–19.

—— (1992) *Jonsonian Discriminations: The Humanist Poet and the Praise of True Nobility*, Toronto: University of Toronto Press.

McKenzie, D. (1973) '*The Staple of News* and the Late Plays', in Blisset, Patrick and van Fossen (1973), 83–128.

McLuskie, K. (1989) *Renaissance Dramatists*, London: Harvester.

—— (1991) 'The Poets Royal Exchange: Patronage and Commerce in Early Modern Drama', *Yearbook of English Studies* 21: 53–62.

McManus, C. (1998) ' "Defacing the Carcass": Anne of Denmark and Jonson's *Masque of Blackness*', in Sanders, Chedgzoy and Wiseman (1998), 93–113.

Meagher, J. (1966) *Method and Meaning in Jonson's Masques*, Notre Dame: University of Notre Dame Press.

Miles, R. (1986) *Ben Jonson, His Life and Work*, London: Routledge.

Miller, S. (1996) 'Consuming Mothers/Consuming Merchants: The Carnivalesque Economy of Jacobean City Comedy', *Modern Language Studies* 26: 73–97.

Miola, R. (ed.) (2000) *The Revels Plays: Every Man In His Humour*, Manchester: Manchester University Press.

Moi, T., (1985) *Sexual/Textual Politics: Feminist Literary Theory*, London: Methuen.

Murray, T. (1987) *Theatrical Legitimation: Allegories of Genius in Seventeenth Century England and France*, New York and Oxford: Oxford University Press.

Newman, K. (1991) *Fashioning Femininity*, Chicago: University of Chicago Press.

Newton, R. (1977) 'Ben Jonson: The Poet in the Poems', in Kernan, A. (ed.) *Two Renaissance Mythmakers: Christopher Marlowe and Ben Jonson*, Baltimore: Johns Hopkins University Press, 165–95.

—— 'Jonson and the (Re-)Invention of the Book', in Summers and Pebworth (1982), 31–55.

Norbrook, D. (1984) *Poetry and Politics in the English Renaissance*, London: Routledge and Kegan Paul.

Orgel, S. (1965) *The Jonsonian Masque*, Cambridge MA: Harvard University Press.

—— (1975) *The Illusion of Power: Political Theatre in the English Renaissance*, Berkeley: University of California Press.

Orgel, S. and Strong, R. (1973) *Inigo Jones: The Theatre of the Stuart Court*, Berkeley: University of California Press.

Ostovich, H. (1994) 'The Appropriation of Pleasure in *The Magnetic Lady*', *Studies in English Literature* 34: 425–43.

—— (1997) 'Mistress and Maid: Women's Friendship in *The New Inn*', *The Ben Jonson Journal* 4: 1–26.

—— (1998) 'Hell for Lovers: Shades of Adultery in *The Devil is an Ass*', in Sanders, Chedgzoy and Wiseman (1998), 155–82.

—— (1999) ' "To Behold the Scene Full": Seeing and Judging in *Every Man Out of His Humour*', in Butler (1999), 76–92.

Parfitt, G. (1976) *Ben Jonson: Public Poet and Private Man*, London: J. M. Dent

Parr, A. (ed.) (1988) *The Revels Plays: The Staple of News*, Manchester: Manchester University Press.

Parry, G. 'The Politics of the Jacobean Masque', in Mulryne, J. and Shewring, M. (eds) *Theatre and Government Under the Early Stuarts*, Cambridge: Cambridge University Press, 87–117.

Partridge, E. (1958) *The Broken Compass*, New York: Columbia University Press.

—— (1973) 'Jonson's "Epigrammes": The Named and the Nameless', *Studies in the Literary Imagination* 6: 153–98.

Paster, G. (1987) 'Leaky Vessels: The Incontinent Women of City Comedy', *Renaissance Drama* n.s. 18: 43–65.

—— (1998) 'The Unbearable Coldness of Female Being: Women's Imperfection in the Humoral Economy', *English Literary Renaissance* 28: 416–440.

Patterson, A. (1984) *Censorship and Interpretation: The Conditions of Writing and Reading in Early Modern England*, Madison: University of Wisconsin Press.

—— (1985) 'Lyric and Society in Jonson's Under-wood', in Hosek, C. and Parker, P. (eds) *Lyric Poetry: Beyond New Criticism*, Ithaca: Cornell University Press, 148–63.

Penniman, J. (1897) *The War of the Theatres*, Boston: University of Pennsylvania Press.

Peterson, R. (1981) *Imitation and Praise in the Poems of Ben Jonson*, New Haven: Yale University Press.

Porter, R. (1994) *London: A Social History*, London: Hamish Hamilton.

Rhodes, N. (1980) *Elizabethan Grotesque*, London: Routledge and Kegan Paul.

Riggs, D. (1989) *Ben Jonson, A Life*, Cambridge MA and London: Harvard University Press.

Rose, M. (1988) *The Expense of Spirit: Love and Sexuality in English Renaissance Drama*, Ithaca and London: Cornell University Press.

Rowe, N. (1994) ' "My Best Patron": William Cavendish and Jonson's Caroline Drama', *The Seventeenth Century* 9: 197–212.

Sanders, J. (1998a) *Ben Jonson's Theatrical Republics*, Basingstoke: Macmillan.

—— (1998b) 'Print, Popular Culture, Consumption and Commodification in *The Staple of News*', in Sanders, Chedgzoy and Wiseman (1998), 183–207.

Sanders, J, Chedgzoy, K. and Wiseman S. (eds) (1998) *Refashioning Ben Jonson: Gender, Politics and the Jonsonian Canon*, Basingstoke: Macmillan

Siddiqi, Y. (1992) 'Dark Incontinents: The Discourses of Race and Gender in Three Renaissance Masques', *Renaissance Drama* n.s. 23: 139–64.

Skinner, Q. (1996) *Reason and Rhetoric in the Philosophy of Hobbes*, Cambridge: Cambridge University Press.

Small, R. (1899) *The Stage Quarrel Between Ben Jonson and the So-Called Poetasters*, Breslau: Marcus.

Smith, B. (1999) *The Acoustic World of Early Modern England*, Chicago: Chicago University Press.

Smith, J. (1998) 'Effaced History: Facing the Colonial Contexts of Ben Jonson's Irish Masque at Court', *English Literary History* 65: 297–321.

Stallybrass, P. and White, A. (1986) *The Politics and Poetics of Transgression*, London: Methuen.

Summers, J. and Pebworth, T. (eds) (1982) *Classic and Cavalier: Essays on Jonson and the Sons of Ben*, Pittsburgh: University of Pittsburgh Press.

Swann, M. (1998) 'Refashioning Society in Ben Jonson's *Epicene*', *Studies in English Literature* 38: 297–315.

Sweeney, J. (1985) *Jonson and the Psychology of Public Theatre*, Princeton: Princeton University Press.

Trimpi, W. (1962) *Ben Jonson's Poems: A Study of the Plain Style*, Stanford: Stanford University Press.

Van den Berg, S. (1987) *The Action of Ben Jonson's Poetry*, Newark: University of Delaware Press.

—— (1991) 'Ben Jonson and the Ideology of Authorship', in Brady and Herendeen (1991), 111–37.

Van Fossen, R. (ed.) (1979) *The Revels Plays: Eastward Ho!* Manchester: Manchester University Press.

Veeser, H. (ed.) (1988) *The New Historicism*, London: Routledge.

Venuti, L. (1989) *Our Halcyon Dayes: English Prerevolutionary Texts and Postmodern Culture*, Madison: University of Wisconsin Press.

Vice, S. (1997) *Introducing Bakhtin*, Manchester: Manchester University Press.

Watson, R. (1987) *Ben Jonson's Parodic Strategy: Literary Imperialism in the Comedies*, Cambridge MA: Harvard University Press.

Wayne, D. (1979) 'Poetry and Power in Ben Jonson's "Epigrammes": The Naming of "Facts" or the Figuring of Social Relations?', *Renaissance and Modern Studies* 23: 70–103.

—— (1982) 'Drama and Society in the Age of Jonson: An Alternative View', *Renaissance Drama* n.s. 13: 103–29.

—— (1984) *Penshurst: The Semiotics of Place and the Poetics of History*, London: Methuen.

—— (1990) 'Jonson's Sidney: Legacy and Legitimation in The Forest', in Allen, M. (ed.) *Sir Philip Sidney's Achievements*, New York: AMS Press, 227–50.

—— (1995) 'The "Exchange of Letters": Early Modern Contradictions and Postmodern Conundrums', in Bermingham, A. and Brewer, J. (eds) *The Consumption of Culture 1600–1800*, London: Routledge, 143–65.

—— (1999) ' "Pox on Your Distinction!" Humanist Reformation and Deformations of the Everyday in *The Staple of News*', in Fumerton, P. and Hunt, S. (eds) *Renaissance Culture and the Everyday*, Philadelphia: University of Pennsylvania Press, 67–91.

Williams, R. (1973) *The Country and the City*, London: Chatto and Windus.

Wilson, E. (1952) *The Triple Thinkers: Twelve Essays on Literary Subjects*, London: John Lehmann.

Wiltenburg, R. (1991) *Ben Jonson and Self-Love*, Columbia: University of Missouri Press.

Womack, P. (1986) *Ben Jonson*, Oxford: Basil Blackwell.

—— (1989) 'The Sign of the Light Heart: Jonson's *New Inn* in 1629 and 1987', *New Theatre Quarterly* 5: 162–70.

Worden, B. (1994) 'Ben Jonson Among the Historians', in Sharpe, K. and Lake, P. (eds) *Culture and Politics in Early Stuart England*, Basingstoke: Macmillan, 67–90.

—— (1999) 'Politics in *Catiline*: Jonson and His Sources', in Butler (1999), 152–73.

Wynne-Davies, M. (1992) 'The Queen's Masque: Renaissance Women and the Seventeenth Century Court Masque', in Wynne-Davies, M. and Cerasano, S. (eds) *Gloriana's Face: Women, Public and Private, in the English Renaissance*, London: Harvester, 79–104.

INDEX

AEI-3591